Short Form American Poetry

Dear Bill: –
I trust you will not hate me for wanting to delete from your poem all the flippancies.

(H.D., letter to William Carlos Williams, 14 August 1916)

Short Form American Poetry

The Modernist Tradition

Will Montgomery

EDINBURGH
University Press

Edinburgh University Press is one of the leading university presses in the UK. We publish academic books and journals in our selected subject areas across the humanities and social sciences, combining cutting-edge scholarship with high editorial and production values to produce academic works of lasting importance. For more information visit our website: edinburghuniversitypress.com

© Will Montgomery, 2020, 2022

First published in hardback by Edinburgh University Press 2020

Edinburgh University Press Ltd
The Tun – Holyrood Road,
12(2f) Jackson's Entry
Edinburgh EH8 8PJ

Typeset in 10.5/13 Adobe Sabon by
Servis Filmsetting Ltd, Stockport, Cheshire,

A CIP record for this book is available from the British Library

ISBN 978 0 7486 9532 4 (hardback)
ISBN 978 1 3995 0054 8 (paperback)
ISBN 978 0 7486 9533 1 (webready PDF)
ISBN 978 1 4744 7640 9 (epub)

The right of Will Montgomery to be identified as the author of this work has been asserted in accordance with the Copyright, Designs and Patents Act 1988, and the Copyright and Related Rights Regulations 2003 (SI No. 2498).

Every effort has been made to trace the copyright holders, but if any have been inadvertently overlooked, the publisher will be pleased to make the necessary arrangements at the first opportunity.

Contents

Acknowledgements	vi
Abbreviations	viii
Introduction	1
1. Ezra Pound, H.D. and Imagism	15
2. William Carlos Williams	42
3. George Oppen	67
4. Lorine Niedecker	90
5. Robert Creeley	118
6. Larry Eigner	139
7. Robert Grenier	159
8. Rae Armantrout	180
Coda	204
Bibliography	208
Index	219

Acknowledgements

Permission has been granted to cite the following material:

By H.D. (Hilda Doolittle), from COLLECTED POEMS, 1912–1944, copyright ©1982 by The Estate of Hilda Doolittle. Reprinted by permission of New Directions Publishing Corp.

By Ezra Pound, from PERSONAE, copyright ©1926 by Ezra Pound. Reprinted by permission of New Directions Publishing Corp. and Faber & Faber Ltd.

By William Carlos Williams, from THE COLLECTED POEMS: VOLUMES I & 2, copyright ©1917, 1921 by the Four Seas Company, 1934 by The Objectivist Press, 1935 by The Alcestis Press, 1936 by Ronald Lane Latimer, 1938 by New Directions Publishing Corp., 1930, 1931, 1933, 1935, 1937, 1938, 1939, 1951, 1952 by William Carlos Williams, 1957, 1966, 1974 by Florence H. Williams, 1982, 1986, 1995 by William Eric Williams and Paul H. Williams, 1986 by A. Walton Litz and Christopher MacGowan. Reprinted by permission of New Directions Publishing Corp. and Carcanet Press.

By George Oppen, from NEW COLLECTED POEMS, copyright ©1960, 1961, 1962, 1963, 1964, 1965, 1967, 1968, 1969, 1970, 1971, 1972, 1973, 1974, 1975, 1976, 1977, 1978, 1981 by George Oppen, copyright ©1985, 2002, 2008 by Linda Oppen. Reprinted by permission of New Directions Publishing Corp. and Carcanet Press.

By Cid Corman. By permission of Bob Arnold, Literary Executor for the Estate of Cid Corman.

By Louis Zukofsky. All materials copyright © Musical Observations, Inc. Used by permission.

By Lorine Niedecker. Collected Works, by Lorine Niedecker and edited by Jenny Penberthy, © 2004 by the Regents of the University of California. Published by the University of California Press.

By Robert Creeley. The Collected Poems of Robert Creeley (1945–1975), by Robert Creely, © 1982, 2006 by the Regents of the University of California. Published by the University of California Press.

By Larry Eigner. Material from Area Lights Heights (Roof Books, 1989) by permission of the Segue Foundation. Material from *Calligraphy Typewriters: Selected Poems* (University of Alabama Press, 2017), copyright of the Estate of Larry Eigner, and used by permission of University of Alabama Press.

By Robert Grenier. By permission of the author.

By Rae Armantrout. 'Grace', 'View' and 'Anti-Short Story' from *Veil: New and Selected Poems* © 2001 by Rae Armantrout. 'Back' and 'Entanglements' from *Up to Speed* © 2004 by Rae Armantrout. 'Two, Three' and 'Units' from *Next Life* © 2007 by Rae Armantrout. 'Translation' and 'Like' from *Versed* © 2009 by Rae Armantrout. 'Duration' from *Money Shot* © 2011 by Rae Armantrout. 'Vessels' from *Wobble* © 2018 by Rae Armantrout. 'Pinocchio' from *Conjure* © 2020 by Rae Armantrout. All texts published by Wesleyan University Press and reprinted with permission.

This book contains revised versions of parts of my article 'Robert Creeley's Refusals' in *Caliban* 35 (2014). Some passages of my chapter on Rae Armantrout are adapted from the essay ' "Umbilical Stump Still Pulses": Public Language and Number in the poetry of Rae Armantrout', which appeared in the conference-proceedings collection *Poetry and Public Language*, ed. Tony Frazer and Anthony Caleshu (Plymouth: Shearsman/ University of Plymouth Press, 2007).

Thanks to those who have read and commented on earlier versions of the material in the book, especially Adam Roberts and Matt ffytche. Thanks to Allen Fisher. Thanks also to Ersev Ersoy, the production staff at Edinburgh University Press and the copy-editor, Christine Barton. All shortcomings and errors are my own responsibility.

Abbreviations

CPC1	Robert Creeley, *The Collected Poems of Robert Creeley, 1945–1975*
CPW1 and CPW2	William Carlos Williams, *The Collected Poems of William Carlos Williams*, Vols 1 and 2
CT	Larry Eigner, *Calligraphy Typewriters: The Selected Poems of Larry Eigner*
CW	Lorine Niedecker, *Collected Works*
NCP	George Oppen, *New Collected Poems*

For Harry and Tessa, and for Jess

Introduction

This is a book about poetic form. The book concerns itself with brevity rather than form per se, or such specific formal features as metre or stanza organisation. Shortness is a category that does not belong to the lexicon of prosody, but various versions of brevity, whether achieved through curtailment, compression or simply finishing early, are central to the poetry of modernism. Discussion of the modernist tradition in American twentieth-century and contemporary poetry has been dominated by such long-form monuments as Ezra Pound's *Cantos*, William Carlos Williams's *Paterson*, and Charles Olson's *Maximus*. This study analyses a countervailing tradition of short-form work. Beginning with Imagism, it argues that the short and short-lined poem is a central feature of American twentieth-century poetry, lacking neither the intellectual ambition nor the expressive range of the well-known epics.

One motivating factor in the book's composition derives from Charles Altieri's nuanced and largely enthusiastic description of Robert Creeley's 'poetics of conjecture' in his important 1984 survey *Self and Sensibility in Contemporary American Poetry*. Altieri concludes that, for all the poetry's strengths, there is a formal defect in Creeley's work.[1] At fault is the 'myth of lucidity' that Creeley inherits from Williams's Objectivism and its attendant commitment to short form. This, writes Altieri, fatally undermines the poetry's ability to map self-consciously the movements of consciousness:

> In his poetics of thinking Creeley becomes a victim of what had been his greatest strength: his taut, ascetic language. In short personal lyrics the spare style both intensifies emotional concentration and twists drama toward abstraction. But when the abstraction becomes the site of poetic activity, the same asceticism inordinately narrows the field and impoverishes the sense of self we need to connect the abstractions to experience. Because it lacks conventional modes of concentration and creates its own world, the rhetoric of conjecture must be a lush one.

In Altieri's view, Adrienne Rich and John Ashbery offer suitably 'lush' ways out of this impasse. Creeley, on the other hand, 'cannot introduce into his reflections much sense of history or a broad enough range of concerns to keep the conjecture a complex philosophical movement'.[2] There is a lack of fit between the evacuated spaces of 'abstraction' and 'asceticism' on the one hand, and the plenitude offered by 'self' and 'experience' on the other. My point of departure is to query Altieri's dismissal of Creeley's 'spare style' and to claim for it a 'complex' cognitive status. I will argue that, in Creeley's work and that of others, there *is* a 'sense of history' folded into the formal contours of this writing, however unlikely that may seem. The style of these small poems is motivated by an aesthetic that cannot be anything but historically specific. The poems may, in 'complex' ways, serve as an index of social experience refracted into language. Sometimes the apparent refusal of this poetry to accommodate 'history', whether as as a determining abstraction or more local motivation, might be a mark of a deeper-lying, non-conceptual aligment with forms and patterns of thinking that is anything but ahistorical. Something of conjectural substance may, in short, be said by this poetry's refusal to say. An ascetic, reduced form may harbour dense clusters of cognitive and affective experience that cannot otherwise be registered in language. And, in any case, Creeley's poetry and that of the post-Imagist line, may not be so beholden to Altieri's 'myth of lucidity' as might at first appear – the relationship between perceiver, object and textual representation may, indeed, be anything but clear, and the poetry may resist the neat separation of such terms.

In discussing form, I do not seek to return to an airless, ahistorical model of criticism that deals primarily with the 'poem on the page'. Nor, on the other hand, do I find it useful to discuss this poetry through 'surface reading' or to align my readings with recent challenges to the 'hermeneutics of suspicion'.[3] While I do not mine the texts in the hope of revealing the concealed, I do find that certain formal qualities we can attribute to short-form verse can help us think about both literary form and the intricately formed cultural and political environments from which the writing emerges.

Tom Eyers has written recently, as he articulates a theory of 'speculative formalism', of how such formal features of a text as repetition, rhythm, metaphor or metonymy may generate a 'nonmimetic kind of reference'. He argues that 'literary texts, insofar as they are able to at least partially break free from their prior determinants and refigure those determinants anew, embody a formal speculative capacity that prevents their final absorption or neutralization by those prior conditions'.[4] My argument is similarly preoccupied with the non-representational and with the ways in which literary form structures and enables thought, enabling it to give shape and substance to experience. Many of the poets I discuss are concerned with the objects or things of the world. Terms such as 'clarity' and 'directness' often appear to guide a poetics in which the unvarnished depiction of the object-world flourishes. However, as Rae Armantrout has argued, the attempts of Williams and the early Imagists to 'put things in dialogue with mind' often bump up against a problem: '*thing* and *idea* don't really merge'.[5] I am curious about the communicative potential of the non-'merging' that is opened by this insight. Indeed opacity, blockage and non-statement are frequently properties of writing that uses the foreshortening techniques I discuss. For Eyers, the term 'impasse' is helpful as he seeks to build a bridge between particular formal instances and what he calls a 'general logic of form, or formalization':

> this logic ... concerns the creative capacity of impasses. Literature stages better than most phenomena the manner in which, far from shutting down the possibility of meaning, the impossibility of any final, formal integration of a structure and its component parts is the very condition of possibility of that structure.[6]

This generative opacity is important to the arguments I make. This book often concerns itself with the recursive qualities of short-form writing that turns from the encounter with the world towards the parsing of that world into literary form. Such poetry often involves or implies a self-aware contemplation of the shape of utterances in the moment of their enunciation. My aim is not to discuss this poetry's exquisite self-consciousness as poetry, or to suggest that such meta-manoeuvres are of intrinsic value. On the contrary, I seek to present such moments as specifically poetic kinds of thinking, not available to more directly communicative or expository kinds of language use. The styles of thinking modelled by such poetry imply a usefully sceptical orientation towards everyday language use. At the same time, much of the poetry I discuss is grounded in quotidiana. Short-form writing often brings a critical orientation towards the presentation of the simplest of materials, finding complexity within that simplicity. The narrowed temporality and the fiction of the merely observational that many of these poems employ does not limit the scope of the writing. Short-form poetry obtains a critical purchase on more fully elaborated methods of utterance. My argument, sometimes explicit, sometimes implicit, is that certain kinds of poetic thinking can be aligned with a broader social orientation that is at once vigilant about false models of closure and optimistic about the communicative reach of condensation.

I argue in what follows that the interruptedness of short-form poetry has affinities with the discontinuities of everyday experience. However, I locate this writing's value in its closeness to the hesitant, self-monitoring, revisionary and vagrant movement of thought. Such cognitive experience is, notwithstanding many attempts to render it, not straightforwardly available to literary depiction. The writing I discuss is not mimetic of experience or the world, but it does communicate the centrality of rupture, impasse and discontinuity to thinking. The directness of representation to which some of the poets aspire is a chimera. The poem's status as aesthetic object is in continuing tension with the objects it names, and the potential for obliquity thus installs itself at every turn. Long-form poetry, however fragmentary, nearly always has a relationship to narrative. Even when indirect in its methods, it cumulatively implies a reading of the world that is ultimately consecutive and bound to a discernible past and future. The temporal scope of short-form poetry is both narrower and, because the micro- and macro-temporalities of the poem are often unfixed by syntactical uncertainty, broader. I concur with Eyers's suggestion that poetry,

> with its self-conscious disruption of [the] narrative impulse... can act as a fever-chart of asubjective, even materialist impulses that are not so easily pinpointed in narrative, but that sit nonetheless at the eccentric centre not only of all literary forms (narrative surely included), but also of variants of political and historical form.[7]

My discussion of short-form writing does not oppose an understanding of lyric to the supposedly epic or collective ambitions of the long-form poem.[8] I do not agree with those who impute to lyric poetry a straw-man model of unitary subjectivity or a circumscribed field of attention that precludes large and complex thoughts that are responsive to the historical moment. However, while recent critical discussions of lyric have been rich, I find the term, and its accompanying baggage, unhelpful in describing the writing discussed in this book.[9] While many of the poems I discuss explore subjectivity and poetic address in various provocative ways, and while I am curious about the acoustic dimensions of the poetry I discuss, I do not think it possible to characterise modernist short-form poetry as essentially a version of lyric. The enduring diffuseness of the lyric category, its embeddedness in a long continuum of prosodic reflection and the precarious associations with voice and song that cling to the term, even in its more radical acceptations, all make it ill-suited to my analysis of poetic brevity.[10]

The most recent example of the disparagement of short-form writing that I have encountered comes in an essay by the poet and critic John

Wilkinson (whose work I have often found inspiring). Discussing the 'substantial' quality of W. S. Graham's poetry, notwithstanding the apparent lack of political, historical or moral content, Wilkinson points to the shortcomings of certain (unnamed) poets who admire Lorine Niedecker or Creeley's work and who, while 'serious', lack the substance he admires in Graham. The verse of such poets 'skates the edges of inconsequentiality, so signalling an aesthetic of attentive care, a phenomenology of small changes, linguistic calls and responses from beyond the linguistic arena, as though poetry might sponsor ethical conduct by example'.[11] Wilkinson provides, albeit from a different vantage point, a contemporary re-statement of Altieri's position on the restricted scope of short-form poetry, setting up an opposition between the 'substantial' and the 'inconsequential' mode he associates with Niedecker and Creeley and those who follow their respective (though surely very different) examples.

This book argues that Niedecker, Creeley and the others I discuss are poets of consequence. This does not depend on a metaphysics of the extra-linguistic (which, as I argue in Chapter 1, would be to replicate a form of pathos that was mined to little effect in British post-symbolist verse) or on the busted-flush of claiming ethical agency for radical formal methods. Instead, I argue that the various experiences of condensation, curtailment and hesitancy that I discuss in this book are not limited in reach just because they appear to lead to dead ends. I believe that such barriers to the narrative development of thought are, on one hand, richly productive literary experiences, and, on the other, that they shadow wider, culturally embedded styles of interruption that structure contemporary experience.

One way to address the relationship of the poetic artefact to the world from which it emerges is by reconsidering Altieri's 'myth of lucidity': the aspiration to a plain and clear-eyed depiction of the object that is free of the deceiving lures of a more conspicuously poetic mode of writing. It is not difficult to find in Williams, Niedecker, George Oppen or Creeley a commitment to clarity that ultimately derives from the various injunctions against superfluity and excess in Pound's writings on Imagism. The poetics of modernist brevity often appears to be motivated by the desire for an uncomplicated encounter with the object world. Many poets in the tradition I discuss seem to want to treat the thing directly. This book, however, is more interested in the possibility that the object may be most communicative at the point of its disappearance – its subsumption into the formal arena of the poem. This disappearance is most acutely felt in the short-form poem. However, none of the major statements of Imagism or Objectivism focus on the quality of brevity, even though their primary commitments (i.e. compared to romanticism or symbolism, for example) are to an understanding of form that necessarily implies a cutting-back.

Peter Nicholls has usefully complicated the term 'thing' in Pound's desire for 'direct treatment of the "thing"', which is usually taken to mean something akin to T. E. Hulme's quasi-empirical 'things as they really are' – an unvarnished representation of external reality. Nicholls points out, with reference to other contemporaneous uses of the word 'thing' by Pound, that the inverted commas around 'thing' align it not with the objects of the world, but with a dynamic perceptual constellation that encompasses both outward and inward: 'these "things" are not single objects, but arrangements in social and psychic space which the poem delicately conjoins'.[12] In light of this reading of the Poundian 'thing', I have read some of the poets in this book against the grain of their own statements on both clarity and the object. Lucidity, in my arguments, is, as it is for Altieri, a myth. This book argues that the directness that Pound and his peers aspire to is short-circuited by the impulse to economy. Indeed, the urge to reduce ultimately takes post-imagist poetics far from the clarity of 'direct presentation' (as anyone who has taught Objectivism to undergraduates will be aware). The poets I discuss go far beyond merely cutting out rhetorical excess. Indeed, they go beyond directness to a poetry that is notable for its indirectness.

The French thinker Judith Balso has written usefully about obliquity in the poetic text, describing the coexistence in the poem of 'what it thinks and the dense, more or less compact, presentation of what it thinks'.[13] She proposes a quality of 'the indirect' that is produced by the short-circuiting relation between what a poem thinks and how it reflects on what it thinks. For Balso, a poem is a style of thinking, producing what she calls the 'figure of thought':

> The figure of thought is not a figure *of the thought*; nor is it a *thought formatted into figures*. It is a new element produced by the poem and it must be seized as such. Yet, grasping it requires a non-interpretative grasp of the poem. Once again, it would not be a question of grasping the 'sense' of the poem, no more so than it would be a question of explaining its 'meaning,' one must grasp the 'indirect' of the poem as the organizer in the poem of some figures of thought specific to it.[14]

I argue that short-form poems produce distinctive 'figures of thought'. This is necessarily plural. The many kinds of obliquity, indirectness and condensation I discuss are examples of the variousness of the generally reduced formal mode that forms the subject of this book. The obstructions to thought that many of the poems trade in are themselves figures of thought, sometimes spurs to thinking the unthought. While I do not discuss the work of Gertrude Stein at any length in this book, her commitment to the intransigence of the unfamiliar is important to the particular strand in modernist poetry that I am describing. That unfamiliarity is no less productive of critical debate than writing that offers the reader more straightforward access to its goals. If one turns to critical responses to poetry of the modernist line, one finds that certain signal texts – Williams's 'Red Wheelbarrow' or Creeley's 'A Piece', for example – have generated considerable light and heat. One might argue that these famous Williams and Creeley examples are so generative of thought precisely because they refuse to do their thinking in more extended and prosaic fashion. Or, to take another example from Williams, the ironic blandness of the phrase 'This is just to say' conceals a spiky reappraisal of all that 'just saying' (to co-opt the title of a book by Rae Armantrout) might imply.

The short-form poem meets the social by encountering how it speaks. Its commitment to the expressive resources of form is not a shutting-off of the historical. On the contrary, it can offer an alert embrace of the linguistic strictures of the moment from which it emerges. The poem is not true to the object in any straightforward way, whatever the poet's aspirations to directness. It can, however, be true to a way of thinking in the world and in this respect it retains a dynamic speculative potential. The short-form poem, moreover, is not merely a symptom of non-resolution – an index, for example, of conceptual aporia. It is capable of exerting traction of its own, offering means of grappling with the existent, ways of thinking around and beyond specious claims to coherence. In this way, its formal arrangements harbour spaces for non-conformist refusals of the existent.

Many of the poems I discuss reflect more or less explicitly on the relationship between poet, world and poem. In this consideration of apprehension and representation, I find Mutlu Konuk Blasing's account of the 'stubborn opacity' of Wallace Stevens's 'Thirteen Ways of Looking at a Blackbird' helpful: 'The poet is concurrently arranging the sounds of words and articulating a natural object/scene and a speaking subject in relation to it. In this triangular relationship, the subject and the object are termini written by the words.'[15] Blasing's materialist account of a lyric subjectivity in which personal and collective experience interpenetrate has influenced some of the readings in this book, even if I have fought shy of the term 'lyric'.

Another theorist of lyric, Jonathan Culler, has written persuasively of rhythm as 'a force operating independently of what we usually call meaning'.[16] In an account that draws on Blasing's writing on lyric, he argues for a split between meaning and rhythm, stressing the somatic origins of the latter and insisting on the experiential specificity of the rhythmic. My book locates its commitments, however, not in the pulse of rhythm (and not, either, in the play of expectation and retrospection engendered by rhyme). I argue that the poetics of condensation is one of interruptedness, and that the pause or cut that we encounter at the ending of the line is no less somatic for the reader than the experience or rhythm or rhyme. While the latter terms depend on iteration, the foreshortened line depends on the cut, and is predicated on withholding. Language is encoded somatically, and the linebreak intervenes in that ordering.

The linebreak foregrounds the relationship between the syntactical unit and the line: it is an intervention in the flow of words that may or may not coincide with the clause. In many of the poems I discuss, syntax is itself disrupted. There is play, therefore, from line to line between different qualities of incompletion. But this is a book about poems that are both short-lined and short. The interruptedness of the short line is compounded in many of the poems I discuss by a larger interruptedness. Few of the poems in this book extend over more than a page, and many are only a few lines long. How can such concise verbal artefacts be in any sense substantial? In my view, substance is not coterminous with a fully articulated world view, a nuanced and self-sealed politics or a close fit with a major branch of philosophical poetics. My argument is that substance can (but need not) be found in the various versions of interruptedness – hesitancy, impasse, micro-collage, elision, for example – that I discuss. (This is not at all to say that all short-form poetry necessarily fulfils these ambitions: often it is trite, picturesque, throwaway or quietly metaphysical.)

My discussion of the poems in this book, therefore, is in accord with Giorgio Agamben's suggestion that 'the poem is an organism grounded in the perception of the limits and endings that define – without ever fully coinciding with, and almost in intermittent dispute with – sonorous (or graphic) units and semantic units'.[17] This book often discusses 'limits and endings' of various kinds. I extend the play of units to include the presence of syntactical units and the trace of more conventional verse units that is left by their conspicuous erasure through truncation. In some poems, line and phrase or sentence and stanza may coincide: in others there is a rippling interplay of different, non-coinciding units of poetic measure.

This book begins with modernism: it does not explore the long tradition of short forms such as the epigram, popular both in the classical world and in the English-language verse tradition. Such poems as Pope's epigrammatic couplet 'I am his highness's dog at Kew; / Pray tell me, sir, whose dog are you?' and Landor's eight-line elegy 'Rose Aylmer' are both examples of short-form poetry that depend for their effect on their completeness as utterances. This book is grounded in phenomena of incompletion. H.D.'s confrontationally terse use of epigrams translated by J. W. Mackail from the ancient Greek is salutary. Pound's 'Papyrus' (1916) is a four-word creative translation of almost-lost words from Sappho. These recovered texts, however, are simply starting points for a practice that is thoroughly modern and that soon detaches itself from classical materials. The otherness of early Greek culture, like the oriental examples also popular with certain of the imagists, offered a means of sidestepping the weight of anglophone literary history. The nearest precedent for modernist incompletion lies in the fad for the fragment in the late eighteenth and early nineteenth centuries, especially Schlegel's 'poetry of becoming' and, in the anglophone tradition, various of Coleridge's poems. While some of the texts I discuss share with the Romantic fragment a quality of self-reflection, and some early modernist examples, such as 'Papyrus', explore the effects of re-presenting incomplete source materials, the modernist practice of fragmentation hosts far more thoroughgoing methods of formal dislocation and discontinuity while holding back from the philosophical idealism implicit in Schegel's schema.[18] The writing I discuss explores, through syntax and linebreaks, techniques of compression that, while related to the long history of the fragment, establish a new field of meaning for poetry. The paradoxical communicativeness of non-statement is integral to the repertoire of the short-form poem in the tradition I describe.

I have argued that, although informed by contemporary discussions of lyric, this is not a book about lyric. Neither is it a book about minimalism. The poet and critic Charles Bernstein has written about the role of the linebreak in Creeley's work. In doing so, he takes the opportunity to distinguish Creeley's poetry from minimalism:

> Creeley reimagined the poetic line as a means of registering microtonal inflections. His achievement, in this respect, is just the opposite of the 'minimalism' that was often used to mischaracterize his work. Creeley's exquisitely precise lines measure the pressure of reality through their articulation of emotional rupture or turbulence. Breaking every two or three words, his lines also – and in contrast – can be read as materializing the language (making it linguistically concrete, heard as words as much as for what the words might mean). What from one perspective is an extremely fragmenting prosody is, from another, a highly charged music of felt intensities. The experience is one of rhythmically charged, exhilarating oscillation, as waves of thought break into particles of sound. While this achievement is present in his earliest work, it reaches its initial height in two collections, *Words* (1967) and *Pieces* (1969).[19]

In Bernstein's reading, then, Creeley's 'music of felt intensities' is replete: he clearly intends the echo of Pound in his use of the word 'charged'. I agree with Bernstein about the way short-form verse foregrounds the oscillation between sense and non-sense. I am less persuaded by the link between linguistic and emotional rupture that he argues for, and I find that the description of 'rhythmically charged' 'waves of thought' assigns a propulsive momentum to writing that is often hesitant and halting. Similarly, the word 'charged' suggests that feeling fills gaps in meaning or syntax. I suggest that what Eyers calls the 'creative capacity of impasses' may offer a way of thinking about both interruptedness and condensation as experiential qualities that, rather than opening the door to feeling, stand for nothing more than themselves. I find Bernstein's argument persuasive on the topic of 'minimalism'. I would make a distinction, however, between the poetics of reduction I identify in Creeley and other of the poets discussed in this book, and poetic minimalism, by which I understand the kind of writing in which brevity is an end in itself. I take the writing of Aram Saroyan as a prime example of this tendency, which I see as a kind of conceptual poetics. For all its virtues, Saroyan's writing is not motivated by the complex interactions between sense, line-ending, syntax, world and words that informs the poetry I focus on.

This book seeks to make an argument about the poetic efficacy of brevity through particular attention to the lineage that, in my reading, best exemplifies short-form techniques. I have sought to address what for me are the salient figures in this tradition. However, in focusing on this lineage, I have omitted to discuss a number of significant practitioners of short-form verse, besides Saroyan. Clearly, a different kind of book on this topic might have said more about Louis Zukofsky's verse. Instead I discuss the influence of his thinking on Oppen and Niedecker, the poets I consider to be the prime examples of the drive to post-imagist reduction in the Objectivist 'nexus'.[20] Zukfosky's example is clearly also important to Grenier. Cid Corman was a vital presence as an editor and publisher and as a friend and interlocutor of Niedecker. His editorial work on *Origin* magazine was essential in establishing the framework in which some of the poetry I discuss could flourish. However, I find that his Zen-influenced para-haikus lack the range and ambition of the writing of Niedecker, Oppen or Creeley. The work of Tom Weatherly, Clark Coolidge, Robert Lax, Thomas Merton, Stephen Jonas and Frank Samperi, all lies to one side of the argument I make in this volume, whether because they focus less stringently on what Blasing calls the 'triangular relationship' between subject, object and words, or because of a fundamentally theological poetics. (The latter, in my reading, is a variant of the symbolist investment in the trope of unsayability.)The short-form writing of Barbara Guest's later period (*Miniatures* and *The Red Gaze*, in particular) shares some characteristics with the writing discussed in this book.[21] However, despite her scrupulous commitment to a variegated modernist tradition, her work lives most fully in relation to a densely textured and interdisciplinary form of intertextuality. Of the Language generation, both Ted Greenwald and P. Inman have produced significant short-form work, and I draw on Ron Silliman's work as editor and critic when discussing the writing of Robert Grenier and Rae Armantrout. I mention some contemporary practitioners of short-form verse in my conclusion.

* * *

I will very briefly outline the contours of this book's argument. In my first chapter I discuss a topic that has received a great deal of attention in the past hundred years or so: Imagism. Even if the poetry of Imagism is patchy in practice, it is hard to overstate the impact that Pound's thinking on compression, and its various adaptations by Williams, Zukofsky, Creeley, Niedecker and others, had on the trajectory of the poetry of the twentieth century. The focus of my chapter is the equivocal status that brevity had for the odd ragbag of writers that Pound brought into the orbit of Imagism. I touch on Imagism's relationship to symbolism and oriental verse (topics that have been extensively covered by other critics), but do so with an eye to the question of short form. I describe what I call the 'pathos of insufficiency' and its role in the often mediocre verse that emerged under the imagist banner. I describe the successes of Pound's orientalist experiments with translation, but present H.D. as the poet who, through a re-encounter with a far more distant tradition, wrote the most rigorous short-form verse of the period.

In my chapter on Williams, I consider his relationship to Pound's writing and to the question of poetic economy. I argue that Williams's attention to line and stanza breaks is integral both to his concept of measure and his desire to write a specifically American kind of verse. I consider his preference for lower-case line-openings and I discuss the ways in which he addresses the things of the object-world. His poetry, like that of Oppen and Creeley, is often implicated in cognitive processes that are not fully acknowledged in the poets' critical writings.

I devote two chapters to Objectivism, in which my focus is on George Oppen and Lorine Niedecker. Zukofsky's short-form poetry and poetics are, of course, crucial to the writing of both poets, but I believe that Oppen and Niedecker practice more thoroughgoing versions both of the aesthetics of brevity and the encounter between word and object-world. Certain of Niedecker's works explicitly reflect on condensation as a poetic technique. I discuss her handling of short-form methods principally in relation to her very short poems, but also as it appears in some of the later serial poems. I discuss Oppen's differences from both Imagism and Zukofsky, and I consider Oppen's attitude towards sentence construction. I argue that his elliptical syntax removed his poetry far from the ideals of clarity, simplicity or directness that he was ostensibly committed to. I devote the bulk of the chapter to his early work *Discrete Series*, but I also discuss the later poetry's thinking about the making of poetry.

My chapter on Creeley begins with an analysis of the role that anger plays in his writing. I argue that Creeley's poetry of the 1960s shows an increasing self-awareness about poetic utterance, even as the diction of the writing itself becomes more immediate and colloquial. I assert that his treatment of issues of power and masculinity is inflected by his commitment to a conspicuously hesitant poetic style. The linebreak becomes a miniature crisis in such writing, and the lack of formal resolution in the work promotes a mode of being-in-the-world that is predicated on the refusal of holistic patterns of thought.

I then discuss the writing of a poet for whom Black Mountain's field poetics provided a powerful model: Larry Eigner. Eigner had a highly distinctive attitude towards both the space in which he moved (restricted by his disability) and towards page-space. I discuss his attitude towards the page and the line-by-line movement of his writing, with a focus on texts in which the line is reduced to a single word. Taking birds as an example, I discuss the blank, generic qualities of the objects in his apparently observational poems. I consider how brevity functions as an organising principle for a thoroughgoing and original poetics of perception.

My next chapter is devoted to a poet who was Eigner's carer in his later years: Robert Grenier. Grenier was strongly influenced by Creeley's 1960s work and the way he built on Creeley's innovations was crucial in establishing a bridging point between the New American Poetry and Language writing. This is the only chapter that does not discuss poetry that appears in book form: I focus on Grenier's 1975 work *Sentences*, discussing the implications for the idea of the series in this work, which is composed of 500 index cards bearing brief typewritten texts. I compare Grenier's innovation to the event scores of the Fluxus movement, I outline the relation of his poetry to imagination, and I describe the diversity of approaches to writing in *Sentences*.

In my final chapter, I discuss a writer who was part of the West Coast Language writing community from the 1970s until she recently moved away, and yet has always seemed at an odd distance from the poetics of this movement. Rae Armantrout has, from her very earliest published work, consistently written in a condensed, short-line mode. I discuss texts drawn from throughout her long career, focusing on the ways in which equivocation is built into the writing at the most fundamental levels. I address her treatment of the question of number, considering how Armantrout complicates the relations between line, stanza and poem units by dividing many of her poems into semi-autonomous sections.

Short-form writing belongs to a poetic disposition that cannot fully be accounted for by the poetics articulated by categories such as modernism, Imagism, minimalism, Objectivism, or lyric. While brevity is an obvious feature of the writing of now-canonical writers such as Williams and Creeley, its effects remain insufficiently appreciated. I argue that the poetry I discuss is writing of substance and moment. Techniques of foreshortening are integral to a mode of poetic experience that makes a virtue of the pause. The willed encounter with incompletion, impasse and non-resolution that characterises short-form writing amounts to a forceful and far-reaching style of poetic thinking.

Notes

1. Charles Altieri, 'Robert Creeley's Poetics of Conjecture: the Pains and Pleasures of Staging a Self at War with its own Lyric Desires', in *Self and Sensibility in Contemporary American Poetry* (pp. 103–31). Altieri has written extensively on Creeley and, while I differ on the point discussed here, I am indebted to his sensitive readings of Creeley's poetry.
2. Altieri, *Self and Sensibility*, p. 130.
3. A reappraisal of Ricoeur's term is central to Rita Felski's work on critique. Elsewhere, as in the work of Stephen Best and Sharon Marcus, 'symptomatic reading' (the critical tradition that pursues the latent or concealed within the text) is rejected in favour of what is evident rather than hidden. See Best and Marcus, 'Surface Reading: an Introduction' and the essays collected in the 2009 special issue of *Representations* that Best and Marcus co-edited.
4. Tom Eyers, *Speculative Formalism*, p. 1.
5. Armantrout, 'Chesire Poetics', in *Collected Prose*, p. 55.
6. Eyers, *Speculative Formalism*, p. 8, p. 1.
7. Eyers, *Speculative Formalism*, p. 32.
8. The term became a rallying point on both sides of the Atlantic in the 1990s for both radical and conservative poets and critics sceptical about Language Writing, and remained so for some of those hostile to Conceptual Writing.
9. For provoking thought about lyric, see criticism by Jonathan Culler, Mutlu Konuk Blasing and John Wilkinson (all of whom are mentioned this introduction), Gillian White's *Lyric Shame* and the online journal *Thinking Verse*.

10. Culler points to the range of theories of lyric, ultimately finding lyric value in such descriptors as 'incantatory', 'ritualistic, hyperbolic', 'abrupt' and 'disjunctive' (pp. 350–1). The hesitant movement of many of the poems I discuss places them at a considerable remove from any simple relationship with song, as does the care many of them take to avoid the conventionally sonorous.
11. John Wilkinson, 'The Weight of Words', p. 40.
12. Nicholls, 'Poetics of Modernism', p. 57. Pound, in his 'Affirmations: As for Imagisme', distinguishes between two kinds of image: one that is 'subjective' and changed when perceived by the mind, and one that is 'objective' and that remains 'intact' when it is drawn into the mind (pp. 374–5). Pound prioritises neither. In both cases, the image is 'a vortex or cluster of fused ideas and is endowed with energy' (p. 375).
13. Judith Balso, *Affirmation of Poetry*, p. 98.
14. Balso, *Affirmation of Poetry*, pp. 100–1.
15. Mutlu Konuk Blasing, *Lyric Poetry*, p. 147, n15.
16. Jonathan Culler, *Theory of the Lyric*, p. 168.
17. Georgio Agamben, *The End of the Poem*, p. 110.
18. Peter Osborne draws provocative parallels between Schlegel's fragments and Sol LeWitt's *Sentences on Conceptual Art*, arguing that, in the light of Schlegel's ideas of poetic becoming, Sol LeWitt's version of 'conceptual art appears as a further radicalization of the concept of Romantic poetry' (p. 67). The ideas of poetry that motivate the authors discussed in this book, however, tend to resist assimilation to the discourse of philosophical aesthetics.
19. Charles Bernstein, 'Hero of the Local: Robert Creeley and the Persistence of American Poetry', p. 374.
20. In the introduction to Rachel Blau DuPlessis and Peter Quartermain (eds), *The Objectivist Nexus: Essays in Cultural Poetics*, the editors explain their choice of the term 'nexus' to describe this diffuse non-movement (p. 19).
21. I discuss this period in Guest's work in my essay 'Sound Leads to Structure: Dissonant Lyricism in Barbara Guest's *Miniatures*'.

Chapter 1

Ezra Pound, H.D. and Imagism

While Imagism is typically given foundational status in the modernist line of anglophone poetry, it was produced by a grouping as confected and irregular as any in the long history of twentieth-century avant-gardes. Ezra Pound, obviously, is central to this conversation, but in this chapter I will also pay close attention to H.D., whose poetry was the most rigorous exemplar of imagist practice (even if Pound remained for many poets of the modernist line the pre-eminent model). I discuss austerity, clarity and directness in this writing, and the complex relationship that Imagism has with figures of the inexpressible, both in its highly mediated adaptations of poetry of the French symbolist tradition and in the literature of ancient Greece, China and Japan.

The relationship between the empirical and short form is usually taken as implicit by poets of the imagist and post-imagist line: a reduced style becomes an inevitable concomitant of this mode of writing. Yet the use of ellipsis and the handling of the linebreak in this poetry go a long way beyond the eschewal of ornamentation. There is a contradiction between the reduced style and the empirical ambitions of such poets – the desire for direct statement as a means of forging a relationship between object and artwork that is unmediated by the artifice of poetic language. The compression and ellipsis that characterises such writing, even at the level of the sentence, works against conventional sense-making, preventing the poetry from representing the things of the world with anything approaching directness.

However, the presentation of a demystified and unvarnished image of the world – Pound's ambition for a literature of 'precision' in the rendering of 'external nature, or of emotion'[1] – remained integral to the stated ambitions of many poets of the post-imagist line. In 1934, Pound wrote as though lack of precision in language use was ultimately responsible for the political catastrophes of his time:

As language becomes the most powerful instrument of perfidy, so language alone can riddle through the meshes. Used to conceal meaning, used to blur meaning, to produce the complete and utter inferno of the past century . . . against which, SOLELY a care for language, for accurate registration by language avails.'[2]

Language, in this view, was both the problem (the blur) and the solution (accuracy). The goal of the new poetry was to achieve an austere clarity that was at odds with the 'rhetorical din and luxurious riot' that characterised (to his eyes and ears) late Victorian verse.[3] Such restraint was rarely achieved by the imagists, even at their early best. In what follows, I will focus on the period 1914–16 that corresponds to the first two anthologies of imagist writing – *Des Imagistes* (1914, edited by Pound) and *Some Imagist Poets* (1915, edited by Richard Aldington and H.D.) – Pound's *Cathay* (1915) and H.D.'s first poetry collection *Sea Garden* (1916), which contains most of her contributions to the two early anthologies.

How can we assess 'direct treatment' when ellipsis is a key principle of the poem's operation? If the poet goes beyond excising 'rhetorical din and luxurious riot' and cuts into the syntactical and referential integrity of the poem, then, of necessity, the constituent elements of the poem, and the relationships between them, communicate meaning in a way that depends as much on what is missing as on what is present. For many of the early imagists, this missing element is a fundamental part of the poem, the unsaid coming to stand for the unsayable. Compression becomes a way of gesturing at extra-poetic emotional or even spiritual content that is otherwise felt to be inexpressible. In such writing, the spaces in the text soon become charged with an air of ineffability. However, the most valuable impetus of Imagism and the ensuing tradition discussed in this book is to potentialise opacity in ways that are not susceptible to such mystificatory co-option. The effects of ellipsis are undeniably hard to define or to assign a use to. Often they arise from the points at which the poem's communicative mission fails. They emerge as expressive residues left behind by acts of excision. The writers discussed in this study go far beyond the rejection of superfluity, reaching a point at which intelligibility – and thus any criterion of redundancy – is itself at issue. This is not, however, the point at which this line of poetic thought collapses in self-contradiction. Rather, it is where the poetry's more enduring strengths lie.

The critic and occasional poet Hulme, an early theorist of Imagism, called for economy in poetry. His 1908 'Lecture on Modern Poetry' emphasises clear definition: 'This new verse resembles sculpture rather than music; it appeals to the eye rather than to the ear. It has to mould images, a kind of spiritual clay, into definite shapes.'[4] And, in his 'Romanticism and Classicism', he called for 'accurate, precise and definite description'.[5] Pound admired Hulme enough to include five poems by the English poet-critic at the end of his own *Ripostes* (1912), albeit under the career-terminating heading of 'Complete Poetical Works' (Hulme was still in his twenties). Hulme was a member, with F. S. Flint, of the Poets' Club that met in 1908 and the subsequent 'school of images' grouping, whose meetings Pound began to attend in spring 1909). Like Pound, Hulme had a distrust of a formlessness and excess, which he aligned with a feminised emotiveness: 'I object to the sloppiness which doesn't consider that a poem is a poem unless it is moaning or whining about something or other.' Hulme advocated a return to a particular conception of classicism: one whose hard lines stood out against the 'sloppiness' of the romantic legacy. 'It is essential', he argued, 'to prove that beauty may be in small, dry things.'[6]

The word 'thing', corresponding to a kind of enigmatic objecthood, emerges at key points in Hulme's argument against abstraction. 'Poetry', he argues, 'always endeavours to arrest you, and to make you continuously see a physical *thing*, to prevent you gliding through an abstract process. It chooses fresh epithets and fresh metaphors, not so much because they are new, and we are tired of the old, but because the old cease to convey a physical *thing* and become abstract counters.' In this view, poetry aspires to the directness of a physical encounter with the world of objects. Cliché, for Hulme, is located in the disappearance of the physical immediacy of the fresh utterance. 'Images in verse are not mere decoration, but the very essence of an intuitive language', he continues. Whatever the nature of the verse, the poet should avoid 'conventional language' in order to capture the 'exact curve of the thing'.[7] Poetry is a privileged form that can innovate in this way. Conventional sense-making is at odds with the intuitive immediacy that poetry can communicate, and that immediacy corresponds more nearly to lived experience than mere intellectual endeavour. The new free verse has, crucially, a smaller compass of attention and reference than more conventional forms: 'the modern . . . no longer deals with heroic action, it has become definitely and finally introspective and deals with expression and communication of momentary phrases in the poet's mind'.[8]

As Hulme rejects slop in his pursuit of exactness, Pound rejects 'slush' and 'slither'. For Pound, the new poetry 'will be as much like granite as it can be . . . We will have fewer painted adjectives impeding the shock and stroke of it . . . austere, direct, free from emotional slither.'[9] It is striking that directness and emotion are held to be opposites. The concision that is recommended goes beyond the economical use of language, to encompass a rational cast of mind. In Richard Sieburth's reading, 'this passage combines a discernibly American, puritanical suspicion of ornament with a functionalist asceticism that we have come to recognize as a characteristic feature of the international style of high modernism'.[10] Such functionalism would later be evident in Williams's machinic conception of the poem. However, in much of the poetry that appears in the first two imagist anthologies, all of the slither and slop is reassigned to the margins of poems that, although brief, gesture clumsily at unspoken immensities.

It is striking that neither Pound nor Hulme in their various statements specifically encourage either short poems or short lines. Imagist theory aimed to bypass most of the figurative techniques that, for preceding generations, constituted the essence of the poetic. In Sieburth's terms, Pound was hostile to a decorative rhetorical mode that 'turns or tropes the poem away from the "thing" by foregrounding the literariness or intransitivity of the poetic utterance at the expense of its communicative function'.[11] Yet Pound signally fails in this regard, as do many of the poets and theorists he enlisted in support of his cause. For the more effective of Pound's followers, the technique of compression makes a virtue of the very 'intransivity of the poetic utterance' that was supposedly outlawed by his commitment to directness.

* * *

Imagism emerged not merely as an ideology of immediacy, a rhetoric of directness: it was also grounded in a commitment to insufficiency that had origins both in symbolism and in a form of literary orientalism. This dual debt to non-anglophone forebears has been widely discussed in literary criticism of the past half century. Although, of course, concision is noted in passing in almost any discussion of imagist poetics, the question of insufficiency has not received comparable attention. Frank Kermode, in a relatively early study, usefully argues that the Poundian aspiration to immediacy, a revelatory sympathy between word and object, is obstructed by the impossibility of jettisoning the prosaic and practicing Hulme's 'intuitive language':

> Pound, like Hulme, like Mallarmé and many others, wanted a theory of poetry based on the non-discursive *concetto*. In varying degrees they all obscurely wish that poetry could be written with something other than words, but since it can't, that words may be made to have the same sort of physical presence 'as a piece of string' [Hulme]. The resistance to words in their Image is explained by the fact that words are the means of a very different sort of communication; they are so used to being discursive that it is almost impossible to stop them discoursing.[12]

Words are not enough for these writers, in Kermode's view. Poetic language communicates something incommunicable by other means. Yet this is made present in poetry that, in its most naked form, seeks to share the mute and obdurate qualities of an object in the world. Clearly, there is a contradiction between the impulse to gesture at what words cannot capture (a legacy of Imagism's debt to symbolism) and the aspiration to direct statement. This contradiction is critical for our understanding of the role of concision in the early period of Imagism.

In his influential book *The Symbolist Movement in Literature*, Arthur Symons praises Mallarmé for his attention to the specifically poetic qualities of language and celebrates the precision of Mallarmé's writing: 'Words, he has realised, are of value only as a notation of the free breath of the spirit; words, therefore, must be employed with an extreme care, in their choice and adjustment, in setting them to reflect and chime upon one another; yet least of all for their own sake.'[13] Language here is only a secondary 'notation' of something more profound. The 'extreme care' Symons recommends in choosing and adjusting words might be read as an anticipation both of Pound's call for a 'care for language, for accurate registration' and the avoidance of conventional language counselled by Hulme. Yet for Symons, this care is a conduit to the 'free breath of the spirit': clarity, economy and precision open on to the ineffable.

While Pound and others sought to bypass the hieratic stance and metaphysical freight of symbolism, a symbolist commitment to an especially intense mode of signification became a central feature of early modernist poetics.[14] And, moreover, a metaphysical charge is frequently evoked in the imagist commitment to the conspicuously insufficient utterance. Many readers and students of imagist poetry are struck by the gaping void between imagist theory – as expressed in the famous 'Don'ts' and other now-canonical statements – and the actual writing that was published in *Des Imagistes* and *Some Imagist Poets*. In this poetry, there is a striking prevalence of motifs of solitariness, loneliness, bereftness, abandonment and incompletion. A swooning male sensibility, at once narcissistic and masochistic, persisted well into the twentieth century, with numerous poets signalling access to an elevated literary plane in figures of mournful insufficiency. An example of this voice can be found in the villanelle in James Joyce's *Portrait of the Artist as a Young Man*. In that book the poem's function is parodic, though it stems from Joycean juvenilia dating from 1900. In this poetic study in languid desire, the male speaker communicates unrequited love in language of sacramental intensity:

> Are you not weary of ardent ways,
> Lure of the fallen seraphim?
> Tell no more of enchanted days.
>
> Your eyes have set man's heart ablaze
> And you have had your will of him.
> Are you not weary of ardent ways?[15]

The villanelle is treated ironically in the novel, with much of the force of the irony deriving from the gap between the novel's sophisticated and knowing use of literary form and the outdated tenor of the protagonist's own art. Yet Joyce's contribution to the 1914 anthology *Des Imagistes*, 'I Hear an Army', which evokes a clangorous Celtic dreamscape, ends on a similar note of dereliction: 'My heart, have you no wisdom thus to despair?/ My love, my love, my love, why have you left me alone?' While Joyce never identified himself as an imagist, this quality of despairing solitude is apparent in numerous imagist texts. F. S. Flint's 'A Swan Song' is a case in point, published in his *In the Net of Stars* (1909) and then re-edited along imagist lines as 'The Swan' for *Des Imagistes*. The pre-imagist and imagist[16] versions are often compared as a way of illustrating imagist methods. When the figure of poet-speaker emerges in the first version, he is again weary, languid and sick of life. A brief example will suffice:

> And, Earth! my heart is weary this hot noon
> Of bearing life, your strange and secret gift.
> Lying upon this bank, I hear the rune
> Of springtime music, with my soul adrift
> Upon its stagnant waters, wondering why
> Thus rudderless I float askirt a shore,
> A drear savannah, Death.
>   With ardent eye,
> Inflamed with dreams of death and ancient lore,
> The wild swan watched and waited for the end
> Two hundred years of life its white wings bore.
> And I in weary truth my song would blend, —
> O heart of sombre lilies, why not now? —[17]

This, from Pound's point of view was how *not* to do poetry. The poem exhibits many of the tropes he was attacking when calling for a poetry that is 'austere, direct, free from emotional slither': the symbolism of the swan, the forlorn posture of the poet, the archaisms ('rune', 'drear', 'ardent'), the metaphysics ('my soul adrift') and heavy-handed metaphor (swans, lilies, song, etc). The second version of the poem appeared in *Des Imagistes* (1914), following robust advice from Pound, and it greatly benefitted from Pound's criticisms:

> Under the lily shadow
> and the gold
> and the blue and mauve
> that the whin and the lilac
> pour down on the water,
> the fishes quiver.
>
> Over the green cold leaves
> and the rippled silver
> and the tarnished copper
> of its neck and beak,
> toward the deep black water
> beneath the arches
> the swan floats slowly.
>
> Into the dark of the arch the swan floats
> and into the black depth of my sorrow
> it bears a white rose of flame.[18]

While the poem is a great deal shorter than the original, it seems unable to prevent itself from sinking, after two relatively economical stanzas of free verse, into a quagmire of sacramental melancholia. It depends on a clichéd image of inspiration: the awakening of the sluggish poetic soul in the encounter with the flaming spirit represented by the swan. As in the example from Joyce, the poem speaks from a position of insufficiency, looking outside the poem for completion. This gesture, combining spiritual or emotional lack with terse poetic form, is discernible in numerous texts in the period under discussion.

Flint was both a promoter of contemporary French poetry and one of the first literary critics to argue for the virtues of oriental verse. A preoccupation with the orient was nothing new in early twentieth-century London. Indeed, it was visible in the work of numerous artists, artisans and thinkers, from Horace Walpole through Whistler to Herbert Giles's translations from the Chinese and Lafcadio Hearn's books devoted to the mystique of Japan.[19] In the US, Henry David Thoreau's interest in Confucius provided an American model for the young Pound. Pound would deepen his knowledge of oriental literature through dialogue with Allen Upward, W. B. Yeats, Laurence Binyon and Yone Noguchi, and through his encounter with the unpublished materials on Japanese and Chinese literature passed on to him in 1913 by the widow of the scholar Ernest Fenellosa.

Flint makes the connection between symbolism and short-form Japanese poetry in an important review in the 11 July 1908 issue of the *New Age*.[20] Flint argues that Japanese literature – or rather, a highly orientalist reading of Japanese poetry – was of signal importance to the vanguard of anglophone poetry. Directness and concision are critical to the aesthetic he is seeking to describe. In his review he discusses several new works of poetry, including 'Sword and Blossom Song', by T. Hasegawa. In praising Hasegawa, Flint gives two examples of 'haikai', which he had found in the writings of the French critic Paul-Louis Couchoud and translated himself (thus prefiguring the highly mediated and layered translation-of-translation found in Pound's translations from both Chinese and Japanese):

> Alone in a room
> Deserted —
> A peony.

and:

> A fallen petal
> Flies back to its branch:
> Ah! a butterfly!

Couchoud's writings were an important influence on Flint. The French critic identifies brevity as the key impulse in Japanese poetry and questions the falsifying narrative implications brought by a 'chain' of connected words:

> Above all, Japanese poetry avoids wordiness and explanation. A single flower lies by itself on the snow. Bouquets are forbidden. The poem springs from an instantaneous lyric impulse, that wells up before thinking or passion have directed or made use of it ... Words are the obstacle. The chain of words introduces an elementary order that is already artificial.[21]

Flint's remarks communicate a similar aesthetic of reduction.[22] The figure of the 'single flower' would become a common imagist trope. He repeats Couchoud's assertion that in Japanese poetry, 'the half-said thing is dearest'[23] and then draws a parallel with the work of Mallarmé. Flint shares Couchoud's conviction that in the return to ancient Japanese literature there lies a pathway to the absolutely modern, a fulfilment of Mallarmé's obscure ambitions. He remarks that for 'the poet who can catch and render, like these Japanese, the brief fragments of his soul's music, the future lies open'. It is the idea of curtailment, not the image or symbol or the 'soul's music' that is the greatest innovation. Brevity is held to be indicative of unachievable fullness: a means of gesturing in language at what is inarticulable (in Flint's conventionally metaphysical terminology, the music of the soul – an echo of Symons's 'notation of the free breath of the spirit'). This truncation is imbued with a singular pathos: a solitary flower that is not simply alone but abandoned ('deserted'). In the second example, the fallen petal, the essence of *japonisme*, is resurrected in the butterfly, thus embodying tropes about the cyclical quality of nature, the flight of verse, and the unreliability of human perception. Both poems seem to redirect poetic perception from human subjectivity – the speaker is not psychologised and the apparent goal of each poem is simply to narrate an event in the natural world. Yet the pathos of fragile, forlorn beauty drives each poem, and, significantly, the formal quality of truncation points outside the poem. Something powerful, moving but unsayable is supposedly communicated by the petals delineated with such expressive economy.

Neither of Flint's culturally displaced haikus, of course, follows the formal rules that govern the Japanese haiku. However, it is clear from Flint's surrounding remarks that the short line is held to be instrumental in capturing the glancing instant of epiphanic perception that the poet seeks to communicate. The arrestedness of these lines is, in other words, a means of expressing the 'half-said thing'. Full statement is implicitly equated with the long line. Flint goes on to say that nature will drive the new poetry. He asserts that it will set aside traditional form and 'prefer more subtle rhythms and broken cadences, the song that will come and go like the wind on the leaf or the bourdon of a blond bee hovering over a bank of swaying mignonette' (thus combining both orientalist and French clichés).

The pathos of the solitary flower or petal or leaf can be found in numerous imagist texts. Aldington's 'The River', published in *Des Imagistes*, captures the melancholic super-position of flower and departure:

O blue flower of the evening,
You have touched my face
With your leaves of silver.

Love me for I must depart.[24]

His 'Choriços' draws a masochistic link between flowers and the ministrations of a personified and feminised Death:

And thou, leaning towards us,
Caressingly layest upon us
Flowers from thy thin cold hands,
And, smiling as a chaste woman
Knowing love in her heart,
Thou sealest our eyes
And the illimitable quietude
Comes gently upon us.[25]

Another example is found in the pathos of Flint's '[The grass is beneath my head]':

> Each leaf of the aspen
> is caressed by the wind,
> and each is crying.
>
> And the perfume
> of invisible roses
> deepens the anguish.[26]

And John Cournos's prose poem 'The Rose', also published in *Des Imagistes*, fuses rose, human heart and death:

> I threw the rose into the sea, and watched it, caught in the wave, receding, red on the snow-white foam, paler on the emerald wave.
> And the sea continued to return it to me, again and again, at last no longer a flower, but strewn petals on restless water.
> So with the heart, and with all proud things. In the end nothing remains but a handful of petals of what was once a proud flower ...

Far from approximating the rhythms of the natural world, such writing invests plants with meaningful weight that is dependent on highly wrought post-symbolist artifice. The relative fragility of plant-life serves as a convenient vehicle for a morbid insufficiency that points dolefully towards the inexpressible.

Pound, although a far more accomplished and self-aware poet than those cited above, was not immune to this trope. His 'Δώρια' in 'Des Imagistes' depicts a monochrome antiquity and the shadowy flowers of the underworld. The entire poem reads:

> Be in me as the eternal moods
>   of the bleak wind, and not
> As transient things are —
>   gaiety of flowers.
> Have me in the strong loneliness
>   of sunless cliffs
> And of grey waters.
>   Let the gods speak softly of us
> In days hereafter,
>   The shadowy flowers of Orcus
> Remember Thee.[27]

This text celebrates an inhospitable and grey eternity against the transience of the present moment. The 'shadowy flowers' of the afterlife are compared to the 'gaiety' of the living world. The flowers are the vehicles of subjective emotion, and the primary means of communicating the contrast between the ephemeral present and eternity. And, again, flowers are aligned with a positive depiction of morbidity.

Pound's celebrated 'In a Station of the Metro' is less emotional about the parallel it draws between faces in a city crowd and 'petals on a wet black bough'. However, the pathos of urban anonymity seems to bind the city-dwellers to the starkly individuated petals. For Pound, as for his imagist peers, the trope of the lonely flower allowed him to communicate insufficiency in a way that was co-extensive with the imagist drive towards formal reduction.

In his discussion of 'In a Station of the Metro' in the 1914 'Vorticism' essay, Pound praises the brevity of oriental models (there is little point in separating faux-Japanese from faux-Chinese at this stage in Pound's career).[28] He then cites a version of the butterfly poem that Flint had translated from Couchoud's French six years earlier in the *New Age* article discussed above. Pound praises the excision of metaphor from the haiku, and he discusses the 'super-position of one idea set on top of another'. The genesis of 'In a Station of the Metro', he writes, was a long process of condensation: it was a thirty-line poem, then a poem 'half that length', and finally, a year later, the much anthologised 'hokku-like sentence'. Pound is willing to allow that the poem might be 'meaningless', but the poet is 'trying to record the precise instant when a thing outward and objective transforms itself, or darts into a thing inward and subjective'. Importantly, this immediacy – this 'thing' – can never be fully captured in the verbal utterance, as it is the movement of thought itself.[29]

Imagism communicates the fleeting perceptual gestalt – a moment whose subsequent poetic reconstruction, recollected, as it were, in tranquillity, is quietly suppressed. The orientalised 'instant' is celebrated in more conventionally literary fashion in Flint's brief 'History of Imagism', published in the *Egoist* in May 1915. Flint praises Edward Storer for 'a form of expression, like the Japanese, in which an image is the resonant heart of an exquisite moment'. He remarks that before Pound had even made his entry into proto-imagist conversations, Flint, Hulme and other members of the Poets' Club had become disillusioned with 'English poetry as it was' and 'proposed at various times to replace it by pure *vers libre*' and by 'the Japanese tanka and haikai'. Pound's angry response contrasts the 'Hellenic hardness' of the female poet H.D. with the feminised softness ('custard') of Edward Storer.[30] Yet, while Pound, as we have seen, had sought to expel an excess that was coded as feminine from poetry, in fact such 'slither' is distinctly male-voiced in the writing promoted by Pound.

In his versions from the Chinese, Pound was heavily dependent on earlier translations, especially Herbert Giles's *History of Chinese Literature* (1901). Pound's changes to Giles's translations are instructive. His 'Liu Ch'e' reads as follows:

> The rustling of the silk is discontinued,
> Dust drifts over the courtyard,
> There is no sound of footfall, and the leaves
> Scurry into heaps and lie still,
> And she the rejoicer of the heart is beneath them:
>
> A wet leaf that clings to the threshold.³¹

This poem is an adaptation of a Chinese original, written about 150 BC. Giles's translation reads:

> The sound of rustling silk is stilled,
> With dust the marble courtyard filled;
> No footfalls echo on the floor,
> Fallen leaves in heaps block up the door . . .
> For she, my pride, my lovely one, is lost,
> And I am left, in hopeless anguish tossed.

In the Giles version, metre and rhyme are insistent and they weigh heavily on the movement of the verse. Such ponderous translations came to seem redundant in light of the fluid verses of *Cathay*, even as scholars lamented errors in Pound's translation. This is a poem of regret and loss occasioned, according to Giles, by the death of 'a harem favourite',³² but Pound's version leaves the context unclear. In his poem, the lost lover is compared, with no further explanation, to the wet leaf at the threshold. Pound uses near-identical means to Flint to evoke the pathos, with the leaf (recalling Couchoud's lonely flower) offered as an emblem of sorrow, yearning and unachievable fulfilment.³³

While Pound's heavily mediated translations from the Chinese did open new possibilities in the form and address of anglophone poetry, he was nonetheless susceptible in this writing to an aestheticised insufficiency that was embedded in the late Romantic and symbolist models he sought to reject. The subjective emotion of the Giles translation is replaced by the expressive wet leaf, yet this attempt to make a natural object bear the emotional freight of the poem is compromised by the peculiar cluster of negative affects that it is meant to represent. On this occasion, a poignant regret attaches to the loss of a particular source of pleasure. The pathos that stems from the super-position of lost lover and wet leaf is acutely gendered: it is a figure of bereft masculinity. The emotional force of the image depends on non-statement rather than the vaunted direct statement of imagist theory.

In more radical vein, Pound reduced Giles's ten-line version of a poem by the celebrated Lady Pan to a mere three lines.³⁴ Giles notes that the occasion of the poem was the Emperor's replacement of Lady Pan, long his 'chief favourite', with 'a younger and more beautiful rival'. Lady Pan, a favourite of the Emperor, evidently inscribed the poem on a fan which she gave him when he replaced her. Giles observes that 'the phrase "autumn fan" has long since passed into the language, and is used figuratively of a deserted wife'. So, once again, faced with an enormous range of potential source material, Pound chooses to use the tools of concision to communicate the pathos of abandonment. Here is Giles's original:

> O fair white silk, fresh from the weaver's loom,
> Clear as the frost, bright as the winter snow —
> See! friendship fashions out of thee a fan,
> Round as the round moon shines in heaven above,
> At home, abroad, a close companion thou,
> Stirring at every move the grateful gale.
> And yet I fear, ah me! that autumn chills,
> Cooling the dying summer's torrid rage,
> Will see thee laid neglected on the shelf,
> All thought of bygone days, like them bygone.

Pound's version, 'Fan-Piece for Her Imperial Lord', which he published in *Des Imagistes*, goes as follows:

> O fan of white silk,
>   clear as frost on the grass-blade,
> You also are laid aside.[35]

The Giles translation compares the fan to frost, snow and the moon: three natural images of coolness and pallor. Pound's version of the poem retains only one comparison, sharpening this to focus on a close-up of a single grass blade. The parallelism of the discarded fan and the lover, implicit in the Giles translation, is made explicit in Pound's version with the word 'also'. As with 'Liu Ch'e', the emotion of the narrator is projected on to an object described with conspicuous economy. The pathos of loss persists in both poems, and it depends for its effect on half-statement. There is, in both, an assimilation of short lines and various affects of incompletion. The lonely, languid, suffering, male sensibility of post-symbolist anglophone verse, readily discernible in numerous early imagist poems, is conveyed in verse that expresses the wound of separation through severe concision. (Even though the original text was written by a woman, it is ventriloquised by the poetic idioms of the male translators.) Truncation is the non-discursive enactment of loss, a means of communicating the narcissistic contemplation of wounds. Imagist claims to directness are tenuous indeed in Pound's translations from translations, in which effects of immediacy are sought in writing that is doubly (or even triply in the case of some of the Fenellosa derivations) removed from the original.

Almost all of the poems of Pound's *Cathay* express some quality of negative feeling: sorrow at parting, exile, abandonment or displacement. 'Lament of the Frontier Guard' expresses sadness at the futility of war; 'The River Merchant's Wife: a Letter', one of several epistolary poems, is addressed to an absent husband; 'The Beautiful Toilet' describes a courtesan neglected by a drunken husband; and 'The Jewel Stairs' Grievance' speaks of a neglected courtesan in words arrived at, according to Pound, after a 'mathematical process of reduction'.[36] Pound may have expunged emotional 'slither' from his poems, but it is certainly made present through evocation, and concision is the method through which such negative emotion is evoked.

For Pound, via Bunting, 'Dichten=condensare'. Poetry is 'the most concentrated form of verbal expression'.[37] Condensation and concentration are integral to Pound's early poetics. Yet Poundian insufficiency implies a kind of plenitude-to-come. As well as the stripping away of the merely decorative, Pound recommends a form of writing that is 'charged with meaning to the utmost possible degree'.[38] This notion of compression, then, implies not Hulme's 'dry' neoclassical vacuum, but quite the opposite: a potential for repleteness that verges on the explosive. In this highly overdetermined model, the condensed poem must communicate a great deal more than its brevity would suggest. Pound's poetry of this period is more formally inventive and self-aware than that of most of the poets he drew into the orbit of 'imagisme'. Yet even his writing remained indebted to intertwined tropes of melancholic inexpressibility and pathos that had their roots in the appropriation of French and oriental models.

As he moved away from Imagism, Pound was already leaving behind the idea of the short poem. 'I am often asked whether there can be a long imagiste or vorticist poem', he remarks chattily in a note at the end of his 'Vorticism' article. 'The Japanese, who evolved the hokku, evolved also the Noh plays. In the best "Noh" the whole play may consist of one image. I mean it is gathered about one image. The unity consists in one image, enforced by movement and music. I see nothing against a long vorticist poem.'[39]

* * *

The 1915 imagist-themed special issue of the *Egoist* that contains Flint's disputed 'History of Imagism' also contains a review article he wrote about the poetry of H.D. In this piece, he expresses certain reservations about H.D., suggesting that her writing 'owes nothing to common speech'[40] and remarking on her 'loneliness' as a poet committed only to 'what has come to her direct'. Needless to say, this disregards H.D.'s erudition. However, more salient for present purposes is the figure of loneliness, which is held to represent a disavowal of the tacit contract between writer and reader. He considers that her 'ceaseless scrutiny of word and phrase' are a great 'danger' to the comprehensibility of her writing:

> For in the creation of beauty and the simultaneous criticism of what is created, you can cut too far and produce angularity, or too curiously and produce enigma, which was the fate of Mallarmé. In all art, it seems to me, there must be generosity and some pity for the spectator; and you may fall short of generosity by withholding in order that the gift may be finer. The riddle the artist has always to answer is, How much shall he give; and the quality of his pity for the spectator will decide this. An artist cannot be inhuman and be understood. I say this because I think I have detected in one or two of H.D.'s later poems a tendency to pare and cut too far, with a consequent slight feeling, in the result, of bareness and jejuneness. But it is only slight; and there is more danger of her becoming inhuman, in the sense I have indicated.[41]

Flint correctly identifies the impulse to purge the imagist poem of psychologised speaker and addressee, and he is right to notice the scrupulous self-awareness of H.D.'s writing. However, in aligning his own sensibility with generosity and pity, in contradistinction to the lonely 'inhumanity' of her project, he fails to understand the communicative energies that might be unleashed by the impulse to 'pare and cut'. Indeed, the formal features that he isolates for criticism are, for many readers, the greatest strengths of H.D.'s early writing. What if the poem, rather than being 'understood' on Flint's terms, asks the reader for new forms of understanding?

The 'paring and cutting' that troubles Flint is comparable in phrasing to H.D.'s description of Pound's interventionist editing of her early poetic versions of fragments from the *Greek Anthology* – the creation myth of modernist poetry. In H.D.'s words, Pound 'scratched "H.D. Imagiste", in London, in the British Museum tea room, at the bottom of a typed sheet, now slashed with his creative pencil, "Cut this out, shorten this line" '.[42] In another account, H.D. writes that 'Hermes of the Ways' was 'a rough transcription of a short poem from the Greek Anthology', which Pound 'pruned ... into vers libre' ... 'It was one of those early poems that Ezra scrutinized and with a flourish of a large lead pencil, in the British Museum tea-room, deleted and trimmed or pruned or chiselled into the then unfamiliar free-verse.'[43]

Pound's paring and cutting was, according to H.D., crucial to her earliest published poetry, which was written at a time when she and Aldington saw Pound almost every day.[44] Yet her account of Pound's pruning understates her own role in formulating a distinctive poetics. All of the verbs used to describe his role involve cutting text, but, unlike Pound's versions from the Chinese, 'Hermes of the Ways' is an *expansion*, not a contraction, of the fragment entitled, in the *Greek Anthology*, 'The Orchard Corner' by the female poet Anyte. H.D.'s poem is considerably longer than the editor Mackail's translation from the original:

> I, Hermes, stand here by the windy orchard in the cross-ways nigh the grey sea-shore, giving rest on the way to wearied men; and the fountain wells forth cold stainless water.[45]

Perhaps what Pound 'trimmed' into 'Hermes of the Ways' was a relatively long-lined poem based on the fragment from Anyte. Or perhaps his intervention was less substantial than H.D., for reasons of her own, gives him credit for. Or perhaps accentuating the poem's 'free verse' qualities was Pound's chief role. Unlike *The Waste Land* manuscript, the evidence for the collaboration is not available. Whatever happened in that storied tea-room, the enigmatic and fragmentary quality of 'Hermes of the Ways' was achieved through a process of both expansion and contraction. The tiny prose fragment, translated into late nineteenth-century literary prose, is transformed again into a poetic text, and then again, through cutting, into the short, spare lines of the published work. H.D.'s poem inserts an almost featureless speaker who refers to Hermes in both the second- and third-person voices. The original, written in the third-century BC in the genre of the inscription, refers to a crossing point marked with a stone monument (not the messenger god of later Greek mythology). 'Hermes of the Ways' develops this image to make the monument a resilient and enduring feature of a harsh coastal environment in which the trees and fruit endure the battering of the wind. The poem, in other words, is entirely consistent with the poems on similar themes that H.D. would write in the years to come. It is likely, therefore, that while Pound made formal adjustments, the rigour and austerity of the poem's vision was entirely H.D.'s, and that Pound's brief but significant contribution was to help H.D. develop the short-lined free-verse aesthetic that would best communicate the themes of attenuation, resistance and violence that preoccupied her. However, while the impression of 'paring and cutting' is certainly a core feature of H.D.'s verse of this period, it is notably free of the pathos of insufficiency that I discuss above.

Pound, aided by his ignorance of the languages he translated, absorbed and propagated distinctly warped appropriations of Chinese and Japanese texts. H.D.'s source material was similarly inaccessible to the Western reader: the obscure and fragmentary writings of pre-Homeric Greece. On the face of it, H.D.'s poetry might appear to satisfy Hulme's call for a neoclassical return to austerity after the perceived excesses of late romanticism. But, as Carr points out, there is a strong likelihood that Jane Harrison's polemical *The Religion of the Ancient Greeks* shaped H.D.'s version of Greece: 'it is no longer the Victorians' masculine citadel of Homeric heroes or Athenian repose but an earlier, more elemental place where the struggles of the female psyche can be played out'.[46] Instead of an emergent demos, myth as social scaffolding and a heaven populated by a huge cast of demiurges, she was addressing a murky and irrecoverable world that was as foreign to anglophone poetry readers – even those with a familiarity with the Classics – as ancient Chinese.

Pound enthused about H.D.'s writing in the famous covering letter he sent with H.D.'s poems to the editor of *Poetry*, Harriet Monroe: 'Objective – no slither; direct – no excessive use of adjectives, no metaphors that won't permit examination. It's straight talk, straight as the Greek!'[47] However, while Pound's rhetoric is, as so often, forceful, it is by no means clear that H.D. shared either Pound's or Flint's reverence for directness. She would certainly come to question the term, and her later poetry is anything but direct. In a December 1916 review in the *Egoist* of John Gould Fletcher's *Goblins and Pagodas*, she writes: 'In the second section of his book, Mr. Fletcher deals with a more difficult and, when successfully handled, richer form of art: not that of direct presentation, but that of suggestion.' Taking up Fletcher's preface, in which he discusses the decoration of a Greek vase as a model for artistic creation, she continues:

> the images so wrought upon the body of the vase – the maenad, poised for ever, quietly for all the swirl of draperies and of loosened head-band, or the satyr for ever lifting his vine-wreathed cup – are satisfying and indeed perfect. But how much more for the lover of beauty is the wine within the great jar beautiful – how much more than the direct image to him are the images suggested by shadow and light, the flicker of the purple wine, the glint across the yellow, the depth of the crimson and red? Who would stand gazing at a satyr and a maenad, however adroit the composition of fluttering garment and poised wine-cup when the wine itself within the great jar stands waiting for him?[48]

By using such phrases as 'direct presentation' and 'the direct image' H.D. appears, following the publication of her first single-author volume earlier that year, to be marking her distance from the imagist aesthetic with which she had so strongly been identified (and which had been restated in Aldington's preface to the 1915 anthology *Some Imagist Poets*).[49] While she would in later years move towards a distinctly vatic mode of writing, I do not believe that there was an abrupt stylistic volte-face in 1916. Despite the manifesto-like statements that surrounded the early poems' emergence, the wilful inscrutability of H.D.'s writing is at least a salient feature as its directness. The technique of cutting in the writing of H.D., which is everywhere marked by formal incompletion, is integral to its effects. As I have argued, many of the poets associated with Imagism remained committed to a pathos of insufficiency: figures of loneliness, abandonment and exile. The formal parsimony of much imagist writing generates an atmosphere in which understatement is heavily emphasised, inviting the supposition that it is pregnant with unstated meaning. The cut of the linebreak often communicates the wounded sensibility of the male speakers of these poems. Even the poems Pound chose for his *Cathay* volume have, as we have seen, loss, exile and suffering in common – and some convey the male reader's pitying (to use Flint's term) contemplation of the deserted female, who like the solitary flower, is beautiful in her destitution. Imagist poetry typically communicates in a diffusely mournful register, notwithstanding the calls for directness, clarity and objectivity.

H.D.'s early poetry embodies such qualities more consistently, inaugurating a new relationship between form and emotion in anglophone verse. There is no plangent, narcissistic contemplation of a wound (cf. Aldington's 'Beauty Thou Hast Hurt Me Overmuch'); no projection of human feeling on to an isolated and fragile natural object ('The petals fall in the fountain,/ the orange coloured rose-leaves,/ Their ochre clings to the stone' (Pound);[50] and no celebration of unachieved relation as a mourning-motor for the poem (cf. Flint's 'Dear one!/ you sit there/ in the corner of the carriage;/ and you do not know me and your eyes forbid'). These poems, which communicate in what Denise Riley describes as 'spiky girlish hellenics',[51] allow effects of formal attenuation to enact resilience, not fragility. The contemporary moment is energised through contact with a distant historical other, and a long, supervening tradition of poetic self-expression is set to one side. An example of this poetic mode is 'Sea Rose', which appears in *Some Imagist Poets, 1915* and which is the opening poem of *Sea Garden*:

> Rose, harsh rose
> marred and with stint of petals,
> meagre flower, thin,
> sparse of leaf,

more precious
than a wet rose,
single on a stem —
you are caught in the drift.

Stunted, with small leaf,
you are flung on the sand,
you are lifted
in the crisp sand
that drives in the wind.

Can the spice-rose
drip such acrid fragrance
hardened in a leaf?[52]

The sea rose stands at a great distance from the wet petals, damp leaves and solitary blooms that populate the writing of H.D.'s male imagist peers. Although the poem adapts one of the oldest and most worn-out items in the poet's symbolic repertoire – the rose – it immediately takes issue with convention: 'harsh rose'.[53] Effects of compression are integral to the power of the poem. The adjectives to that are applied to the rose – 'meagre', 'thin', 'sparse' – are readily discernible in the form of the text. Yet these qualities, all typically pejorative terms, are here advantages. While the rose is 'caught' by the sea, 'flung' by sand and 'lifted' by wind, it survives and the message of its scent is powerful and singular. *Sea Garden* is a book of borderlands, outlining a seaside environment in which plant-life is hardened to hostile conditions. The rose in 'Sea Rose' is sturdy and enduring. It is compared favourably to the rose of an inland garden, which might correspond to the rose of more 'cultivated' verse convention. The sea rose, battered by circumstances and blown along a vast beach, emits a bitter and concentrated fragrance that is altogether more pungent than the convention of sweet scent would allow. H.D. invents a hardy category of plant: its solitude is a source of strength, not poignant fragility. While one might read the sea rose as an emblem of bruised but triumphant femininity, or as a record of the rigours of H.D.'s own self-actualisation as a poet, my belief is that this writing, while crucially inflected by female experience, is also the record of the emergence of a hard-edged and distinct mode of poetic thought, formed in the teeth of an often quite explicitly gendered form of adversity.

The attenuated form of this writing is not – or not merely – a token of triumph over difficult conditions. The compression and the cutting of the writing are its strengths. These are the conditions of an expressive mode that does not draw on incompletion either as an index of what has been lost, or as a gesture towards an metaphysical and extralinguistic fullness. This writing identifies curtailment as a self-sufficient (not insufficient) medium for cognitive experience. This experience is categorically distinct from what can be communicated by the uninterrupted line. H.D.'s sea wind scours the marine landscape mercilessly, revealing forms that are clear and singular. The poetic representation of this wind is entirely lacking the aestheticised masochism of Aldington's: 'Toothed wind of the seas,/ No man knows thy beginning./ As a bird with strong claws/ Thou woundest me,/ O beautiful sorrow.' The sensibility that animates H.D.'s writing survives the tooth and claw of the natural world, emerging with speech that is marked by the elements but which endures.

The flower poems of *Sea Garden* – 'Sea Rose', but also 'Sea Violet', 'Sea Lily' and 'Sea Poppies' – seem almost programmatically to use flowers to take issue with the pathos of insufficiency in the writing of her peers. The hardened leaf of 'Sea Rose' is very different indeed to the deserted peony or fallen petal of Flint's influential 1908 review; it is distinct, again, from the wet petals of 'In a Station of the Metro' or the 'wet leaf' of 'Liu Ch'e', or the wet petals (again) of 'Ts'ai Chi'h'. As Cynthia Pondrom argues, H.D.'s writing is not merely the example of imagist poetry that best bears out the precepts outlined by Pound, Hulme and Flint, it is the practice that made the theory possible: 'The Imagist poems of H.D. stand in sharp contrast to these early [imagist] poems of Pound and Aldington in clarity, sharpness, precision, objectivity, and the use of a presentational rather than a discursive style.'[54]

Throughout *Sea Garden*, H.D. marks her distance from the pathos of neglect and separation. The atmosphere of *Sea Garden* is not, whatever Flint argues, inhuman. There are minimal indications of human culture in a garden and shipping. H.D. invokes, like countless poetic forerunners, a pre-industrial past but she does not succumb to the lure of benign pastoral. Recurring motifs are flowers, trees, sea, sand, wind, heat, rocks, gods, honey and salt. The principal human figure is the speaker, although others are occasionally invoked. This speaker is resilient in poem after poem. Even the speaker of 'Loss', written for a drowned lover, professes gladness at the bereavement, because the gods have called the lover back. In writing by her male peers, the truncated presentation of such images might trigger a soul-stirring gesture in which feelings of pain and vulnerability are given a positive or even redemptive aesthetic gloss. Truncation in H.D., though, is comparable to the 'thin', 'sparse of leaf' rose: it is wiry and resilient, an attribute of strength. Rachel Blau Du Plessis argues that:

> These flowers of the sea gardens are of a harsh surprising beauty, slashed, torn, dashed yet still triumphant and powerful, despite being wounded, hardened, tested by exposure. These flowers propose an almost contemptuous

defiance of ease, of simple fashions of ripening. H.D. constructs flowers admired in ways and for motives far different from the view of lush ripeness in carpe diem roses.[55]

I would go beyond this remark to suggest that the 'slashed, torn' qualities of the writing are an endorsement of the communicative potential of an aesthetic grounded in cutting back. The flowers are emblems of formal as well as metaphorical power. Pound, in H.D.'s own words, 'slashed' her manuscript to help launch her as a poet, but she does something distinctive and original by insisting on the sturdiness and self-sufficiency of the short-form poem. Indeed, H.D.'s early writing is significant for the ways in which a harsh editing is imaged. The word 'slashed' occurs twice in 'Sea Lily', and the occurrence is significant:

> Reed,
> slashed and torn
> but doubly rich —

And:

> Yet though the whole wind
> slash at your bark,
> you are lifted up[56]

It is hard not to read both the reed and the bark as references to writing. A certain editorial violence is the creative energy that leads to the 'new beauty' in 'some terrible wind-tortured place'. No longer outsourced to Pound, editorial intervention happens in the course of writing. The austere, abrasive qualities of the poetry are evidence of a battered text. However, the foreshortening of the line and the abstention from the rhetorical resources of conventional literary language lead away from a poetics of loss, abandonment and exile. In most imagist writing, innovations in *vers libre* were accompanied with a sensibility that paraded its injuries, finding in them some guarantee of artistic credibility. In H.D.'s early writing, more than in *Cathay*, and more than in the work of the other imagists, the cuts made to the text in the pursuit of concision are presented not as a wound, but as a generative opacity. H.D.'s conspicuously damaged text is sufficient to itself, however oblique and truncated. The slashing and cutting of which it speaks does not point towards restitution, only towards communicating new forms of beauty.

Her repertoire of condensing gestures is broad. Repetition, acoustic echo, and abrupt line and stanza breaks all play a part. Similar effects are discernible in all of the poems to sea species invented by H.D.: 'Sea Violet', 'Sea Lily', 'Sea Iris' and 'Sea Poppies'. In 'Sea Lily', the entire poem is a testament to the endurance of physical assault and, again, the flower is hard: 'sand cuts your petal,/ furrows it with hard edge,/ like flint/ on a bright stone'. In 'Sea Iris', a 'brittle flower' is 'scented and stinging,/ rigid myrrh-bud, camphor-flower, /sweet and salt'. In 'Storm', the motif of the single leaf appears, only without the forlorn connotations we have encountered elsewhere in this chapter. The inhuman addressee of this poem is a violent storm, which batters the trees:

> you have broken off a weighted leaf
> in the wind,
> it is hurled out,
> whirls up and sinks,
> a green stone.[57]

This 'weighted leaf' has substance that causes it to sink. But the 'green stone' simply vanishes from the reader's contemplation. It is not offered as the token of evanescence or as the conduit to Symons's 'free breath of the spirit'. Wind is again an emblem of strength in 'The Sheltered Garden', in which the speaker betrays increasing frustration with the bland pink flowers of a cultivated garden, which represent 'beauty without strength'. In the remarkable conclusion to this poem H.D.'s speaker feels the violence of the elements:

> I want wind to break,
> scatter these pink-stalks,
> snap off their spiced heads,
> fling them about with dead leaves —
> spread the paths with twigs,
> limbs broken off,
> trail great pine branches,
> hurled from some far wood
> right across the melon-patch,
> break pear and quince —
> leave half-trees, torn, twisted
> but showing the fight was valiant.
>
> O to blot out this garden
> to forget, to find a new beauty
> in some terrible
> wind-tortured place.[58]

This is an iconoclastic credo of almost Futurist intensity. H.D.'s poetry of this period is far clearer in its desire to destroy than anything written by Pound, even in his Vorticist period. If the garden becomes a scene of devastation, H.D.'s chosen alternative is far from comfortable. The 'wind-tortured place' might well be within the pages of *Sea Garden*, through which blow a succession of harsh winds, continuations of the scouring wind that 'whips round my ankles' in H.D.'s breakthrough work, 'Hermes of the Ways'. Now the wind is asked to 'rend open the heat,/ cut apart the heat, rend it to tatters'.[59] Beauty lies in incompletion, emerging from the embrace of violent change.

I do not wish to argue that the history of the short-form line in modernist poetry is essentially H.D.'s: her work was, after all, not always easy of access, and Pound is clearly of greater significance to most of the poets I discuss. Many critics, since May Sinclair's 1927 identification of H.D. as the 'perfect Imagist', have observed that her early work is the best example of Imagism in practice.[60] My claim, rather, concerns short form: H.D.'s writing better exemplifies the impulse towards *condensare* in Pound's thought than his own poetry. The consequences of concision have been consistently overlooked in discussion of Imagism in favour of the discussion of directness, objectivity and the image qua image. But there is no reason to conclude that either directness or objectivity lend themselves to short-form poems, or that an image might better be communicated with short lines.

While imagist poems are typically brief and short-lined, that quality of curtailment is, in most cases, bound up with a wounded sensibility. In work that is far from 'objective', the emotional consequences of loss, separation, and absence are of paramount importance. Sometimes, this triumphantly wounded mental state is a mere cliché fed by Decadent or post-symbolist posturing: it is more or less undiluted 'slither'. In other cases, as with the poems of Pound's *Cathay*, the writing may communicate across generic and cultural boundaries in rich and complex ways, while still committed to a poetics that invests incompletion with a positive aesthetic value.

Mallarmé wrote that '*Nommer un objet, c'est supprimer les trois-quarts de la jouissance du poème qui est faite du bonheur de deviner peu & peu; le suggérer, voilà le rêve*' [to name an object is to lose three-quarters of the poem's joy, which comes from the pleasure of guessing little by little; to suggest, that is the dream].[61] Too many imagists were afflicted by the desire to suggest mystery by means of compression. Such elegant short lines allowed the 'thing' to be 'half-said' and thus to open on to inexpressible immensities. Pound's fine poem 'The Return', based on the relatively little-known 'Médailles d'Argile' by the symbolist forebear Reignier, is a case in point: brief, elliptical and steeped in the mystery of returning divinities.[62] Even H.D.'s writing, for all its terse embrace of the hardy, weathered and resilient flora of coastal regions, sought the mysterious resonance of inaccessible pre-Homeric deities. However, H.D.'s poems of this period have a countervailing anti-metaphysical edge, removing the poem far from any historical or cultural moment recoverable by H.D. or her contemporaries, and opening up the possibility of a wild, violent and uncultivated form of beauty. This openness to abandon, which is the antithesis of the poised neoclassicism of Hulme's 'small dry things', is clearly at odds with the severe restraint of the lines. The resulting conflict, between austerity and violence, is the source of the poems' mould-breaking energy.

Imagist theory was a nexus of thought from remarkably different times and places. In the best such work, collage, interruption and incompleteness served to communicate the withdrawal from rhetorical excess. In this way such poems act as a gesture of refusal in the face of a literary culture burdened with ideologies that could not outlast the First World War. The primary impulse behind Pound's desire for directness was to demystify. However, such directness proved a chimera, particularly when the 'charging' of poetic language through condensation militated so effectively against directness. The function of compression in the ensuing tradition is not – as in the earliest imagist work – to suggest lagoons of mournful affect. It is to ask language to contemplate its own self-sufficient unfolding.

Notes

1. Pound, 'A Retrospect', *Literary Essays*, p. 11.
2. Pound, 'Date Line', *Literary Essays*, p. 77.
3. Pound, 'A Retrospect', p. 12.
4. Hulme, 'Lecture on Modern Poetry', *Selected Writings*, p. 66.
5. Hulme, 'Romanticism and Classicism', *Selected Writings*, p. 78. At the end of this essay Hulme distinguishes between ineffability and the unrepresentable: 'The intellect always analyses – when there is a synthesis it is baffled. That is why the artist's work seems mysterious. The intellect can't represent it. This is a necessary consequence of the particular nature of the intellect and the purposes for which it is formed. It doesn't mean that your synthesis is ineffable, simply that it can't be definitely stated' (p. 82).
6. Hulme, 'Romanticism and Classicism', p. 75, p. 78.
7. Hulme, 'Romanticism and Classicism', p. 80 (my emphasis).
8. Hulme 'Lecture on Modern Poetry', p. 63. Helen Carr argues in *The Verse Revolutionaries* that Hulme 'was very taken by [Remy] de Gourmont's argument (a development of Nietzsche's view of language) that poetry introduced fresh and vital metaphors into the language, which would eventually pass as dead metaphors, or in Hulme's terms, "counters", into prose' (p. 161).
9. Pound, 'A Retrospect', p. 7, p. 12. Whether or not by design, Pound's phrasing echoes the apparent argument in George Herbert's 'Jordan (I)': 'May no lines pass, except they do their duty/ Not to a true, but painted chair?'
10. Richard Sieburth, 'In Pound we Trust', pp. 148–9. For Sieburth, there is

a lurking misogyny to Pound's language at such moments. This prefigures both his economic theory and his anti-semitism: 'The phallic metaphors that dominate Pound's imagist and Vorticist polemics clearly designate the Other or the excess that needs to be vigorously eliminated from contemporary art as somehow feminine or excremental – soft, slushy, slithery, ambiguous, indefinite, internal' (p. 149).

11. Sieburth, 'In Pound we Trust', pp. 149–50.
12. Frank Kermode, *Romantic Image*, p. 157. Kermode argues that Hulme is not even successful in his adaptation of French models: 'the Hulmian Image – precise, orderly, anti-discursive, the product of intuition – is the Symbol of the French poets given a new philosophical suit ... once it is granted that Hulme was trying to do much the same thing as Mallarmé, it becomes evident that he did not do it very well' (p. 154).
13. Symons, *The Symbolist Movement in Literature*, pp. 130–1.
14. Pond's imagist period comes after he had moved on, with Ford Madox Ford's help, from an early style memorably characterised by Hugh Kenner as 'Rosettian tosh' (*The Pound Era*, p. 92).
15. Joyce, *Portrait of the Artist as a Young Man*, p. 223.
16. Cyrena Pondrom notes that in an angry letter of July 1915, in which Pound disputed the origins of Imagism with Flint, the American poet cited the difference between the two swan poems as exemplary of Imagism's innovations ('Selected Letters From H.D. to F. S. Flint', p. 563).
17. Flint, *In the Net of Stars*, pp. 21–3, p. 21.
18. Pound (ed.), *Des Imagistes*, p. 35. Flint, according to Pondrom, was not persuaded that this was the better poem (Pondrom (ed.), 'Selected Letters from H.D. to F. S. Flint', p. 563).
19. This environment is sketched in Carr, *The Verse Revolutionaries*, pp. 190–2.
20. Flint, 'Recent Verse', *New Age,* 11 July 1908, pp. 212–13.
21. Couchoud, as translated by Carr, *The Verse Revolutionaries*, p. 172.
22. Carr observes: 'Hulme had the theory; Flint had found the form. The haiku's qualities of simplicity, brevity, fusion and instantaneous impact were all to be central to later Imagism' (p. 172).
23. As translated by Flint ('Recent Verse', p. 212).
24. Richard Aldington, in Pound (ed.), *Des Imagistes*, p. 16.
25. Aldington, in Pound (ed.), *Des Imagistes*, p. 9.
26. Flint, in Pound (ed.), *Des Imagistes*, p. 34.
27. Pound, in Pound (ed.), *Des Imagistes*, p. 41.
28. In 'Vorticism', in *A Memoir of Gaudier-Brzeska*, pp. 81–94. Pound is notably casual about national distinctions: 'The Japanese have had the sense of exploration. They have understood the beauty of this sort of knowing. A Chinaman said long ago that if a man can't say what he has to say in twelve lines he had better keep quiet. The Japanese have evolved the still shorter form of the hokku' (p. 88).
29. Pound, 'Vorticism', p. 89.
30. Cited in Helen Carr, *The Verse Revolutionaries*, p. 766.
31. Pound in Pound (ed.), *Des Imagistes*, p. 44.
32. Herbert Giles, *A History of Chinese Literature*, p. 100.
33. In his book *Orientalism, Modernism, and the American Poem*, Robert Kern describes how Pound uses wilfully awkward phrases such as 'she the

rejoicer of the heart is beneath them'. In so doing, he argues, Pound 'invents Chinese for the English reader, in part, by defamiliarizing his English' (p. 186). Zhaoming Qian, in *Pound and China*, notes the ways in which Pound 'foreignises' his translations more than other translators, including Giles: the bowing of heads over clasped hands in 'Taking Leave of a Friend', for example, is a Poundian invention that depends on received ideas of Chinese behaviour (p. 36). In *Cathay: Ezra Pound's Orient*, Ira Nadel finds that Pound's experimentalism survives the orientalist clichés: 'The basic tension in the collection is, in fact, that between the world imagined by the conventional term "Cathay" and the originality of Pound's English text' (p. 55). Ming Xie's *Ezra Pound and the Appropriation of Chinese Poetry: Cathay, Translation, and Imagism* contains thoroughgoing discussion of Pound's orientalism.
34. The poem is found a page further into Giles's *History* than the source for 'Liu Ch'e'.
35. Pound (ed.), *Des Imagistes*, p. 45.
36. Pound, *Early Writings*, p. 298.
37. Pound, *ABC of Reading*, p. 30.
38. Pound, *ABC of Reading*, p. 30.
39. Pound, 'Vorticism', p. 109.
40. Flint, 'The Poetry of H.D.', *The Egoist*, 1 May 1915, p. 73. Flint is alluding to the preface to *Some Imagist Poets*, 1915, primarily authored by Aldington, which makes the use of 'the language of common speech' the first precept uniting the imagists. His appraisal of H.D. is more nuanced and generous than that of Harold Monro in another article in the issue: 'It is petty poetry; it is minutely small: it seems intended to be . . . Such reticence denotes either poverty of imagination or needlessly excessive restraint' (p. 79).
41. Flint, 'The Poetry of H.D.', p. 73.
42. H.D., *End to Torment: A Memoir of Ezra Pound*, p. 18.
43. H.D. papers, cited in Carr, *The Verse Revolutionaries*, p. 491.
44. Carr, *The Verse Revolutionaries*, p. 424.
45. Mackail, J. W. (ed.), *Selected Epigrams from the Greek Anthology*, p. 207.
46. Carr. *The Verse Revolutionaries*, p. 495.
47. Pound, *Selected Letters*, p. 11.
48. H.D. 'Goblins and Pagodas', p. 183.
49. Rachel Blau DuPlessis, in *H.D.: The Career of that Struggle*, argues that H.D.'s 1920s prose works were a means of rebelling against her ' "canonisation" as Imagist saint (miracle worker and icon)' (p. 31). In a 1929 letter to his estranged wife, Aldington wrote 'Ezra may have "invented" Imagism but, after all, you wrote the poems' (cited in Diana Collecott, *H.D. and Sapphic Modernism*, p. 136).
50. Aldington and Pound, in Pound (ed.), *Des Imagistes*, p. 13, p. 46; Flint in Aldington and H.D. (eds), *Some Imagist Poets*, p. 58.
51. Denise Riley, *The Words of Selves*, p. 96.
52. H.D., *Collected Poems*, p. 5.
53. Comparably noncomformist modernist roses can be found in Pound's 'a rose in the steel dust', from Canto 74; Williams's 'obsolete rose' in *Spring and All*; and Stein's famous 'a rose is a rose is a rose'.

54. Cyrena Pondrom, 'H.D. and the Origins of Imagism', p. 93.
55. Rachel Blau DuPlessis. *H.D.: The Career of That Struggle*, pp. 12–13.
56. H.D., *Collected Poems*, p. 14.
57. H.D., *Collected Poems*, p. 36.
58. H.D., *Collected Poems*, p. 21.
59. H.D., *Collected Poems*, p. 25.
60. May Sinclair, cited in Collecott, *H.D. and Sapphic Modernism*, p. 135. For many of H.D.'s admirers in the years since the revival of her reputation – Robert Duncan, Collecott, Peter O'Leary, Blau DuPlessis – the later work is of greater interest than that of the brief imagist period.
61. Translation mine. Mallarmé cited in Christopher Butler, *Early Modernism*, p. 6.
62. Barbara Guest, in her H.D. biography, *Herself Defined*, speculates that 'The Return' gave H.D. the impetus to develop her early style (p. 45).

Chapter 2

William Carlos Williams

William Carlos Williams's commitment to short form is evident even in his very earliest works. The antiquarianism of that period notwithstanding ('Lady of dusk-wood fastnesses, / Thou art my lady' *CPW*1, 4),[1] there is a more salient commitment to brevity and a concomitant objectivity of perspective.[2] This modernity of tone is more visible than in the early work of Ezra Pound, whose interest in Provençal troubadours, the writers of the Italian Renaissance and Browning – among other influences – caused his writing to be studded with archaisms. In Williams, the second term in Pound's equivocal relation between 'a thing outward and objective' and 'a thing inward and subjective' falls away. The thing or object, the ostensible focus of the poem, is located externally. It is no longer located in the transaction between inner and outer worlds. As a consequence, the action of the perceiving consciousness, or the subjective moment in the act of writing, is communicated through Williams's handling of poetic form. This is especially true of Williams's writing of the 1920s and 1930s, which is the focus of this chapter.

Williams always acknowledged his debt to Pound. He first met him at the University of Pennsylvania while he was a medical student, later remarking, 'before meeting Pound is like B.C. and A.D.'[3] He sustained a correspondence with Pound, part of which features in his important prologue to *Kora in Hell: Improvisations*. While his *Autobiography* indicates that he found Pound an infuriating presence in person, there is no doubt that the elder writer's activity as a poet and editor were crucial to Williams.[4] In his *Autobiography* he remarks that he and his generation 'had followed Pound's instructions, his famous "Don'ts", eschewing inversions of the phrase, the putting down of what to our senses was tautological and so, uncalled for, merely to fill out a standard form'.[5] Above all, however, a renovation of the poetic line was crucial: 'To my mind the thing that gave us most a semblance of a cause was not Imagism, as some thought, but the line: the poetic line and our hopes for its recovery from stodginess. I say recovery in the sense that one recovers a salt from solution by chemical action.'[6] The metaphor suggests a process of transformation through precipitation. Importantly, however, the Williams's attention is on the 'how', not the 'what' of the poetic utterance: the 'poetic line'. In Williams's practice as a poet, it is impossible to separate 'line' from 'linebreak'. His renovating 'recovery' of the line was also a truncation of the line. He excised 'stodginess' and the 'tautological' through a process of reduction that brought simplicity of diction into play with the persistent but irregular mini-jolt of the linebreak.

The second poem in the 1913 volume *The Tempers* (published with a somewhat overheated introduction by Pound), 'Postlude' (*CPW*1, 3), is included in the 1914 anthology *Des Imagistes*. Its language is akin to H.D.'s classicism and its lines are very short ('O, prayers in the dark!/ O, incense to Poseidon!/ Calm in Atlantis' (*CPW*1, 4)).[7] 'Portent', also in *The Tempers*, contains lines of only one and two syllables ('Lo! how/ The winds blow now!' and 'Wild/ In afright!' (*CPW*1, 10)). Williams's 1914 poem 'Aux Imagistes' seems to be a direct response to Pound's 'In a Station of the Metro', published in *Poetry* magazine in 1913. His speaker commends the 'frost bitten blossoms' against the 'envious black branches', continuing:

> Bloom quickly and make much of the sunshine.
> The twigs conspire against you!
> Hear them!
> They hold you from behind!
>
> You shall not take wing
> Except wing by wing, brokenly,
> And yet —
> Even they
> Shall not endure for ever.
>
> (*CPW*1, p. 40)

Williams recasts Pound's opposition between black and white into a more traditional reflection on transcendence and the ephemerality of beauty. The pathos of 'brokenly' and the studied poeticism of 'take wing' indicate that Williams, like most of those associated with Imagism, was far from rigorous in his commitment to the supposedly austere precepts of the movement. However, the severe contraction of the lines lends the poem a prickly dynamism that Williams would exploit in later work. The four complete and closed syntactical units of the first stanza cited are followed by a final stanza containing a single long, broken sentence in which syntactical breaks and linebreaks do not coincide. Williams's experiments with linebreaks and ellipsis clearly gave him the confidence to embrace uncertainty in his work. *Al Que Quiere!* (1917) contains a poem as brief and enigmatic as the four-line 'El Hombre':

> It's a strange courage
> you give me ancient star:
>
> Shine alone in the sunrise
> toward which you lend no part!
>
> (*CPW*1, p. 76)

The poem seems to praise the morning star for its self-sufficiency, claiming it for neither the larger dawn nor the poet's own designs.[8] In 1919 he published a sequence of poems, 'Broken Windows', in *Poetry* that contained some remarkable miniatures, accelerating the drive to reduction in his work. One of these is dwarfed by its humorously excessive title, 'To be Closely Written on a Small Piece of Paper which Folded into a Tight Lozenge will Fit any Girl's Locket'. The poem itself runs to only eleven words over three lines:

> Lo the leaves
> Upon the new autumn grass —
> Look at them well...!
>
> (*CPW*1, p. 123)

The poem, presented as a kind of keepsake, urges an act of attention. Williams's advice is simply to look. Again, it is worth noting that this looking is a sceptical encounter with Nature, a disabused pastoral. Rather than sustaining a plangent Keatsian autumn, the punning 'Lo' of this poem places the emphasis on the contrast between new growth and falling leaves. The reader is urged not merely to contemplate mortality, but to consider it in relation to the relentlessness of new beginnings. In a very compressed way, the text anticipates the bold embrace of the new in the poem later entitled 'Spring and All' – itself a rejection of the threnody on spring that opens Eliot's *The Waste Land*. Also in the 1919 sequence are 'Spring', which has only two lines, and a poem with the Creeleyesque title of 'Lines':

> Leaves are greygreen,
> the glass broken, bright green.
>
> (*CPW*1, p. 159)

Williams is already beginning to associate his shortest poems with an encounter with the natural world. Here the contrast is not between red-brown autumnal leaves and green grass, as in 'To be Closely Written ...', but between 'greygreen' leaves and 'bright green' *glass*. The poem uses an imagistic 'chord', setting two elements against one another, but this miniature is twisted by William's ability to pun with readerly expectations – the disjunct between the bright green 'grass' we might expect and the broken green 'glass' that the poem offers us.[9] The poem invites the reader to weigh the natural world and human artefacts against one another, and, once again, to pay close attention. Yet this paying attention to the world, becomes, despite itself, an analogy for the attention of the reader to the unfolding poem: the shift from 'grass' to 'glass', urging us to look at the minute detail of the text itself.

While 'Lines' makes a bald statement of Williams's interest in compression, his 'Spirit of '76' is a seven-line poem, framed within a prose letter pleading for the use of 'small letters at the beginning of my lines' (as opposed to capitals).The addressee is the editor of *Poetry*, Harriet Monroe, and the letter and the poem it contained were published in the June 1920 issue of the magazine:

> Her father
> built a bridge
> over
> the Chicago River
> but she
> built a bridge
> over the moon.[10]
>
> (*CPW*1, p. 128)

The letter suggests to Monroe that the poem is 'very American' but that it will not be bound by 'prehistoric prosodic rules'. This composite letter-poem recommends a specifically American prosody. For Williams, the focus, once again, is on the line. He seeks to dispense with the convention that erects a typographical barrier between lines. He clearly objects to the way in which initial capital marks the beginning of the line as an emphatic break from the previous line. The removal of the initial capital letter has the effect of quietly accentuating the fact of the linebreak, which now stands alone as the sole demarcation between one line of verse and the next. (Many subsequent poems only use capital letters where Williams specifically wanted to indicate a new sentence in the absence of punctuation.) Lower-case openings to lines allowed for more subtle effects of demarcation and were integral to his project. From 1916 on, Williams dispensed with automatic initial capitals after linebreaks, making his point repeatedly in conversations with Monroe. After the publication of 'Spirit of '76', *Poetry* acceded to Williams's requests on this key formal issue.

One significant feature of Williams's 'very American' mission was to forge a linguistic art form from contemporary materials: he was himself the son of a migrant, seeking to gain access to the polyglot energies lurking beneath the surface of twentieth-century American English – the language 'out of the mouths of Polish mothers'.[11] Critical discussions of his work have often focused on this notion of the American voice, as well as his antipathy towards the acquired Europeanness and pessimism of that 'subtle conformist' Eliot,[12] the inconsistent and confusing idea of 'measure' in his later work, his use of citation, his ideas of locality, and the relationship between ideas and things in his writing. Yet very little has been said about his career-long fascination with the short line as his chosen vehicle for the American idiom.[13]

Sour Grapes, published in 1921, includes poems of mixed forms, even the prose poem 'The Delicacies', along with the imagistic miniatures contained in the 'Broken Windows' series discussed above. The final poem of the volume, 'The Great Figure', is the best known:

> Among the rain
> and lights
> I saw the figure 5
> in gold
> on a red
> firetruck
> moving
> tense
> unheeded
> to gong clangs
> siren howls
> and wheels rumbling
> through the dark city.

(*CPW*1, p. 174)

In this poem, rather than serving the meditative stasis of the Imagist tradition, the short, sub-phrasal lines communicate the dynamism of the urban scene. The poem does not settle on a single moment of quasi-epiphanic insight. Each line is dedicated to a unit of perceptual experience. The fire truck is encountered through the number 5, a bold but meaningless emblem that flashes noisily past. The single-word line 'moving' is placed at the centre of the poem, the seventh of thirteen lines. Yet it is followed by two single-word lines – 'tense/ unheeded' – that suggest that the clangour of the truck's passage means nothing in the streets of the 'dark city'. The tension belongs to the machine and the machinic poem, not to the urban scene. The perception of the single poet-speaker is relativised: other passers-by evidently do not notice the emergency vehicle. The vibrant audio-visual impact of the fire engine becomes an example of art within the everyday. Rather than the pathos of the aestheticised nature represented by the solitary flower, we are presented with a ready-made art encountered in the moment and derived from industrial design (the size, typeface and colouring of the number on a moving background). The 'figure 5' is given a mobile backdrop, producing an entirely different effect to the characteristic static tableau of imagism. The poem appeals both visually – lights, red, gold, dark – and acoustically – clangs, howls, rumbling – yet neither the '5' nor the sounds communicate anything meaningful to either onlookers or the reader.

Williams had a close interest in the visual arts, particularly at this stage in his life. This, rather than Pound or Eliot's literary archaeology, was an important source for the ideas in his writing.[14] He was a member of the New York avant-garde grouping the Others, and an attendee at the 291 Gallery. Figures such as the American photographer Alfred Stieglitz and the painters Charles Demuth and Marsden Hartley were of lifelong significance to him (Demuth, the dedicatee of *Spring and All*, produced a painting in response to 'The Great Figure').

In his Prologue to *Kora in Hell*, the first section of which was published in the *Little Review* in 1919, Williams places himself in the Dada-suffused New York of the 19-teens, referencing Mina Loy, Marianne Moore, Marcel Duchamp, and others. This social context is bolstered by excerpts from his correspondence with Pound, H.D. and Stevens, all of whose letters he cites at length. He remarks that 'Nothing is good save the new', echoing Pound, yet Pound and Eliot are, ultimately, dismissed:

> It is silly to go into a puckersnatch because some brass-button-minded nincompoop in Kensington flies off the handle and speaks openly about our United States prize poems. This Mr. Jepson ... is not half a fool. ... Upon the Jepson filet Eliot balances his mushroom. It is the latest touch from the literary cuisine, it adds to the pleasant outlook from the club window. If to do this, if to be a Whistler at best, in the art of poetry, is to reach the height of poetic expression, then Ezra and Eliot have approached it and *tant pis* for the rest of us.[15]

On the other hand, Williams praises the radicalism of Moore and Loy: 'By divergent virtues, these two women have achieved freshness of presentation, novelty, freedom, break with banality.'[16] However, the closest analogy to the freedom he himself pursues is to be found in his references to Marcel Duchamp:

> According to Duchamp, ... a stained glass window that had fallen out and lay more or less together on the ground was of far greater interest than the thing conventionally composed *in situ*.[17]

This idea of a comparably disarranged and improvisatory text appears in Williams's Prologue:

> If the inventive imagination must look, as I think, to the field of art for its richest discoveries today it will best make its way by compass and follow no path.[18]

Williams objects to a 'scientific' mode of encountering the world, just as he rejects the 'atavistic religionists' he associates with H.D.'s commitment to the 'sacred', favouring a more diffuse and straying mode of attention ('a more flexible, jagged resort'). In this early period, the prose improvisation appealed to him as one means of registering the world of things, 'close to the nose', and representing the 'divergent' onrush of sensations occasioned by the real in a suitably open way. However, the more enduring commitment in his writing is to a short-form mode that, similarly, responds to the 'detail' that is 'immediately before' the senses, but that is purged of the flamboyant associative straying of his early experimental prose.[19]

When Williams writes of bringing a 'more flexible, jagged resort', and a loosened attention to the 'things that lie under the direct scrutiny of the senses', his first response is prose improvisation. Yet it is his poetry, with an intensifying linebreak that served to isolate each 'detail of the world' that best approximates the 'flexible, jagged' representation of the world that he was looking for. Williams approvingly refers in his autobiography to early Duchamp artworks such as 'Nude Descending a Staircase' – a snapshot-by-snapshot parade of sequential moments – and 'Fountain', a foundational gesture of recontextualisation. However – and oddly – nowhere, whether in Williams's own writing or in the contemporary commentary in his writing, is there any extended discussion of the origins of his interest in short lines and short poems.

One significant literary model, however, was another writer immersed in the visual arts, Gertrude Stein. In his *Autobiography*, just after a brief discussion of Objectivism, he refers to his debt to Stein in the following terms:

> It must be the purpose of the poet to make of his words a new form ... [I]t was Gertrude Stein, for her formal insistence on words in their literal, structural quality of being words, who had strongly influenced us . . . It all went with the newer appreciation, the matter of paint upon canvas as being of more importance than the literal appearance of the image depicted.[20]

And, in his 1931 essay on Stein (co-authored, according to Peter Quartermain, with Louis Zukofsky):[21] 'Stein has completely unlinked words ... from their former relationships in the sentence ... she has gone systematically to work smashing every connotation that words have ever had, in order to get them back clean.'[22]

Williams's interest, via Stein, in words *as* words and words decoupled from syntax is brought into contact with the incipient formalism in the new art: the technique of representation being of greater significance to Cubists, for example, than the actual image represented.[23] In his essay on Stein, Williams privileges 'movement' as a category, managing both to praise Stein and to evoke Keats:[24]

> Movement (for which in a petty way logic is taken), the so-called search for truth and beauty, is for us the effect of a breakdown of the attention. But movement must not be confused with what we attach to it but, for the rescuing of the intelligence, must always be considered aimless, without progress.[25]

As with the prose sections of his *Spring and All,* he locates a specifically poetic mode of thought in the quality of dynamism. Writing must preserve its status as 'art' if it is to evade the deadly 'grip' of philosophy, science and 'logic'.[26] It must evade the burden of 'purposed design'. *Spring and All* juxtaposes meandering, improvisatory prose disquisitions on the nature of the poetic imagination with poems written in a remarkable variety of styles. It is clear that Williams wishes to make his way 'by compass', as there is no easy match available between the assertions about poetic imagination and the actual poems, which vary considerably in method and technique. Williams's chief polemical point is that literature remains embedded, to its detriment, in an outmoded model of representation. It must cast off its desire to imitate nature, to represent it, and, as he puts it in *Spring and All,* it 'must be real, not "realism" but reality itself'. Williams's position, restated several times in the circumlocutory prose of the book, is radically anti-metaphorical and anti-mimetic:

> The form of prose is the accuracy of its subject matter — how best to expose the multiform phases of its material
> the form of poetry is related to the movement of the imagination revealed in words — or whatever it may be — the cleavage is complete.
> Why should I go further than I am able? Is it not enough for you that I am perfect?
> The cleavage goes through all the phases of experience. It is the jump from prose to the process of imagination that is the next great leap of intelligence — from the simulations of present experience to the facts of the imagination.
>
> (*CPW*1, p. 219)

Williams, then, wants art to approach experience in factual terms. But this is not a scientific understanding of fact, which belongs to the realm of prose.[27] Poetry's difficult task, struggling to *be* rather than be *like*, is to embody both the 'movement of the imagination' and the 'facts of the imagination'. This can only be a formal question, and Williams indicates that solely poetry can achieve this 'leap'. The facts of the imagination are encountered in how one represents the world, rather than what one represents: 'the imagination is 'not "like" anything but transfused with the same forces which transfuse the earth – at least one small part of them' (*CPW*1, 204, p. 207). The central formal fact of poetry's difference from prose is the linebreak. In ways that Williams never fully articulated himself, short form, the form and line that he had been cultivating from his earliest writings, emerged as the most suitable tool for the capture of 'the movement of the imagination'. As his writing develops, it is the intervention of the linebreak that is increasingly the means of enacting the halting, 'jagged' movement of the imagination 'revealed in words'.

Interspersed among the sometimes comically excessive and otiose prose polemics of *Spring and All* are numerous poetic experiments with short form, as well as his most famous, and most anthologised, statement on brevity, 'The Red Wheelbarrow':

So much depends
upon

a red wheel
barrow

glazed with rain
water

beside the white
chickens.[28]

(*CPW*1, p. 224)

As numerous commentators have made clear since the 1970 re-publication of 'The Red Wheelbarrow' in its original context in *Spring and All*, the exemplary economy of this quietly revolutionary poem takes on new significance in the context of the baggy and repetitive prose that surrounds it. Just before the poem, Williams had aligned the category of prose with various categories of fact. Here, though, he claims the hard-edged objectivity of 'fact' for the imagination. Williams, then, does not oppose the documentary needs of prose to the fictional space of imaginative invention. For him, the products of the creative imagination count as a superior version of reality. It is this kind of absolute facticity, stripped of sacred or transcendental trappings, that leads him to the pointedly anti-metaphorical 'Red Wheelbarrow'. This wheelbarrow is not *like* anything, it does not stand for anything or point outside itself. The poem's glittering and momentary perception is humdrum, free of any epiphanic or numinous overtones. These are the 'facts of the imagination', as Williams makes them available to us.

The only point at which the poem might appear to gesture away from the objects it names, is in the first stanza. The phrase 'so much depends' appears to indicate that there is a weight of significance to attach to what follows. But the significance lies in the very lack of import that we can attach to the scene that is thumbnailed for the reader. The poem's great statement is to achieve an unvarnished presentation of the existent.

The poem might be read as an application of the Poundian 'Don'ts', with their rejection of ornamentation and superfluity. The conventionally poetic – whether that be understood as mystery, transcendence, specialised language use, song, profundity or emotion – is entirely absent from this poem. Yet Williams is not proposing a poetry that simply enumerates the objects of the world. Lineation is critical. The poem might be reconfigured as plain prose: 'So much depends upon a red wheel barrow glazed with rain water beside the white chickens.' What transforms the poem from a humdrum utterance into the sphere of the imagination is form: the line- and stanza breaks. The matter of this poem is its artifice.

The poem is broken into four stanzas of roughly equal length: each has a line of three or four syllables followed by a line of two. The stanzas are of similar appearance on the page, each suggesting the shape of a wheelbarrow. The severe cuts in the flow of the fairly straightforward utterance break each of the three perceptual units into two: the 'wheel/ barrow' (usually one word); the 'rain/ water' (often one word) and the 'white/ chickens'. The preposition 'upon', at the head of the poem, exerts a downward pressure on the words that follow. Yet they cannot flow evenly because of the repeated intervention of the linebreak. So the preposition 'beside' puts the objects in a planar, pictorial relationship, rather than the discursive, narrative one that begins the poem. The poem thus moves, on one hand, towards a two-dimensional pictorialism, while on the other its halting temporal passage persists. It cannot simply be an image, because language happens in time and has its own distinct pictorial physicality in the *mise-en-page*.

Williams reduces the poem to the barest of statements, thus drawing attention to all that it leaves out. At the same time, he levers ordinary language into a space that, through its formal operations and through its own performative attributes, is aestheticised. His primary means of doing this is the breaking-up of a discrete unit of language into smaller units. The apparently simple gesture of breaking lines and arranging clusters of words into stanzas become powerfully resonant. The poem has the foundational, paradigm-shifting qualities of early Duchamp. Just as a ready-made such as 'Fountain' located the aesthetic in the recontextualisation of the everyday, so Williams's poem succeeds in the feat of turning a poem that is devoid of abstract or literary language into a performative manifesto-poem. While Duchamp's gesture initiated the conceptual turn in art, Williams shows us that language is *always* conceptual, even when it appears most bound to the material.

There is a great deal more, of course, to *Spring and All* than 'The Red Wheelbarrow'. There is the disgusted social observation of 'To Elsie', and the anti-Eliotic sentiments of 'Spring and All' – a poem that, as the prose text later has it, hymns the 'perfection of new forms as additions to nature' (*CPW1*, p. 226). There is the reflection on Stein and Juan Gris in 'The rose is obsolete', and the immersion in popular communal experience of 'The crowd at the ball game'.

All of these very different poems work with the short line as a fundamental expressive tool. 'To Elsie' is a short-lined poem, but not uniformly so. The second line of each three-line stanza is very short, typically two or three syllables. Many of the short lines contain nouns, but there is no syntactical pattern. For the reading eye, the effect is to draw attention to the short lines: the *mise-en-page* sets up a discrete pattern of emphasis that runs both with and against the sense-bearing movement of the sentences. The syntax of the poem is open-ended: the only punctuation comes from dashes. Three lines begin with capital letters, which gestures towards a breakdown of sense into sentences. The precarious 'no-one to drive the car' is experienced by the reader in the delicate balance between line, phrase and clause. Not only is lineation a prominent feature of the reading experience, but its presence greatly amplifies the distinction between phrasal and clausal word-groups.[29] Sentences do not really exist in the poem, which begins with two very long, meandering, parenthetical thoughts that stray across line and stanza breaks. It finally contracts to three brief ones, the final two coinciding with the stanza unit, though only the penultimate one is a clause:

> the stifling heat of September
> Somehow
> it seems to destroy us
>
> It is only in isolate flecks that
> something
> is given off
>
> No one
> to witness
> and adjust, no one to drive the car

(*CPW1*, pp. 218–19)

It is easier to see now why Williams was so stringent in his requirements for upper- and lower-case letters. On this occasion, the capitals that open the final stanza play a large role in giving them their conclusive quality. The poem moves from a mood in which equivocal, open-ended syntax is in tension with the short lines to one in which stanza and syntax are aligned. However, the rather dogmatic, dismissive tenor of the pronouncements that characterise the bulk of the poem is replaced by uncertainty. The cramped, hesitant movement of the compressed stanzas is the only persistent pattern in the poem as sense moves from the definite to the indefinite, while syntax moves in the opposite direction.

In 'The rose is obsolete', the short lines have a very different effect. The lines are longer and the stanzas strikingly irregular in length, ranging from eight lines to a single word. Each bundle of words is organised into a stanza that is sufficient for the unfolding thought. The linebreaks are not obtrusive in themselves but they reinforce the jagged contemporaneity that Williams describes: 'The edge/ cuts without cutting/ meets – nothing – renews/ itself in metal or porcelain –' (*CPW1*, p. 195). Taken together, stanza and linebreaks convey the impression of what Williams's admirer Robert Creeley would describe as form considered as an 'extension' of content. In this case, content emerges in an improvisatory way. The parcelling of words, line by line, is integral to this effect.

In 'The crowd at the ball game', there is a long sequence of two-line stanzas. The first line is typically longer than the second, and there is a loose congruence between stanza and unit of thought. Again, initial capitals indicate sentence breaks, and these carry as much weight as the other breaks in the poem. The poem is ambivalent about the absorption of the crowd in the grace and beauty of the spectacle, finding in it both a lucid presentness and a 'terrifying' potential for violence: a tense relationship between aesthetics and power. The breaking of the poem into short and short-lined stanzas helps support the poem's attention to the moment: the repeated versions of 'it is' in the poem need reassertion in small, emphatic bundles of words. The poem is situated at a temporal tipping point: the summer solstice of the occasion, and the moment isolated and experienced as permanence. The brevity of the lines allows for a unit-by-unit unfolding of dense thought that is in contrast to the rapturous immediacy that is described: 'So in detail, they, the crowd,/ are beautiful// for this/ to be warned against' (*CPW1*, p. 233). The irregularity that the incursion of the linebreak underlines, in other words, acts as a counter to the state of entranced fascination that the poem both celebrates and fears.

* * *

A relation to the real is prominent Williams's 1931 review of Pound's *A Draft of XXX Cantos*, in which he announces that Pound's writing needs to be considered in relation to the 'principal move in imaginative writing today – that away from the word as symbol toward the word as reality'.[30] This key perception reads as an extension of the various remarks in *Spring and All* to the effect that poetry was 'new form dealt with as a reality in itself' (*CPW*1, p. 219). Form itself, then, has a structuring role in our encounter with reality. I would argue that a fuller understanding of social and political forms can be reached through the encounter with the necessarily partial and attenuated forms of poetic utterance. The chronic interruptedness of the poetry I am discussing serves, I suggest, to illuminate our experience of less visible discontinuities that conceal themselves as false coherence.

A characteristically disenchanted version of Imagist investment in directness is clear in Williams's rejection of the poetry of symbolism, which one might align with both Yeats and Eliot, as well as the elements of French symbolist theory that each, in his way, drew on. In his review Williams inveighs, in words that recall Pound's objections to 'slither', against verse that is 'muzzy, painty, wet'.[31] Like Pound, Williams rejects softness, which for Williams means a lack of formal rigour. He praises Pound for a 'dry, clean use of words' (recalling Hulme's predilection for dryness). He remarks that 'the word has been used in its plain sense to represent a thing – remaining thus loose in its context – not gummy – (when at its best) – an objective unit in the design – but alive'.[32]

In such remarks the kinetic energies of *Spring and All* are married with an austere drive for the 'plain sense'. This would imply a notably straightforward mode of expression. While in some early prose texts Williams cultivates an improvisatory muzziness that retains the 'loose' quality of a first draft, his drive increasingly becomes oriented around a version of the 'thing'. This is a notion of objective reality that words correspond to in one way or another. He is clear in his commitment to words used simply 'to represent a thing'. This recalls his oft-repeated phrase 'no ideas but in things', a slogan that would first appear in 1927's early version of 'Paterson' (*CPW*1, pp. 263–6) and that would thenceforth be crucial to his work, notably to the long-form version of *Paterson*. Yet, as I argue below, the phrase 'no ideas but in things' is itself less straightforward than might be supposed. Moreover, it is not clear that Pound's 'thing' was ever the same thing as Williams's thing. As Peter Nicholls has argued (see my introduction), Pound's 'direct treatment of the "thing", whether subjective or objective' places the thing in scare quotes, suggesting that Pound's 'thing' is akin to his 'intellectual and emotional complex' – a perceptual event that forms part of poet's encounter with the world of things. Pound's 'thing', in other words, is not a thing.

Williams's emphasis is different, and Creeley would go on to interpret the thing in Williams's terms. When Williams writes 'no ideas but in things' he is, first of all, making a commitment to an anti-metaphysical position, stated most clearly in his introduction to *The Wedge*: 'Let the metaphysical take care of itself, the arts have nothing to do with it.'[33] Does he mean that poets should confine their activities to this materialistic sphere of operation, or does he mean to entirely reject the ideal, asserting an unsparingly empirical position? Is he arguing, in other words, that there *should be* no ideas in poetry but those found through things, or, more broadly, that there *are* no ideas but in things?

We can find an answer, perhaps, in the note on his own poetry that Williams wrote for *The Oxford Anthology of American Literature* (1938):

> since the senses do not exist without an object for their employment all art is necessarily objective. It doesn't declaim or explain; it presents. A poem is a whole, an object in itself ... The whole poem, image and form, that is, constitutes a single meaning. Times change and forms and their meanings alter ... Their forms must be discovered in the spoken, the living language of their day.[34]

Read this way, 'no ideas but in things' becomes clear: for Williams, there is nothing but the encounter with the objective. There is no value at all in the 'subjective' speculation or theorisation that he finds in explaining, or in abstraction. The imperative is simply to 'present' in the 'living language' of one's own time and language, of course, is collective, not subjective. This is, on the face of it, a surprisingly narrow and empiricist vision, given the indirectness and speculative range that, notwithstanding his apparent ambitions, are to be found in the poetry. However, it is easy to forget that the context for Williams's argument is poetics. The doggedly nonmimetic stance that informs his poetry finds literary expression in poems that take determinate shapes. It is in these shapes, these forms, that what is most valuable in his thought lies, rather than the prosaic exposition that Williams has in mind when he rejects the impulse to 'declaim or explain'. Turning again to his praise for Pound, we find that what Williams seeks to recommend is a kind of immanent intellectual energy to the local detail of poetic language:

> All the thought and implications of thought are there in the words (in the minute character and relationships of the words — destroyed, avoided by ...) — it is *that* I wish to say again and again — it is there in the technique and it is that that is the making or the breaking of the work. It is that that one sees, feels. It is that that *is* the work of art — to be observed.
>
> ... the material is so molded that it changed in *kind* from other statement. It is a *sort* beyond measure.[35]

Williams's argument on Pound's enormously allusive project, which clearly refers outside itself by repeatedly gesturing at entire bodies of thought that lie outside the poem, is really a way of reading Pound against the grain. For Williams, unlike many Poundians, what is most valuable in the poetry is formal – 'there in the technique'. This is what he meant when, in his introduction to *The Wedge* he wrote that 'the poet thinks with his poem', a perception that is critical to the argument I am advancing in this book.

While Williams builds on and extends the precepts of early Imagism, he finds the rejection of ornament of fundamental value. He reorients Pound's thing-complex towards the things of the world in the name of a kind of imaginative realism. Yet, this is in tension with the desire to isolate the value of 'technique', for surely technique might easily become the kind of literary sophistry that Williams deplores. There is nothing in such statements to connect this notion of representation with brevity or short form. Why *should* poetry of formal austerity correspond better to the manifold that is experience than prose? What is there, then, in this line of thinking that might lead to a commitment to brevity?

In setting so much store by the 'minute character and relationships of the words', Williams reads Pound's epic against its epic ambition. Williams shows not the slightest interest in – say – Malatesta, Sordello or Odysseus. Dante is mentioned, but Williams notes that Pound succeeds in replicating Dante's attention to 'popular language'. This is of more value than the 'rhapsodic swoon induced by his blinding technical, aesthetic and philosophical qualities'.[36] Williams praises the movement of thought in the texture of Pound's lines – language use that has not been 'violated by "thinking"'. This movement is apparent in the smallest detail. He cites two-word composites – 'sun-dazzle', 'vine-trunk', 'wave-runs' – rather than long passages when he praises Pound. He argues that it is in the 'small make-up of the lines that the character of the poem definitely comes – and beyond which it cannot go'.[37] It is possible to see from this eccentric but strong reading of the Poundian line how Williams himself might value in his own work what Pound himself had long ago discarded – the intensifying impact of a technique that necessarily draws attention to the 'small make-up of the lines'.

I am not seeking to argue that Williams was a formalist of the kind for whom there is nothing in the poem but technique. His poetry is clearly too grounded in the social and the local for that to be the case. However, I do want to argue that in his reading of Pound, he locates value in the kind of precisely demarcated detail that is amplified in the short-form poem. Short-form writing, of its nature, amplifies the formal or technical aspects of the writing, and this is where Williams locates Pound's success (he utterly disregards Pound's grand syntheses, claiming that Pound 'succeeds against himself').[38]

Williams's reading of Pound, then, lays the foundations for a mode of writing that foregrounds the 'minute character and relationships of words'. This kind of poetry is not anti-intellectual or hostile to the conceptual dimensions of prosody, but it finds that these operate at the optimum level when immanent in the poetry. The poet should, in Williams's view, ground his or her writing not in Pound's 'subjective or objective' but in the objective. Poetry should concern itself with objects, not ideas.

At the time Williams was writing these words, the loose coalition of writers known as the Objectivists was coming into being. Before considering Objectivism and Williams's influence on them, however, I wish to dwell a little longer on Williams's work, considering the writing that followed the belatedly seminal *Spring and All*. I wish to discuss the development of a particular kind of compressed pastoral poem. This is a mode of writing in which he seemed to find a particular satisfaction, perhaps because in addressing himself to the 'natural' world he could emphasise his own artifice and the peculiar rigour he brings to observation and expression.

The 1928 sequence *Descent of Winter* contains, like *Spring and All*, a mixture of prose and poetry. Each of the poems is dated, which lends the writing a journal-like immediacy (the text was begun as Williams travelled back on a liner from a trip to Europe in which he had spent time with Pound, H.D., Robert McAlmon and the surrealist Philippe Soupault).[39] The mood is more melancholy than that of *Spring and All* and the text more radical in its absorption of Steinian methods than any he had yet written. The sequence took up much of the fourth (and last) number of Pound's little magazine *Exile*, which he published from Rapallo.

One of the strongest poems focuses on a canna, a flamboyant flowering plant:

Monday
          the canna flaunts
its crimson head

crimson lying folded
crisply down upon

                  the invisible

darkly crimson heart
of this poor yard

the grass is long

           October tenth
   1927

                                                        (*CPW*1, p. 293)

The poem plays with the vocabulary of Blake's 'The Sick Rose', with its 'invisible worm', its 'bed/ Of crimson joy' and 'dark secret love'. While this indigenous American plant, therefore, does not bear the symbolic freight borne by the rose, it is nonetheless acknowledged as part of a long poetic tradition, with one foot on either side of the Atlantic. In his 'introduction' to the sequence, written three weeks later, Williams cites a few lines on a rose, and remarks, 'poetry should strive for nothing else, this vividness alone, *per se*, for itself. The realisation of this has its own internal fire that is "like" nothing. Therefore the bastardy of the simile. That thing, the vividness which is poetry by itself, makes the poem' (*CPW*1, p. 302). His canna poem is just such a poem, in which sheer vividness trumps metaphor. The poem uses allusion as an emptying-out gesture, rather than one of thickening texture. The Blakean material leads nowhere at all, with no reckoning with the past or with poetic forebears. The poem emerges into a bare and anti-metaphorical moment in the 'poor yard'. Towards the end of the poem, the line 'the grass is long' leads the reader away from the darkly symbolic 'heart' of the poem and to a simple experience of presence.

The brevity of the lines is notable – typically four, five or six syllables per line. The lines coincide with the sub-clausal phrasal divisions of the sentence. The omission of punctuation makes the concluding 'the grass is long' appear even more isolated and unrelated to the foregoing. The poem is bookended by a statement of the date of composition – 'Monday' . . . 'October tenth/ 1927'. Unlike other poems in the series, the date of composition is incorporated into the poem itself. The compression of the poem is severe, with the word 'crimson' repeated three times. The poem resists visualisation, because the 'darkly crimson heart' is 'invisible'. There is sparse use of half rhyme (head// folded) and (heart/ yard). Williams admits a degree of uncertainty into the poem – the uncertainty about the nature of the 'heart' he refers to, and the dissonance between the extravagance of 'flaunts' and the restraint of 'folded/ crisply down'. The poem places itself in a tradition that might include Blake, and, closer to Williams, Emily Dickinson, but its inconclusiveness and its insistence on making the occasion of the poem's composition an integral feature of the work make it a highly self-conscious and sceptical manipulation of nature poetry. Williams's austere pastoral first conjures and then resists the symbolic freight of 'heart', 'rose' and 'crimson'. The poem is scrupulously inconclusive and uncommunicative: no lesson or conclusion is drawn from the flamboyant plant. The metaphor of the heart is evacuated and deadpanned into incommunicativeness, leaving the simple presentation of a colourful object, as urgent as Williams's red fire truck.

This tendency to reduce and to compress remained a salient feature of Williams's writing. His 1935 book *An Early Martyr and Other Poems* contains a poem that allocates one word to each line, most of them monosyllabic. The compression is severe. The poem is not even syntactical:

'The Locust Tree in Flower'

Among
of
green

stiff
old
bright

broken
branch
come

white
sweet
May

again

(*CPW*1, pp. 379–80)

This experiment sits jaggedly beneath the relative opulence of the five-word title (which refers to another tree indigenous to the US). The elision is such that little but a loose impression of the arrival of May is given. The tension between the opulent associations of a tree flowering in spring and the linebreaks is considerable. The 'sweet/ May' may allude to Wordsworth, but, as with the canna poem, the allusion is a dead end.[40] This severe style of representation is some way from the 'intellectual and emotional complex' or the 'direct treatment of the "thing"' that Pound had recommended more than two decades earlier. Poetic form itself is presented as a means of encountering the real: there is no direct conduit from this halting poem to the spreading fecundity of the flowering tree.

The poem is a radically compressed version of a poem published in *Poetry* in 1933.[41] In what follows I have italicised the words that Williams has retained. The experiment is not simply an act of deletion. There is some re-ordering; 'sweets' becomes 'sweet'; and the words 'bright' and 'again' are added to the poem.

Among
the leaves
bright

green
of wrist-thick
tree

and old
stiff *broken*
branch

ferncool
swaying
loosely strung —

come May
again
white blossom

clusters
hide
to spill

their *sweets*
almost
unnoticed

down
and quickly
fall

(*CPW*1, p. 366)

This version of the poem is also asyntactical, though it is much clearer. The reader is led on a journey through the foliage: the key entrance is 'come May/ again', though it is ungrammatical. The poem has a trajectory that ends with the petals falling to the ground. This version of the poem does quite different things with short form. The leaves of the first stanza look forward to the 'ferncool' of the fourth stanza. The May blossom 'come[s]' amid these leaves. Williams appears to be seeking the jostling visual effect of branches and blossom moving in the breeze. However, the shifting and half-fulfilled implications of the syntax lead the reader towards an impression of the ephemerality of the spring moment within the larger cycle of the months and seasons. While the 'fall' is another form of bathos, the dynamism of the poem lies in the interplay between linebreak and syntax, not in the observation itself or the splendours of foliage or blossom.

Prompted by a puzzled reader of the 1935 version, Williams explained what he had done: 'It's the recurrence of the season – the whole history of May . . . I cut out everything except the essential words to leave the thing as simple as possible and to make the reader concentrate as much as he can. Could anything be plainer?' (*CPW*1, p. 538). It is hard to take these remarks seriously. The 1935 version is not, by any standards, a 'plain' or 'simple' representation of the essentials of May flowering. The disjunctiveness of the poem presents a challenge to any reader. The poem cannot be read without attention to its own methods. It derives much of its energy from the mismatch between the cutting of the lines and the flowering of spring. While Williams claims that the pruning of the longer text facilitates direct perception of the tree, encountered as part of the 'whole history of May', the real claim of the poem is for using literary form as a distinct means of knowing the world. The poem enacts a fracturing of a pastoral trope as old as the rose.[42] Its mode of 'recurrence' is to acknowledge the past but to turn towards the communicative potential of barely rendered form.

Another kind of elliptical pastoral is found in 'Silence', published in *The Wedge* (1944). Colour, again, is important – red and green are opposed, as in several of the poems discussed above. There are red, yellow and green leaves, and a single action is observed. There is a suggestion of natural abundance in the peach tree. On this occasion the parsimony of the lines does not coincide with a disruption of syntactical norms. The poem telegraphs the intensity of looking, focusing on one almost imperceptible action: the bird's disturbance of a single twig. The short lines lend themselves to the carefulness of the perception described. Indeed, although the title of the poem is 'Silence', it is not clear whether the poem is concerned with looking or listening.

'Silence'

Under a low sky —
this quiet morning
of red and
yellow leaves —

a bird disturbs
no more than one twig
of the green leaved
peach tree

(*CPW*2, p. 91)

The sounds of the first stanza are various, but in the second stanza the poem is driven by assonance, moving from the first line's 'bird disturbs' to the four-fold chiming of 'green leaved/ peach tree'. The poem therefore makes a point of sounding, even though it announces itself as 'Silence'. The vanishingly quiet sound of a bird disturbing a single twig could well be imaginary, and the insignificant action might well be seen rather than heard. The poem's concision draws attention to what Williams admired in his review of Pound, 'the minute character and relationships of the words'. But at the same time it enacts the 'minute character and relationships' of attention itself.

The poem produces an Imagistic snapshot: a moment that is narrated across linebreaks in time; and a sounded enunciation that is far from silent. The poem depends on two shifts. The first is the movement from large to small, the vastness of the 'low sky' providing the backdrop for the central detail of the bird's tiny movement of the twig. The second is the movement from the diffuse 'red and/ yellow leaves' that communicate the general character of the morning to the specific instance of the green leaves of the tree containing the bird. The small sound of the twig is available as a sound only because the morning is so quiet and the perceiver's attention is so sharpened. The poem captures a particular kind of attentiveness that finds revelatory vividness in the tiniest detail – it is, in its quiet way, almost a manifesto for reading, and its own condensation is offered as the best vehicle for this kind of readerly attention.

Williams's poems put the machinic efficiency of the industrial age in the service of an ideal economy of literary action. At the same time, they remain committed to the generative possibilities of the encounter between poet and nature. Williams develops a kind of pastoral that draws on oriental tradition, but which transposes this from meditations on natural order to the starker question of the relationship between word and thing. For Williams, neither the natural world nor the individual speaker has anything to disclose about themselves. With this narrowing of expressive possibility, the arrangement of words on the page structures perception in new ways. The short-form technique that Williams uses is a kind of magnifying glass. With the symbolic axis of literary expression stripped down to the barest essentials, other factors come to the fore. Chief among these are those that concern breaks of various kinds: lineation, syntax, stanza breaks, the space between individual words. Sonic features such as assonance, consonance and rhyme gain greater force in these reduced circumstances, constituting another order of association that exists alongside the purely textual.

Williams's achievement was to build on Imagism and, in his most austere work, to strip it even further of ornament. Imagism, in practice, often betrayed a debt to the symbolism it sought to rebel against: a numinous field of poignant stirrings that accords significance to its own willed inarticulacy. Williams purges Imagism of any residual symbolism, leaving the reader with words, things and the cognitive processes that mediate between them. I will discuss one more example from Williams, as I wish to consider the magnifying qualities of the linebreak.

'The Hurricane'

The tree lay down
on the garage roof
and stretched, You
have your heaven,
it said, go to it.

(*CPW2*, p. 158)

This example of short-form pastoral, from 1948's *The Clouds*, endows nature with a speaking voice. It reads almost as a parable. The tree becomes a destructive agent in the poem, abstracting the power of the hurricane. The key break in the poem is the comma after 'stretched', where we would expect a full stop and, perhaps, quotation marks. The lack of punctuation and the run-on into the next sentence leave the reader uncertain who is speaking until the final line's 'it said'. The poem might be read as a precursor of Creeley's better known 'I know a man', where there is similar uncertainty around the final stanza: 'drive, he sd, for/ christ's sake, look/ out where yr going'.[43]

In 'The Hurricane', the tree is the figure for a kind of anti-pastoral. This is a vision of nature that is not inclined to guide and nurture the mind of the poet, or to provide the seedbed for the poetic imagination. The violence in the poem is languid and unthinking: the tree 'lay down .../ and stretched'. This image of casual destruction is followed by the voice of the tree. Initially we assume that the voice is the speaker's, but this is overturned with the final line's 'it said'. The spurious metaphysics that Williams found so troubling is dismissed by the tree as a curious custom of mankind: 'You/ have your heaven'. The final words, 'go to it' are both menacing and dismissive.

What does it mean to say that the poet 'thinks' with a poem such as this? The poem invokes a dark vision of nature: human vitality is crushed by a tree in an alarmingly offhand manner that is quite striking. The tree is given human characteristics, first through the verbs used to describe its actions, which impute intent; and second through the tree's own voice, which is hostile, perhaps even vengeful. Yet how different this brief poem might be with longer lines, or with no lineation at all. The grouping of words into lines of roughly equal length on the page decisively colours the information that it conveys. Despite the characteristically demotic language, the linebreaks insist on the specifically poetic nature of the utterance. This is a special form of speech, it asserts, even as it stresses how colloquial it is. The informal language masks the use of rhymes: 'down/ on', 'roof/ you', 'have/ heaven'. The final line's repetition of 'it' in two of the line's five syllables has an effect that would be lost in a longer line. It is possible to find an anticipation of Creeley here, too:

his ' "Time" is some sort of hindsight',[44] discussed in my Chapter 5, ends with a dramatically doubled use of 'it'.

Even the words of the poem are short: all are monosyllables bar 'garage' and 'heaven'. There is a pulse of uncertainty in the condensed thought of the poem. Each line-unit contains an unexpected turn, chief among these being the unannounced change of speaker. The poem only makes sense retrospectively, when the reader comes to the final line. This line is, on the page, the shortest, with four of its five syllables given to two-letter words. The poem's brutality is accentuated by the succinctness of the poem's articulation. Form thus comes to the fore. To attribute an unthinking violence to Nature would be a fairly small gesture. To do so in a way that is so tightly arranged makes the point far more forceful.

In the poems I have discussed in this chapter, Williams continues the Imagist impulse to rid the poem of unnecessary abstraction and ornamentation, succeeding where most Imagists failed. The freeing gesture of 'The Red Wheelbarrow' allows the poem simply to enact 'the vividness which is poetry by itself'. Every linebreak, in such constrained verse, I believe, contains a trace of violence because a thought is interrupted. This quality of truncation has a negligible effect in more capacious lines, where the line may extend with the thought. Similarly, in prose poetry, the particular kind of disjunction enacted in the prose work of Stein or the New Sentence experiments of the language-writing era, the train of thought is broken by the sentence: the reading eye is not required to move down the page by the intervention of the linebreak. In the short-form mode that Williams did so much to establish, the line is typically shorter than the unit of thought. This is a recurrent thought-break. The potential of cognition to stall and stutter is both revealed and enacted, and we cannot entrust ourselves to the narrative development of a thought in motion. The thought is caught and interrupted at the point of articulation and the reader of the poetry is unable to separate the breaks from the supposed object of the utterance itself, whether it be flower, tree or wheelbarrow. Williams instates a separation between the gradual building of dialectical blocks that marks a complex thought, and the non-narrative other to coherence, which continually threatens to turn the thought elsewhere: towards a refusal of the concept, towards self-reflexive self-questioning, towards an atomisation of the sense-making process. He does not need to work with a radically splintered or asyntactical language in order to do this. The latent energies of dissolution in the short line are enough for him both to think and unthink his poem.

Notes

1. References to the two volumes of Williams's *Collected Poems* are given parenthetically as *CPW*1 and *CPW*2.
2. In his autobiography William Carlos Williams writes that Keats was a 'God' to him when he was a medical student (p. 53). However, he burnt his long-form homage to 'Endymion', and the antique diction of some of the early writing soon fell away.
3. Williams, *I Wanted to Write a Poem*, p. 5.
4. Williams remarks in his *Autobiography*, for example, that 'I never (so long as I kept away) got tired of him' (p. 58).
5. Williams, *Autobiography*, p. 148.
6. Williams, *Autobiography*, p. 148.
7. In a letter cited in Williams's Prologue to *Kora in Hell*, H.D. describes 'Postlude' as 'supreme among your poems' (*Imaginations*, p. 13).
8. Stevens wrote a response to this poem, 'Nuances of a Theme by Williams', that begins by citing the entire poem and goes on to amplify its sentiments. The Stevens poem is explicitly anti-Romantic: 'shine like bronze/ that reflects neither my face nor any inner part/ of my being' (Stevens, *Collected Poetry and Prose*, pp. 14–15). The poem was first published in the *Little Review* in December 1918.
9. In 'A Lecture on Modern Poetry', Hulme writes: 'Two visual images form what one may call a visual chord. They unite to suggest an image which is different to both' (p. 64).
10. The editor of Williams's *Collected Poems*, Christopher MacGowan, notes that Williams's first published poem in which the first lines do not begin with capital letters is 'Metric Figure (Veils of clarity)', published in *Others* magazine in 1916. However, Harriet Monroe insisted on capitalising the first letters of lines for a further three years. Williams complained about this practice in several letters. The first poem published in *Poetry* after 'Spirit of '76', 'A Goodnight', contained lower-case initial letters (*CPW*1, p. 491).
11. Williams, *Autobiography*, p. 311.
12. Williams, Prologue to *Kora in Hell*, *Imaginations*, p. 24.
13. There are significant long-form exceptions that explore a more expansive poetics, of course: 'Desert Music' and *Paterson*, for example.
14. Surveyed in Williams, *A Recognizable Image: William Carlos Williams on Art and Artists*.
15. Williams, Prologue to *Kora in Hell*, *Imaginations*, p. 23, p. 25. The English critic Edgar Jepson's extravagant praise of Eliot had caused controversy in the *Little Review* and elsewhere (known as the 'International Episode'). His essay 'The Western School', originally published in the *English Review* and republished by Pound is cited in the Williams Prologue.
16. Williams, Prologue to *Kora in Hell*, *Imaginations*, p. 10.
17. Williams, Prologue to *Kora in Hell*, *Imaginations*, p. 8.
18. Williams, Prologue to *Kora in Hell*, *Imaginations*, pp. 13–14.
19. Williams, Prologue to *Kora in Hell*, *Imaginations*, p. 14.
20. Williams, *Autobiography*, p. 265.
21. Peter Quartermain, *Disjunctive Poetics*, p. 67.

22. Williams, 'The Work of Gertrude Stein', *Selected Essays*, p. 116.
23. Clive Bell's influential notion of significant form was propounded in his 1914 book *Art*.
24. Quartermain, *Disjunctive Poetics*, p. 91.
25. Williams, 'The Work of Gertrude Stein', p. 117.
26. Williams, 'The Work of Gertrude Stein', p. 116.
27. The prose/poetry opposition should not be taken, incidentally, to mean the opposition between his own prose poetry and the poems in the book.
28. As with other of the poems in this edition, the poem as originally published is untitled.
29. James Longenbach discusses the relationship between syntactical units and lineation in Williams's poetry in his book *The Art of the Poetic Line*.
30. Williams, 'Excerpts from a Critical Sketch: A Draft of XXX Cantos', p. 107.
31. Williams, 'Excerpts from a Critical Sketch', p. 111.
32. Williams, 'Excerpts from a Critical Sketch', p. 111.
33. Williams, CP2, p. 54.
34. Williams, 'A Note on Poetry', pp. 1313–14.
35. Williams, 'Excerpts from a Critical Sketch', pp. 107–8.
36. Williams, 'Excerpts from a Critical Sketch', p. 107.
37. Williams, 'Excerpts from a Critical Sketch', p. 108.
38. Williams, 'Excerpts from a Critical Sketch', p. 111.
39. See Noel Riley Fitch's 'Voyage to Ithaca: William Carlos Williams in Paris'. Williams later translated Soupault's novel *Last Nights of Paris*.
40. See 'Ode: Intimations of Immortality from Recollections of Early Childhood', 'Ode: Composed on May Morning', and 'To May'.
41. Williams chose to publish the two poems alongside one another in his *Collected Earlier Poems*.
42. Perhaps, by the 'whole history of May' Williams has in mind his *In the American Grain*, with the 'gambol on the green' of the 'Maypole at Merry Mount' chapter (p. 94) or his description of the Puritans as 'the seed of Tudor England's lusty blossoming' in his 'Voyage of the Mayflower' chapter (p. 78).
43. Robert Creeley, *Collected Poems, 1945–1975*, p. 132.
44. Creeley, *Collected Poems, 1945–1975*, p. 391.

Chapter 3

George Oppen

The exemplary work of Objectivism is George Oppen's *Discrete Series*, published in 1934 by the Objectivist Press. Shortly after publication, the book received a review in the pages of *Poetry* magazine from William Carlos Williams.[1] The review presents Objectivism in ways that happen to coincide fairly closely with Williams's own views.[2] Williams discusses the importance of form, remarking, 'technique is everything'.[3] He draws a distinction between merely 'good' poems, which 'constitute necessary corrections of or emendations of human conduct', and those which themselves effect such changes through 'a direct liberation of the intelligence'. Williams contends that the great importance of such poems 'cannot be in what the poem says, since in that case the fact that it is a poem would be a redundancy'. He continues: 'The importance lies in what a poem *is*. Its existence as a poem is of first importance, a technical matter, as with all facts, compelling the recognition of a mechanical structure.'[4] He is, therefore, making a large claim for the singular efficacy of poetic language as a tool of intellectual 'liberation'.[5] The poem *as poem* has a potential reach that far exceeds that of mere concepts. In his opinion, Oppen's short book achieves this level of 'importance'. If seen from a narrowly political point of view, Williams's larger claims about the liberatory potential of technique may seem invidious from contemporary perspectives, given the acute attention devoted to the politics of poetic form in recent decades. However, for Oppen and other of the Objectivists, issues of form and technique were a manifestation of, not a retreat from, political convictions. Such convictions were broadly shared with poet-contemporaries such as Muriel Rukeyser and John Wheelwright, in whose very different work directly political content was readily apparent.[6] Indeed, when Language writer Ron Silliman laments the aesthetically 'conservative' implications of Oppen's increasing focus on what a poem 'says' in his later work,[7] he is revoicing a difference of opinion about the value of content in poetry that had been at issue in the relationship between Wallace Stevens and Williams.[8]

The title of William's review, 'The New Poetical Economy' is playful. On one hand, it co-opts the discursive authority of 'political economy'. On the other, it advocates economy as the strategy through which poetic 'importance' is achieved. 'Economy' may mean the circulation of cultural value, but the language of the review suggests that the stronger meaning lies in the economical use of language. What the poem 'says' will count for little or nothing, if the poetic technique does not achieve the machinic economy that Williams recommends. Williams makes his case, both figuratively and literally, by appealing to a poetics of reduction. 'Surely an apprentice watching his master sees nothing prosaic about the details of technique', he writes. 'Nor would he find a narrow world because of the smallness of the aperture through which he views it, but through that pinhole, rather, a world enormous as his mind permits him to witness.'[9] In this view, an economical technique can open up an 'enormous' perspective on the world. Such restricted means of operation are founded, remarkably, on the discipline required by any serious model of political change:

> An imaginable new social order would require a skeleton of severe discipline for its realisation and maintenance, thus by a sharp restriction to essentials, the seriousness of a new order is brought to realisation. Poetry might turn this condition to its own ends. Only by being an object sharply defined and without redundancy will its form project whatever meaning is required of it. It could well be, at the same time, first and last a poem facing as it must the dialectical necessities of its day. Oppen has carried this social necessity, so far as poetry may be concerned in it, over to an extreme.[10]

Williams's review takes the rejection of 'redundancy' favoured by Imagism and rethinks it in a social context, as a means of harbouring the complexities and contradictions – the 'dialectical necessities' – that the work confronts. The impersonal efficiency of the machine, anathema to any variant of romanticism, becomes the model, not the antithesis, of poetic thought.[11] Oppen's poems, writes Williams 'seek an irreducible minimum in the means for the achievement of their objective'. Poetry of any value will rest on a 'craftsmanlike economy of means'.[12]

Williams's essay allows a bridge to be thrown up between the Imagism of nearly two decades earlier and the more sophisticated considerations of technique and the social in the work of the Objectivists. Although he is, like many poets writing on other poets, ultimately discussing his own preoccupations, he also provides an effective summary of the imperative to short form in the Pound-Williams line leading to Oppen and his peers. Williams advocates a technique that requires great concision, and he deploys a battery of terms to reinforce his point: 'smallness of ... aperture'; 'a skeleton of severe discipline'; 'sharp restriction'; 'without redundancy'; 'irreducible minimum'; 'economy of means'.[13] More than a language of realism,[14] or a call for poems to be rather than to say, there is unequivocal support for a poetics of reduction, not merely as an aesthetic imperative, but as a conduit to writing that contains the seeds of intellectual 'liberation'.

In contrast to the sharpness of Williams's definitions, Objectivism itself is notoriously hard to define. As Rachel Blau DuPlessis remarks, 'There was no such movement ... no "-ism" – no manifesto, no like-minded mutually supportive grouping, no headline magazine, no performances, no excommunications – all characteristics of literary movements. An objectivist ethos is fundamentally a poetics without a movement.'[15] There is, moreover, enduring confusion about how such an 'ethos' might be constituted. In discussing the genesis of Objectivism, the usual reference points are the February 1931 issue of *Poetry* magazine, edited by Louis Zukofsky after Ezra Pound had lobbied *Poetry* magazine's editor Harriet Monroe, and the subsequent An 'Objectivists' Anthology. The key theoretical statements are held to be the two essays contributed by Zukofsky to the 1931 issue of *Poetry*, in which he outlined the concepts of 'sincerity' and 'objectification' (this latter term is also understood as 'rested totality'). As Peter O'Leary has argued, however, Zukofsky's handling of the key arguments is vague to the point of mysticism.[16] Zukofsky later rejected the term Objectivism, and it seems clear that the special issue and the anthology were generated as more through necessity than through conviction.[17] Indeed, there is even less cohesiveness in the February 1931 of *Poetry* than in the publications that announced the arrival of Imagism. Jeffrey Twitchell Waas, for example, points to the lack of shared ground even between the core Objectivists, finding that the two poets most strongly associated with Objectivism, Oppen and Zukofsky, had 'little in common'.[18]

In discussion of the poetics of that early 1930s modernist moment, consideration of short form tends to be sidelined by elucidation of the terms 'sincerity' and 'objectification'. Zukofsky's 'the objectification which is a poem, or a unit of structural prose, may exist in a very few lines' does hint at the possibilities for compression but it is given as possibility rather than a central principle or aim.[19] Of more interest to commentators is the notion, which appears to derive from Williams's commitment to the dispassionate operations of the poem, that the poem itself is an object. Zukofsky writes of the 'apprehension satisfied completely as to the appearance of the art form as an object' and of a poem 'which is an object or affects the mind as such'. Oppen would echo this distinction between the poem as aesthetic object and the object itself with his phrase 'a poem is concerned with a fact which it did not create'[20] but more straightforward is his: 'the necessity for forming a poem properly, for achieving form. That's what "objectivist" really means.'[21]

Zukofsky does not have a great deal to say about form, even though it is a key term for his argument, in his discussion of Charles Reznikoff in his 'Sincerity and Objectification' essay. He refers to the specifics of metre and syllable-count in Reznikoff in ways that cannot be generalised into a larger theory, and no broader conclusions can be drawn from the other poems that he mentions: works by Pound, Williams, Eliot and Moore. While Zukofsky wrote superb examples of short-form poetry, and while he sometimes addresses compression in his critical writing, I believe that the *condensare* impulse that informs this particular study is not best exemplified by his poetics. Sound is crucial to the poems' unfolding, but they do not show the consistent preoccupation with elision that can be found in the early writing of Oppen or in the poetry of Lorine Niedecker. His short-form writing often explores a kind of errant sound-play that trumps other formal issues, as in the variations in 'Songs of Degree':

> Hear, her
> Clear
> Mirror,
> Care
> His error.
> In her
> Care
> Is clear[22]

For my purposes, Oppen and Niedecker are the optimal practitioners of short-form poetry among the Objectivists. Zukofsky's influence on both is acknowledged, and, of course, he retained strong personal ties to Williams and to Robert Creeley, both of whom are central to this book's argument. The austerity, ellipsis, foreshortened lines and equivocal syntax in Oppen and Niedecker indicate a belief that concentration might give access to a specific kind of poetic attention. Michael Davidson finds an affinity between Zukofsky and Oppen's various post-Imagist enactments of cognitive events, but identifies in the latter a turn away from the image and towards language itself:

> Oppen ... places his faith in parts of speech and speech acts rather than images, because it is only in its reduced, functional state that language may reveal its complicity in the production (rather than reflection) of reality. The image is a means to an end, not an end in itself.[23]

This 'reduced' linguistic state is everywhere apparent in Oppen's writing, and he was aware of it. 'I stripped myself bare', he wrote, comparing himself to Zukofsky, 'while you, Louis, have hung on yourself every fancy rag you could find.'[24] Oppen certainly saw his writing's affinity with Imagism. However, he was worried about the contrived quality of 'sloppy American imagism', favouring a 'test of truth'.[25] This truth, oddly enough for a poet renowned for his opacity, had to do with seeing the world clearly: 'That lucence, that emotional clarity, the objectivists wanted, and by that they are related to Imagism. But not the falsity of ingenuity, of the posed tableau, in which the poet also, by implication, poses.'[26] He is even clearer about the value of clarity in a draft of 'Latitude, Longitude': 'I want, if I can find it, the essential/ clarity, plain glass' (*NCP*, p. 401). And, speaking to L. S. Dembo, he remarked on his desire to 'construct a meaning by empirical statements, by imagist statements'.[27]

Syntactical indeterminacy in Oppen is inseparable from the drive to reduction. In a letter to the younger poet Paul Vangelisti, Oppen suggests: 'I wonder how you would feel about omitting the stage directions ... would not the white space carry more ... than the indication of "staging"?'[28] Whatever the complications surrounding his desire for clarity, his commitment to the communicative potential of ellipsis is clear. In the years since his death, however, the study of Oppen has been greatly enriched by interest in something akin to 'stage directions' – the clues offered up by the material features of Oppen's papers, held in the archive at UCSD, and the various insights that can be gleaned from his daybooks.[29] Pressed on these peripheral materials by Burton Hatlen and Tom Mandel, Oppen asks, 'Are these things really interesting?'[30] The desire to strip away all extraneous material – to encounter what Oppen often called, citing, or rather misciting, Reznikoff, 'the girder/ Still itself among the rubble' – has perhaps been sidelined in the recent tendency to probe the compositional rubble that lies around this recalcitrant poetry.[31] Of more interest is the way that Oppen – unlike Olson, the Pound of the Cantos, or the Williams of *Paterson* – makes the suppression all this extraneous matter an integral part of his creative process as he moves towards a final draft.

How could a writer who valued clarity above all produce poetry of such apparent opacity? The tangled relation between perception, language and world is in his poems may ultimately be true to a particular conception of experience. However, the 'fact that [the poem] did not create' implies a Williamsian empiricism that does not ring true as a gloss of Oppen's dense, refractory poetry. Nowhere in his writing is there an equivalent of the red wheelbarrow. Language – the self-questioning language of the poem – is always felt to mediate this encounter with the world outside the poem. Indeed, it might have been more accurate for Oppen to have said that 'the poem is concerned with the facts that it creates'. Yet clarity in the depiction of an object in the world is not the same as the clear depiction – through enactment – of a complex cognitive process. The following argument is informed by the supposition that clarity in the necessarily complicated representation of representation is Oppen's goal.

Oppen himself held that the substantive, or noun, was at the heart of his enquiry. However, this pursuit of the substantive does not lead to a writing of plain statement. Rather, he remains unwilling to disentangle the noun from the grammatical context in which it is inevitably embedded:

> I had trouble with syntax in this undertaking and, as a matter of fact, I still have trouble with verbs. It's not exactly trouble; I just didn't want to put it too pretentiously. I'm really concerned with the substantive, with the subject of the sentence, with what we are talking about, and not rushing over the subject matter in order to make a comment about it. It is a principle with me, of more than poetry, to notice, to state, to lay down the substantive for its own sake.[32]

By this, he means not that he wants to suppress the effects of parts of syntax other than the noun in the framing of the substantive, but that the statement of an object should not be obscured by commentary – and, by extension, metaphorical or symbolic weight. However, questions of sequence are integral to his writing, whether at the level of phrase, line, stanza or poem-series. Oppen remarked of *Discrete Series* that his aim had been to construct poems consisting of 'a series of empirically true terms'. The term he draws from mathematics, 'discrete series', refers to a series that only makes sense as a series through reference to an external classifying or unifying term. For Oppen, it counts for the 'fragmentary character of those poems'.[33] He mentions in a letter to Blau DuPlessis the numbers 14, 28, 38, 42 as an exemplary discrete series because they are unified by their status as stops on the New York subway system.[34] In Andrew Crozier's neat gloss of the title, the world itself is the external reference point that brings the poems in the series together – he refers to 'the inferred continuum of the world accessible to empirical knowledge, however full of gaps that world might be'.[35]

The 'inferred continuum' we find in Oppen's writing is a lattice of subtly interrelated terms. The nuance of those relations is ultimately of greater importance, notwithstanding Oppen's own remarks, than the named objects around which Oppen, Objectivism and much American modernist poetry of the Pound-Williams line hovers. The drive to reduction, in Oppen's writing, seeks to represent a world 'full of gaps' by means of a poetry of elision. Space, indeed, is full and communicative in this writing. Oppen's 'Net of branches' presupposes both disjunction and connection, rupture and association.[36]

'Party on Shipboard' both encapsulates the reduced mode of *Discrete Series* and looks forward to the concerns of Oppen's work in the 1960s:[37]

'Party on Shipboard'

Wave in the round of the port-hole
Springs, passing, — arm waved,
Shrieks, unbalanced by the motion —
Like the sea incapable of contact
Save in incidents (the sea is not
    water)
Homogeneously automatic — a green capped
    white is momentarily a half mile
      out —
The shallow surface of the sea, this,
Numerously — the first drinks —
The sea is a constant weight
In its bed. They pass, however, the sea
Freely tumultuous.

(NCP, 15)

One of the immediately striking features of this poem is the uncertainty about whether certain words are verbs or nouns – the substantive itself is in question. How do we understand the poem's first word, 'wave', for example? Or 'springs', 'shrieks', or 'drinks'? 'Wave' would seem to describe the moving sea – until the next line's 'arm waved'. The twin impulses of motion and stasis, often in opposition in these early poems, are captured in the equivocation between verb and substantive.

This poem has an inside and an outside. The inside is the world of a shipboard party. From this perspective, the sea is out of reach, 'incapable of contact', and its motion is denatured, 'homogeneously automatic'. From outside, the poem implies a calamity. The arm is not waving but drowning, the sea encroaches, resonant with the memory of the *Titanic*. The word 'shrieks' perhaps recalls the feminised frivolity of Prufrock's dismissive 'ladies who come and go', perhaps sheer panic. Either way, the instability of the scene is grounded in syntactical incompletion. There is no straightforward sentence linking subject, verb and object in the poem until the inscrutable 'The sea is a constant weight in its bed.' Predication is attempted but largely forestalled. Much of the poem belongs to elucidatory dependent clauses that lack anything to depend upon. Fragments such as 'The shallow surface of the sea' are syntactically unmoored and thus deprived of any means of representing a world. Instead, they pursue a more oblique ambition: to represent the apprehension of a world through a network of words of phrases that are only contingently related to one another. No discernible or visualisable object can be recovered from this encounter. Neither is the poem indeterminate. Instead, the poem coheres around an identifiable set of themes: solid and fluid, countable and uncountable, stasis and motion, celebration and disaster.

Oppen's equivocal syntax bears a complicating relation to the encounter with the 'empirical'. Sense data is not parsed into a recognisable order: Oppen resists such an organising impulse. This translation of the empirical urges a 'reduced' method of working that opens new lines of semantic and syntactical possibility. Oppen's use of destructured syntax is an expansion of relation rather than a suspension of relation. This steers his writing towards a layered and multivalent encounter with the poet's assembling of a world. The empirical itself is thus never directly accessible.

The relationship between the empirical and short form is usually taken as implicit by poets of the Imagist and post-Imagist line. Since the famous Imagist precepts, the rejection of ornamentation is held to facilitate an increased focus on the bare 'object'. A reduced style becomes an inevitable concomitant in this mode of writing. Yet the use of ellipsis and the radical handling of the linebreak in this poetry go a long way beyond the mere eschewal of ornamentation. Moreover, as we have seen, such techniques of compression are at odds with the representation of the apparently empirical. Davidson's editor's introduction to the *New Collected Poems* points out that Oppen greatly prizes the 'experiential grounding of the poem', which is a means of 'linking the phenomenal object with an experiencing, language-using subject'.[38] This linking of subject, object and word is more persuasive than Oppen's own remarks about clear depiction of the substantive.

In his 'Statement on Poetics', Oppen writes that prosody 'is a music, quite simply, of image and honest speech – *image* because image is the moment of conviction. It cannot be altered and it cannot be falsified without one's knowing it.'[39] The directness of visual perception is invoked by Oppen, then, to convey a moment of truth or sincerity, a direct realisation of the unfolding experience of consciousness in the moment. Yet, immediately after this, Oppen writes, 'Prosody is a language, but it is a language that tests itself.' This gap is significant: I do not think the doubling-back involved in that testing is compatible with the immediacy, clarity, conviction or honesty that Oppen assigns to visual perception. The depiction of the 'moment of conviction' in the perceptual process achieves something different to the compression and temporal effects of Oppen's syntax. A gap opens up, therefore, between the empirical ambitions of the writing and the effects of the syntactical contingency that Oppen constructs with such care.

Crozier suggests a potential response to this problem when he observes that in *Discrete Series*, 'language itself is treated as an empirical datum, in which reference is inextricably combined with its terminology; language cannot, on such assumptions, mediate neutrally between the reader and some other matrix of empirical knowledge'.[40] It is certainly the case that language does not 'mediate neutrally' in Oppen's writing, and that the poetry shows itself to be aware of this. However, the perception of language – or indeed a poem – as itself an empirically available object is misleading as it suppresses language's conceptual moment. Oppen's suggestion that for him Objectivism sought 'to make the poem an object' should be met with scepticism because materiality does not exhaust language's potential.[41] When, for example, Oppen speaks of the 'pulse of the thought which is given by the lines',[42] he is describing a necessarily reflexive process, not a moment of visual apprehension and not a process of linear unfolding. Oppen's equivocal syntax is amplified by equivocal linebreaks – lines that often look both backwards and forwards. The temporal movement of the writing is intrinsically uncertain.

Oppen's orientation towards empirical observation, an inclination that appears in different ways in Pound, Williams and Zukofsky, is tempered by speculative thought that derives not from the *moment* of empirical encounter with the world but from the manifold of potential pathways made possible by the fissures of Oppen's open-ended syntax and linebreaks. The opening poem of *Discrete Series* contains the following quote from Henry James, 'approached the window as if to see/ what really was going on'. Oppen is quoting Henry James's 'The Story in It', in which the character Maud Blessingbourn (without the final 'e' that Oppen gives her) appears. Many years later he would again reference this moment in James in section 37 of his *Of Being Numerous* (NCP, p. 186). For my purposes, it is helpful to note that Oppen begins his first book with a character looking out of the window. Glass is one of the running themes of the book. Yet the conditional mood of the phrase lifted from James is critical. Oppen does not present someone looking at the real. His figure does not even look. She approaches the window 'as if' to see. The action, typically for Oppen, is held at arm's length by its framing in the conditional mood. Nothing of what follows in the book is as straightforward as the first poem's scene – a woman at a window – and even then the prospect of seeing is made provisional. The next poem in the series is given the title '1', though the implied sequence soon peters out. This poem is far more broken. There is not a single complete sentence in the poem:

> White. From the
> Under arm of T
>
> The red globe.
>
> Up
> Down. Round
> Shiny fixed
> Alternatives
>
> From the quiet
>
> Stone floor . . .
>
> (NCP, p. 6)

The poem begins with a line that might refer to a T-shirt, but then juxtaposes the T shape with – after a line's space – a red globe. There is no apparent relationship at all between these two groups of words. Nor is there any indication why the red globe might take a definite article. The prepositions that follow bring movement into the poem, though it is not clear whether this movement is potentially the property of the objects in the poem, or of the perceiving eye. The 'round' may or may not refer to the globe. The 'alternatives' are qualified by the adjectives 'shiny' and 'fixed', neither of which makes an easy fit with the noun. The concluding two lines are separated by a line's space but might easily be run together. There is no indication which absent object is the agent of the absent verb that conveys moving 'from', or whether there is a destination to which it is moving.

I choose this poem because, as the notes to the *New Collected Poems* point out, it has been identified with a specific visual image: the logo used by a popular manufacturer of lifts. The image, Oppen wrote in a letter to Charles Tomlinson, would have been recognisable to his 1930s readers: 'So familiar at the time that I don't think anyone was puzzled'. The movement of the poem, the globe, the stone floor, all become comprehensible read through this lens. Oppen's further remarks extend the description of the scene to include a veiled criticism of alienated white-collar labour: 'The office building evoked by its lighting effects in those dim days. And it limited alternatives, the limited alternatives of a culture' (cited in *NCP*, p. 359). However, this reading of the poem exemplifies the limited perspective offered by what Williams, in his review, calls 'what the poem says', as opposed to what it *is*. What makes the poem work, in Williams's terms, is its formal arrangement. The 'irreducible minimum' that Williams identifies leads to the extreme brokenness of presentation. The possible meanings opened up by the uncertain relations between word and word, line and line, in the poem are far more complexly expressive than the unification of the fragments through the visual image of a lift. The Oppen we reach through Williams's prism is one in which both perception and language are contingent on the historical circumstances in which they take place. The enduring communicative power of this clipped arrangement of twenty-one words lies, in other words, in its ability to express in formal terms what Williams called the 'dialectical necessities of its day'.

Conferring a determinate shape on the poems of *Discrete Series*, as we may with the lift logo, is to lead them towards an Imagistic directness that they quite clearly resist. Once again, it is necessary to read Oppen against his own stated desire for clarity. If we compare, say, 'The Red Wheelbarrow' to '[Under arm of T]', we see that the later poem depends on an ellipsis so severe that the visual image it addresses is inaccessible to the reader. So, while the poem clearly aspires to contemplate the material world, the reader is bounced into a contemplation of the language through which perception and representation are mediated. The urge to reach an 'irreducible minimum' is carried to the point at which the communicative potential of the words is entirely changed.

While it extends a tradition that has its roots in early Imagism, *Discrete Series* nonetheless dismantles the Imagist 'direct perception'. The urge to visualise founders on Oppen's syntax. We cannot imagine the relation between the 'T' and the 'red globe'. Prepositions and adjectives are detached from their substantives. The 'shiny' may refer to the globe but it also appears to refer to the 'fixed alternatives', and it is very hard indeed to make the leap from 'fixed alternatives' to the narrowness of office life, as Oppen suggests we might. The poem appears to fail in the terms that he himself claims for it. The richly communicative outcome of Oppen's techniques of reduction is to amplify the crosstalk produced by the encounter between subject, object and text.

In this writing, a desire to bring a world into being on the printed page is confronted by the great difficulty of doing so. The poems' truthfulness lies not in direct representation but in their faithfulness as a record of thought. Oppen remarks that: 'I was, even in 1929 [ie *Discrete Series*] consciously attempting to trace, to re-produce, the act of the world upon the consciousness.'[43] He is drawn to the unadorned facticity of the substantive, but his substantives are set in such equivocal signifying contexts that they become vehicles for questioning the processes of perception and representation.

As elsewhere in this study, the 'thing' is at issue. One of the best-known poems from his later period, which began twenty-five years after the poems of *Discrete Series*, is 'Psalm', from 1965's *This in Which* (NCP, p. 99). In the most useful interview we have with Oppen, L. S. Dembo asks what the 'faith' is in the lines 'The small nouns/ Crying faith/ In this in which the wild deer/ Startle, and stare out'. Oppen replies:

> Well, that the nouns refer to something; that it's there, that it's true, the whole implication of these nouns; that appearances represent reality, whether or not they misrepresent it: that this in which the thing takes place, this thing is here, and that these things do take place. On the other hand, one is left with the deer, staring out of the thing, at the thing, not knowing what will come next.[44]

This is a remarkable aspiration: truth and representation, a match between thing said and thing meant. Yet the terms are hazy, particularly the 'thing' – a word that has been at a focal point of equivocation since Pound's early statements on Imagism. The 'thing' under discussion appears to be at once an object, a scene, and an action that 'takes place'. The remark is complicated by the deer in the poem, which is both of the thing (construed as 'scene') and distinct from it, an uncomprehending consciousness that looks out of the poem and 'at the thing'.[45] This proliferation of versions of thingness may, perhaps, be understood as 'that which is represented'. There is a desire for a revelatory, even transcendental, coming together of word and referent. Yet, the word will not simply convey meaning in a one-to-one way. Syntax nuances the perception in ways that are almost uncontrollable. The poem will stand as the tangled evidence of a perceptual incident in which neither word nor thing can be known independently.

In his editor's introduction to the *New Collected Poems*, Davidson argues that, in Oppen's poetry, '[o]ne finds oneself in a world of intersecting particulars, no one of which may be isolated for purposes of scrutiny. Oppen is less interested in *what* is discovered than he is in the condition or mood in which things can be apprehended, in which things constellate a world.'[46] This remark, although it runs counter to Oppen's stated views on appearance and reality, better captures the workings of Oppen's writing. Yet it does not account for methods that go beyond spareness and economy to a warping ellipsis that, as we have seen with the elevator motif, places a near-opaque veil between reader and scene.

Williams's 'the poet thinks with his poem' is desubjectivised with Davidson's suggestion that 'For Oppen the poem does not represent the mind thinking; it *is* the mind thinking itself.'[47] This staging of the 'mind thinking itself' is encountered as a wary, hesitant, self-correcting linguistic process that is consistent with Oppen's various techniques of abbreviation. The faithfulness that the writing achieves is not to the world of objects and nor is it to a notionally preverbal state of thought, somehow gestured at in language. Rather, it communicates a highly self-aware contemplation of the mutual embeddedness of world and thought.

To take an example from one of the less well known poems in *Discrete Series*:

> As I saw
> There
> Year ago —
> If there's a bird
> On the cobbles;
> One I've not seen

(NCP, p. 22)

In this condensed poem, Oppen relates a moment of perception. As often in his work, we begin *in media res*, as if in the middle of a discussion. Something was seen a year ago. Oppen then makes present a bird – hypothetically, with the word 'if'. It is located in a particular place, 'On the cobbles'. The poem concludes by apparently refuting its first line, with 'One I've not seen'. Does the speaker mean a *kind* of bird he has not seen? Perhaps. But the poem seems more likely to turn on a problematisation both of perception and statement. This is not the baldly stated face in the city crowd or the wheelbarrow. Oppen's bird is both made present and withheld by the conditional syntax and the extreme compression of the little poem.

As with 'Party on Shipboard', this poem maintains a persistent tension between part and whole, singularity and collective, past and present, subject and object. The instability of these relationships is specifically linguistic. Oppen's beloved 'little words' cannot help but insert themselves into relationships – and so the work's empirical aims are undermined by a conceptual mediatedness that is far richer than the bare logging of sense-impressions.[48]

Oppen's later work is various, and the 25-year gap between *Discrete Series* and *The Materials* troubles any attempt to think of poetic continuities or genealogies. Oppen's most famous poem, the Pulitzer-winning 'Of Being Numerous', is a long one. However, even this is broken into smaller units: it is a serial poem. The tenor is meditative and the thought more sequential than in most of Oppen's work. While Oppen's writing is more or less long and more or less consecutive, and his use of page-space varied, there is a remarkable consistency of register. Oppen continually sought to punch holes in his writing, strewing his poems with communicative gaps. These are at once spaces for speech and figures for looking.

This motif of the hole is evident in the second poem of 'Five Poems about Poetry' from 1965's *This in Which*, in which Oppen references Williams:

> The little hole in the eye
> > Williams called it, the little hole
> > > Has exposed us naked
> > > To the world.
>
> > And will not close.
>
> (NCP, pp. 101–2)

The hole that Oppen refers to is found in the second part of Williams's 1955 poem 'Shadows':[49]

> > > Save for the little
> > central hole
> > > of the eye itself
> > > > into which
> > we dare not stare too hard
> > > or we are lost.
>
> (CPW, p. 310)

Williams's hole 'of the eye' and Oppen's hole 'in the eye' are different in emphasis. Williams writes of the pupil as something that we cannot look too closely at, as if it were the sun. The pupil becomes a perilous void, both as a window on to the world, and in the person into whose eyes we are gazing. For Oppen, the issue is perception, not interaction. The pupil is like the hole in a pinhole camera (like that referred to in Williams's review of *Discrete Series*), and it makes humans vulnerable. Being open to the world – perceiving – entails risk as well as reward. Human consciousness, in this poem, receives impressions like a screen, as 'Blankly, the world/ Looks in'. Williams goes on to valorise the 'instant', which is 'all we have'. But for Oppen the focus is on those who feel 'violent' and 'alone' and are unable to 'rest'. In 'Parousia', the fourth poem in the sequence, the world is 'fierce' and 'solitary' and the 'fact' that it is 'irrevocable' is 'lethal'. More than this, though, the 'little hole' speaks of the one's openness – willed or unwilled – to the things 'which one cannot/ Not see' (*NCP*, p. 185). This, Oppen remarks in interview, is the 'base of my metaphysic'.[50]

I would like to turn to Williams to develop this point in a more formal direction. Oppen said that 'What I learned from Williams was ... what Zukofsky meant by "objectification": the question of form.'[51]

For Oppen, one has no choice but to see, and the facts of the world are irrevocably present. The on-off movement of sense, line by fractured line, becomes in Oppen a way of parsing perception. The need for a particularly condensed idiom springs from the desire to use poetry as a speculative device, not as a record of the known. As he remarks, 'the line is a limitation . . . a unit, a solidity, something to stand on. It derives from the fact . . . that I wouldn't bother to write something which I already knew. The lines are line by line the achievement and the meaning of the image.'[52]

While Oppen sometimes spoke of facts, the empirical and the actual, his poetry is really oriented towards the unknown. Incompletion is the means through which mental phenomena that are not amenable to articulation are made available to the reader. Oppen's poetic sense-making is grounded in small particles. The 'little hole in the eye' stands for a prosody that finds expansive speculative range through, not in spite of, the drive to reduction.

At this point, it would be useful to turn to a quality that is a long-running preoccupation of Oppen's: clarity. In section 22 of his poem 'Of Being Numerous' he appeals to a visionary clarity that, paradoxically, is aligned with silence.

> Clarity
>
> In the sense of *transparence*,
> I don't mean that much can be explained.
>
> Clarity in the sense of silence.

(*NCP*, p. 175)

The clarity that the poem imagines is an unusual one. For most, terms such as 'clarity' and 'transparence' would correspond to an instrumental use of language, in which message takes precedence over medium. For Oppen, though, clarity leads not towards clear meanings but towards a clearing-away of meaning to reach a silence that teems with expressive potential. The move is comparable to his desire to celebrate 'facts' and the 'actual'. What might, in the hands of some poets, involve a turn towards a prosaic realism, involves, in Oppen's work, a commitment to a strenuously difficult poetry grounded (albeit in different ways at different stages of his career) in ellipsis and condensation. Indeed, the terms 'clarity' and 'transparence' might just as well be replaced with 'opacity' (to take a term favoured by his most thoroughgoing commentator, Peter Nicholls).[53]

'Route', which appears in the same 1968 volume, begins with the epigraph 'the void eternally generative', which is attributed to the Chinese poet and literary critic Lu Chi. This long multi-form poem expands on many of the preoccupations of work written three decades earlier. It ranges from two-word lines to prose narrative. The lines are typically longer than in *Discrete Series* but they are mostly single or grouped in twos or threes. While the work of the 1960s is less radically committed to brevity than in very early or very late Oppen, the communicative potential of endings remains a powerful formal and thematic principle. As with 'Of Being Numerous', the poem ruminates on the nature of clarity:

> Clarity, clarity, surely clarity is the most beautiful
>   thing in the world
> A limited, limiting clarity
>
> I have not and never did have any motive of poetry
> But to achieve clarity
>
>   (*NCP*, p. 193)

Oppen here he makes clarity the defining ambition of his writing. What is initially surprising, though, is the phrase 'a limited, limiting clarity'. The clarity that Oppen admires derives its force from constraint. It is narrow itself and it elicits a narrowing of focus. It is clear that in this period, the 'limited, limiting clarity' embraces a broader range of poetic and cognitive states than is envisaged in *Discrete Series*. In 'Route', coming to an end is a theme as well as an effect of lineation. There are numerous references to roads and accidents, and, towards the end of the poem, to apocalypse: 'cataclysm of the plains, jungles, cities' (*NCP*, p. 201). Reference is made to the use of napalm in Vietnam, and to Oppen's own wartime experience in the Alsace region of France. In a forceful anecdote, he tells the story of a local man drafted into the German army who committed suicide by riding his bicycle fast downhill into a tree. The poem begins with the chromosomal beginning of life, but coming to an end is felt at the level of line, the human life, colonial genocide, war and humanity itself. The poem aspires, on one hand to Oppenesque plainness: 'The purity of the materials, not theology, but to present/ the circumstances'. On the other, it acknowledges 'Words cannot be wholly transparent. And that is the/ "heartlessness" of words' (*NCP*, p. 194).[54] The poem begins and ends with nothingness – Lu Chi's generative void – and the dream that gives way to the real:

> These things at the limits of reason, nothing at the limits
> of dream, the dream merely ends, by this we know it is the real
>
> That we confront
>
>   (*NCP*, p. 202)

With a 'Prufrock'-like awakening to death, Oppen's poem considers ending as a form of clarity.[55] The 'limited, limiting' quality that he admires allows him to bring a clear eye to bear on the unstructured psychic experience – dream, unreason – that poetry classically privileges. The final phrase, with its three isolated words, shows limitation to be enabling, a void that is 'eternally generative'.

Such scrupulous attention to psychic experience is one expression of Oppen's interest in consciousness, which is a notable feature of both his daybooks and his 'Statement on Poetics': 'Impossible to doubt the actualness of one's own consciousness: but therefore consciousness in itself, of itself, by itself carries the principle of ACTUALNESS for it is actual beyond doubt.'[56] This thought finds poetic revoicing in 'Who Shall Doubt', from *Myth of the Blaze*:

'Who Shall Doubt'

consciousness

>   in itself

of itself carrying

>   'the principle
>   of the actual' being

actual

itself ((but maybe this is a love
poem

Mary)) nevertheless

>   neither

the power
of the self nor the racing
car nor the lilly

>   is sweet but this

(*NCP*, p. 259)

In a letter to John Taggart, Oppen suggests that the thought about consciousness 'should have been the meaning of "objectivism" '.[57] The phenomenological or ontological weight of 'the principle/ of the actual' and its revelation to itself through the consciousness of consciousness is important to Oppen's late poetics (its seeds can be found in the earlier writing). The word 'actual' seems to refer both to an experience of the moment and of the real. Clearly, there is a difference between the phrase, found in the 'Statement' – 'consciousness in itself, of itself, by itself carries the principle of ACTUALNESS for it is actual beyond doubt' – and the poetic formulation. Indeed, the fracturing of the phrase by means of linebreaks, syntax and punctuation brings a quality that is integral to the argument of this book: that poetry's meanings are not co-extensive with the meanings of words and phrases that constitute it.

The spacing and interruption in 'Who Shall Doubt' enact the turning-back of consciousness upon itself, bringing a reflexive hesitancy to the thought. Oppen gives a distinct representation of the movement of consciousness by standing outside the process he is describing and framing it in the particular movement of the poem. Thus, while the poem advances a rhetoric of immediacy, it achieves its effect – *can only* achieve its effect – through the mediation of poetic form. In prose, the thought is unexceptional. The poem, moreover, moves beyond the 'actual// itself' to develop complicating perspectives. It considers whether it is a love poem, and moves to a conclusion in which such poetic subjects as the self, racing cars (a rare Oppen joke?) and flowers are discounted in favour of 'this'. With the 'little word' this the poem refers to the haecceity of the poem itself. Yet, the encounter gestured at so confidently by 'this' is only notionally direct. The 'actual', in other words, is actually far from actual.

The poem 'The Little Pin: Fragment', also in *Myth of the Blaze*, is dotted with the puncture marks mentioned in my discussion of the pinhole above. When Oppen writes of 'the intricate// veins in the stones and the rock/ of the mountains wandering// stars in the dark ...', (NCP, p. 254), he seems to find patterning in non-human timescales – geological and cosmic time – that can be only be discerned with the closest of attention to the smallest of scales. At the end of the poem come the remarkable lines:

>   Song?
>
> astonishing
>
> song?   the world
> sometime be
>
> world the wind
> be wind o western
> wind to speak
>
>   of this
>
> (NCP, p. 255)

Oppen frequently refers to Shelley's destructuring west wind. Yet such lines also attest to his fascination with Blake's world-encompassing 'grain of sand'.[58] The meeting of 'world' and 'wind' resembles that between world and poetry, and all that it is possible is to say of 'this'. Again, Oppen's poem ends with a pronoun without a referent. The thisness of 'this' is ultimately the subject of the poem. While many poets of the modernist era sought to comprehend complexity through large, synthesising visions, Oppen's drive is always towards the small and the particular. In his poetry, the loquacity of the small is only fully encountered in the broken, miniaturist, pinpricked collage that he cultivated.

In Oppen's treatment of smallness I find a demystifying attachment to uncertainty. In his poetry the objects of the world are the beginning not the end of thought. The contingency he brings to the smallest act of attention to the world, the minutest nuance of phrasing offers a world-renewing openness to the strangeness of poetic articulation.

This apparent narrowness of focus does not preclude the collective, social dimension of the poetry, which is sometimes glancingly invoked and sometimes an absent presence, discernible by implication. There is a Whitmanesque concern with the relation between the one and the many, the small and the large, in the early 'Party on Shipboard', and in 'Of Being Numerous'. In the very late work this mutates into a preoccupation with relatedness. The public role of the poet is at issue in such poems as 'Res Publica' (the last poem of *Myth of the Blaze*), and in 'Disasters' and 'Populist'. In these poems, the collective is experienced through the small, not the large. He closes the short poem 'The Natural', which appears towards the end of *Primitive*, with an echo of 'Populist's 'I am of their people':

> help me I am
>
> of that people the grass
> blades touch
>
> and touch the small
>
> distances the poem
> begins
>
> (*NCP*, p. 281)

'If it all Went up in Smoke' ends with a near-repetition of these words, preceded by:

> the poem begins
>
> neither in word
> nor meaning but the small
> selves haunting
>
> us in the stones and is less
>
> always than that
>
> (*NCP*, p. 274)

In both poems the possibility of relatedness is imaged in the blades of grass that touch. In 'If it all went up in Smoke', the 'small/ selves' sit alongside the 'small// distances', and the poem is still 'less' than that. The linebreak or stanza-break that follows the word 'small' serves to amplify the effect of reduction. The interplay between very small and very large is repeated in *Primitive*'s Halloween poem, 'Strange are the Products', with its reference to the 'small/ huge dark' (*NCP*, p. 283). This makes comedy of the impenetrability that Oppen's poems so often circulate around.

'Neighbours', the penultimate poem in *Primitive*, begins (like the first poem of *Discrete Series*) with an act of perception, someone gazing through a window. It ends with the barest commitment to communication, however much words will 'fail' us: 'we/ will speak// to each/ other we/ will speak' (*NCP*, p. 285). Poetry, here as in his earliest collection, is found in the minute detail, the 'small// distances'. The poetry offers no hope of a collective political subject, but this late work nonetheless reflects on political agency through the pinprick openings it locates in the verbal fabric. Such poems recommend an attentiveness to being in the world that is always on the point of atomisation as the tiny salient details multiply. What truth there is, in late Oppen, is to be found in an accumulation of tiny points of experiential data that, held together in the contemplative frame of the poem, hold out the hope of a renewal of perception.

In George Oppen's writing, poetic thought ultimately cannot ultimately escape impenetrability, notwithstanding the poet's commitment to 'clarity'. The poems, to borrow Nicholls's formulation, enact a 'resistance to conceptual resolution, leaving a remainder which thought cannot penetrate'.[59] Yet Oppen's needles, pinpricks, and 'little hole' lead towards a liberatory acuity of perception. Williams was prescient in his 1934 review to locate in Oppen's writing not a vapid minimalism, but a sightline, through the 'pinhole' to a 'world enormous as his mind permits him to witness'.[60] What emerges, ironically, from the palimpsest-like layering through which Oppen elaborated his poems,[61] is a poetry whose narrow vistas open on to an 'astonishing// song'. This, in Oppen's peculiarly abstract mode of lyric, celebrates a 'this' without object. His microcosmic vision far surpasses the little elements from which it is assembled.

Notes

1. Williams, 'The New Poetical Economy', pp. 220–5.
2. Jeffrey Twitchell-Waas draws the following conclusion in his article 'What were the "Objectivist" Poets?' ' "Objectivist," then, designates little more than an affiliation with the Imagist legacy as practiced by Pound and Williams' (p. 325).

3. Williams, 'The New Poetical Economy', p. 222. Pound's 'Credo', part of 'A Retrospect', foreshadows the critical language of objectivism: 'Technique. – I believe in technique as the test of a man's sincerity' (p. 9).
4. Williams, 'The New Poetical Economy', p. 221.
5. Williams's essay 'Caviar and Bread Again: A Warning to the New Writer' has more to say about poetry as the catalyst for change: 'On the poet devolves the most vital function of society: to recreate it – the collective world – in time of stress, in a new mode, fresh in every part, and so set the world working or dancing or murdering each other again, as it may be' (p. 103).
6. In her essay 'Objectivist Poetry and Poetics', Rachel Blau DuPlessis, a key figure in the reception of Oppen's work, writes: 'Though Objectivists were a late modernist set of leftists and realists, objectivist work is not Popular Front poetry, but rather a transposition of a Poundian sensibility to a leftist vision. . . . The complex materialist *world* as represented by the complex materialist *word* formed the rigorous dialetic of objectivist practice' (p. 91).
7. Ron Silliman, 'Third Phase Objectivism', p. 90.
8. Stevens writes in a 1946 letter: 'Williams is an old friend of mine. I have not read *Paterson*. I have the greatest respect for him, although there is the constant difficulty that he is more interested in the way of saying things than in what he has to say.' And, in a 1953 letter, he remarks: 'Williams . . . rejects the idea that meaning has the slightest value and describes a poem as a structure of little blocks' (Stevens, *Letters of Wallace Stevens*, p. 544, p. 803).
9. Williams, 'The New Poetical Economy', pp. 222–3.
10. Williams, 'The New Poetical Economy', pp. 223–4.
11. The prose of *Spring and All* (1922) drew on organic metaphors for poetic creativity.
12. Williams, 'The New Poetical Economy', p. 224, p. 225.
13. Williams, 'The New Poetical Economy', pp. 222–5.
14. Williams's move 'away from the word as symbol toward the word as reality' ('Excerpts from a Critical Sketch', p. 107) clearly diverged from Zukofsky's praise of the 'absolute symbol' in poems of reduced form: 'The economy of presentation in writing is a reassertion of faith that the combined letters – the words – are absolute symbols for objects, states, acts, interrelations, thoughts about them' ('An Objective', *Prepositions*, p. 14).
15. Blau DuPlessis, 'Objectivist Poetry and Poetics', p. 89.
16. Peter O'Leary, 'The Energies of Words', n.p.
17. Zukofsky and L. S. Dembo, 'Interview', p. 203. See Scroggins, *The Poem of A Life: A Biography of Louis Zukofsky*; O'Leary, 'The Energies of Words'; Blau DuPlessis's 'Objectivist Poetry and Poetics'; and Twitchell-Waas for accounts of the 'Objectivist' number of *Poetry* magazine.
18. Twitchell-Waas, 'What Were the "Objectivist" Poets?', p. 318.
19. Zukofsky, 'Sincerity and Objectification', p. 274.
20. Oppen, *Selected Letters*, p. 146.
21. Oppen and L. S. Dembo, 'Interview', p. 160.
22. Zukofsky, *Anew: Complete Shorter Poetry*, p. 145.
23. Michael Davidson, introduction to George Oppen: *New Collected Poems*, p. xxxiii. Subsequent references are given parenthetically as *NCP*.

24. Cited in Peter Nicholls, *George Oppen and the Fate of Modernism*, p. 36.
25. Oppen and L. S. Dembo, 'Interview', p. 161.
26. Oppen, *Selected Letters*, p. 146.
27. Oppen and L. S. Dembo, 'Interview', p. 161.
28. Cited in Nicholls, *George Oppen and the Fate of Modernism*, p. 152.
29. Oppen, *Selected Prose, Daybooks and Papers*, p. 49.
30. Oppen, Mary Oppen, Burton Hatlen and Tom Mandel, 'Interview', p. 233.
31. The line derives from Reznikoff's 'Jersualem the Golden', and should read 'a girder still itself among the rubbish' (Reznikoff, *Poems 1918–1975*, p. 107). The error is repeated on the rear cover of the book.
32. Oppen and L. S. Dembo, 'Interview', p. 161.
33. Oppen and L. S. Dembo, 'Interview', p. 161.
34. Letter to Blau DuPlessis, *Selected Letters*, p. 122. Oppen suggests that this series of numbers should have appeared on the flyleaf of *Discrete Series*.
35. Andrew Crozier. 'Inaugural and Valedictory: the Early Poetry of George Oppen', p. 207.
36. The phrase 'Net of branches' comes from 'Some San Francisco Poems' #6, *New Collected Poems*, p. 228.
37. In a 1934 letter to Pound, Oppen writes: 'The book'll be named DS. Tricky, but I want a name out of statistics for 'Party Aboard' [*sic*] and some others particularly, and the term describes my hon. intentions pretty accurately.' *Selected Letters*, p. 4.
38. Davidson, introduction to *New Collected Poems*, p. xxix, p. xxx.
39. Oppen, *Selected Prose, Daybooks and Papers*, p. 49.
40. Crozier, 'Inaugural and Valedictory', p. 151.
41. In a February 1961 letter to Mary Ellen Solt, Oppen writes, 'We [i.e. the 'Objectivists'] were all very much concerned with poetic form, and form not merely as texture, but as the shape which makes the poem possible to grasp. . . . Objectivist meant not an objective viewpoint, but to objectify the poem, to make the poem an object. Meant form' (*Selected Letters*, p. 47). Cf. Zukofsky's 'the apprehension satisfied completely as to the appearance of the art form as an object' ('An Objective', p. 13). Nicholls, *George Oppen and the Fate of Modernism*, p. 7, n10, notes Davidson's 'counter-view', the suggestion that Zukofsky's practice 'exposes the object-status of the poem as a delusion'. See Davidson, 'Dismantling "Mantis": Reification and Objectivist Poetics', p. 522.
42. Oppen and L. S. Dembo, 'Interview', p. 167.
43. Oppen, in Davidson (ed.), 'An Adequate Vision: A George Oppen Daybook', p. 30.
44. Oppen and L. S. Dembo, 'Interview', p. 163.
45. Nicholls is the best resource for discussion of Oppen's debt to Heidegger.
46. Davidson, in *NCP*, p. xxxi.
47. Davidson, *Ghostlier Demarcations*, p. 70.
48. On the 'little words', see L. S. Dembo and George Oppen, 'Interview', p. 162.
49. The lines cited also contain an allusion to *Spring and All*'s 'They enter the new world naked'.
50. Oppen, Charles Amirkhanian and Don Branning, 'Interview, 1973', p. 52.
51. Oppen, Charles Amirkhanian and David Gitin, 'Interview, 1970', p. 43.

52. Oppen, and Charles Tomlinson, 'Interview, 1973', p. 58.
53. For discussion of the ethics of 'opacity', see Nicholls's article 'Of Being Ethical: Reflections on George Oppen'.
54. These two lines occur in a sympathetic remark on Cid Corman in a 1966 letter (*Selected Letters*, p. 144).
55. The last poem in his last collection, *Primitive* (1978), which contains glancing references to life events such his war experience and the composition of his 'series empirical' is entitled 'Till Other Voices Wake Us'. It ends 'till other voices wake us/ and we drown' (*NCP*, p. 286).
56. Oppen, *Selected Prose, Daybooks and Papers*, p. 49. The The question of consciousness in Oppen is addressed in Peter Nicholls's *George Oppen and the Fate of Modernism*; Matthew Carbery's *Phenomenology and the Late Twentieth-Century American Long Poem*; and Tim Woods's *The Poetics of the Limit*.
57. Oppen, *Selected Letters*, p. 290.
58. Oppen, *Selected Letters*, pp. 19–20; *Selected Prose, Daybooks and Papers*, p. 127. Oppen and L. S. Dembo, 'Interview': 'Blake is more important to me than Williams' (p. 171).
59. Nicholls, *George Oppen and the Fate of Modernism*, p. 129.
60. Williams, 'The New Poetical Economy', pp. 222–3.
61. Davidson, *Ghostlier Demarcations*, pp. 64–78.

Chapter 4

Lorine Niedecker

Lorine Niedecker's handling of brevity is different to that practised by either George Oppen or her friend and long-term correspondent Louis Zukofsky. All of her best poems are short-lined and many of them are also short, though in later life she produced some admirable serial poems that explore large and small scales. The Wisconsin poet has been read in many ways: as surrealist, modernist recluse, Objectivist, ecologist, feminist, folk author, and a writer of place. Early accounts of her writing tended to dwell on her rural isolation and her close relationship, poetic and personal, with Zukofsky. The range of her work was not really appreciated until, thirty-two years after her death, a reliable collected edition of her poetry became available.[1] Since the publication of the *Collected Works*, recent scholars have found new ways of reading Niedecker and she has gradually emerged as a key figure in American post-war poetry.[2] Niedecker's poetry shows a debt to the naturalism of Thoreau and the taut asceticism of Dickinson, but much of her work draws on the compression of the post-Imagist tradition, even in the long-form (but still short-lined) work of her later years.

She viewed herself as an Objectivist, though on the 'periphery' of that loose association of writers.[3] From the outset, brevity was a key feature of her work. Her poetry, as Rachel Blau DuPlessis has argued, shows a changing relationship to Objectivism as it develops.[4] The Objectivist issue of *Poetry* magazine was certainly central to her beginnings as a poet,[5] announcing a constellation of writing that she considered 'the centre of literature in this country and in the world'.[6]

Her relationship and correspondence with Louis Zukofsky, in particular, helped shape her poetics. Yet, although she often acted on his editorial suggestions, her poetry itself is very different to Zukofsky's, both in form and subject matter. Where their attitudes towards writing converge is on the issue of compression. For Zukofsky, 'Condensation is more than half of composition', 'simplicity of utterance and song go together' and 'good poetry is the barest – most essentially complete – form of presenting a subject'.[7]

These positions, which echo some of Ezra Pound's early injunctions, are strongly evident in Niedecker's writing. However, notwithstanding the importance of her conversations with Zukofsky and a few others, detailed and explicit discussion of poetry in her correspondence is scarce. Her longest statement on writing comes from a letter to a Wisconsin friend, Gail Roub, a history teacher who lived within a mile of Niedecker.[8] In it, she expands on her relationship to Objectivism, complicating it with a notion of 'reflection':

> how to define a way of writing poetry which is not Imagist nor Objectivist fundamentally nor Surrealism alone ... I loosely called it 'reflections' or as I think it over now, reflective, maybe. The basis is direct and clear – what has been seen or heard, etc ... – but something gets in, overlays all that ... The visual form is there in the background, and the words convey what the visual form gives off after it's felt in the mind. A heat that is generated and takes in the whole world of the poem. A light, a motion, inherent in the whole. Not surprising since modern poetry and old poetry if it's good, proceeds not from one point to the next linearly but in a circle. The *tone* of the thing. And awareness of everything influencing everything. Early in life I looked back of our buildings to the lake and said, 'I am what I am because of all this – I am what is around me – those woods have made me ...' I used to feel that I was goofing off unless I held only to the hard, clear image, the thing you could put your hand on but now I dare do this reflection.[9]

One way of viewing this rare statement on poetics from Niedecker, is as a commitment to interconnectedness, a state of anti-narrative holism – 'everything influencing everything'.[10] What Niedecker means by 'reflection' is rather elusive, though it is clear that she uses the concept to distance herself from both Imagism and Objectivism. She seems to view the 'hard, clear image' as one stage in the compositional process, but to attribute to 'reflection' and 'words' a secondary process that greatly complicates what was once 'direct and clear'. The 'heat' thus generated is linguistic. 'Light' and 'motion' are felt through the concatenation of linguistic representations in the unfolding of the poem, not the presentation of a literary snapshot. Language, then, becomes not a conduit to the image, but the very matter of the poem.

Another perspective on her poetics is found in a letter to Mary Hoard:

> I conceive poetry as the folk-tales of the mind and as creating our own remembering. And no creature puts idiom on anything at all except by putting himself on it, and to me, that means, inchoate thought, the Self association of nervous vocables coloured by the rhythms of the moment ... this would be of course what no one else has written – else why write?[11]

While 'inchoate thought' may evoke the surrealism of her earlier writing, the 'Self association of nervous vocables coloured by the rhythms of the moment' suggests a partially directed process in which sound and rhythm give colour and shape to spontaneous thought. Niedecker attaches value to 'unrecognisability' and the 'non-expressive, unconscious part' of memory, which we access as 'a nerve-sense, a vibration, a color, a rhythm'. Her goal in this letter is to 'reconcile energy with unrecognizability'.[12]

In my view, Niedecker's poetry is at its best when the 'hard, clear image' is blurred by the various cultivated intensities and uncertainties of the form and syntax of her writing: what she means by 'unrecogizability' or 'a nerve-sense, a vibration, a color, a rhythm'. The notion of Objectivist lucidity was a chimera, as was the idea of conceiving the conceptual-material construct of the poem itself as an object. She, like William Carlos Williams, is much preoccupied by the movement of non-semantic elements in poetry – by what they both called measure. The term is discussed in her remarks to Cid Corman, and twinned with a Poundian emotional charge:

> I get for the first time that meaning has something to do with song – one hesitates a bit longer with some words in some lines for the thought or the vision – but I'd say mostly, of course, cadence, measure make song. And a kind of shine (or sombre tone) that is of the same intensity throughout the poem. And the thing moves. But as in all poems, everywhere, depth of emotion condensed.[13]

It is notable that Niedecker admires 'light' in her letter to Roub and 'shine' in her remarks to Corman. It is a quality that accompanies song and that is at once 'sombre' and shining. Her reference to the 'thing' echoes Pound, and one might find in her remarks about emotion something comparable to Eliot's thinking on the objective correlative. Yet Eliot's 'a set of objects, a situation, a chain of events which shall be the formula for that particular emotion' is, in its expansiveness, very different to Niedecker's 'emotion condensed', which depends, above all, on compression. I interpret the sombre 'shine' that Niedecker values not as an epiphanic gleam, but, more prosaically, as a consistent 'intensity' of poetic thought.

Measure, consistency of tone and compression are intrinsic to the successful poem, for Niedecker. All of these features are evident in a famous poem from 1962, 'Poet's Work':

> Grandfather
>   advised me;
>   Learn a trade

> I learned
>   to sit at desk
>   and condense
>
> No layoff
>   from this
>   condensery
>
> <div align="right">(<i>CW</i>, p. 194)</div>

In this poem, Pound's '*condensare*' is viewed as the work of condensation. Poetry is self-consciously reduced to the art of reduction. The simple act of sitting at the desk is the condition of possibility for this art form. But it is also labour, and now a life-sentence. There is no 'layoff' from this work. The reference is not merely poetic: a 'condensery' is a condensed-milk production plant, of which there were many in Wisconsin.[14] This ability to play across both the real-world referent and abstract or figural content is typical of Niedecker's writing.[15] The poem is not a self-propelling machine, autonomous from the world. Neither does it set itself the task of simply and sincerely stating the world. It is an agile, compressed sequence of words on the page in which representation and reflection have equal status. More than this, the 'shine' or 'light' or 'motion' that Niedecker attributes to the poem lies above all in technique: the craft of arranging words on the page in ways that bring readerly attention to bear on the process of compression. The intervention of the linebreak and the acute economy that she brings to the thoughts she formulates communicate a formal commitment to austerity. This willed paucity of means forms, on one hand, a poetics, and on the other – as the subject matter of the poetry sometimes makes clear – serves as a formal analogue for the unwilled material poverty of Niedecker's life. In what follows, I will discuss the relationship between poem and world in Niedecker's work through the prism of two pressing real-world themes in her work: property and plumbing.

The term 'foreclosure' plays a prominent role in Niedecker's poetic treatment of property. A deliberate poverty of diction contributes to the power of Niedecker's writing in the late 1950s and early 1960s (she worked as a cleaning woman at Fort Atkinson hospital from 1957 to 1963). These were not particularly good years for Niedecker. She tried to sell the two small houses she had inherited from her father but could only sell on land contract (meaning that the buyers borrowed from the seller rather than the bank), leaving her with the obligation to foreclose on the deals if the buyers defaulted on their repayments (which they did).[16]

At a time of material difficulty, Niedecker makes a gesture of withdrawal or non-compliance that might be called a poetics of foreclosure. To foreclose is primarily understood in the legal sense: to bar a mortgage holder from redeeming a mortgage because payments have been missed. However, for Niedecker, foreclosure signifies more than reluctant expropriation and the resulting feeling of 'Venom against property'.[17] Indeed, it has a generative dimension. In her three foreclosure poems she draws a parallel between reduced poetic speech and the loss of material wealth. In both cases, loss is experienced as a gain. Here is the first of these poems, from 1962. Like many of Dickinson's poems, it begins with a definition:

> Property is poverty —
> I've foreclosed.
> I own again
>
> these walls thin
> as the back
> of my writing tablet.
>
> And more:
> all who live here —
> card table to eat on,
>
> broken bed —
> sacrifice for less
> than art.

(CW, pp. 194–5)

In this complicated poem, the house offers the barest conditions of shelter. Material wealth is compared, in a gesture of quasi-religious asceticism, to the superior 'wealth' of poverty. The speaker makes the gesture of foreclosure on her rental properties herself. She thus 'owns' these very reduced circumstances. The house is compared to the writing tablet, thus blending material circumstances with the preconditions for writing poetry, and offering shelter for that activity. Writing, rather than being aligned with the poet at her desk, is bound up with the fabric of the building. Compositional space, in the sense of *mise-en-page*, fuses with the physical location of composition.

The second half of the poem begins with the buried blessing of 'all who live here', which invokes the familiar formula 'Bless this house and all who enter'. Eating will take place on a flimsy card table; sleeping in a broken bed – the poem almost revels in its embrace of insufficiency. The paratactic movement of the close of the poem makes it hard to read the last four lines as either the completion of 'all who live here' or as a consequence or continuation of 'broken bed'. As a result of this uncertainty, the poem can be understood as either celebration or complaint. On one hand, the poem leads us to believe that Niedecker is making a fairly conventional act of artistic renunciation, choosing art over wealth and

worldly success; on the other hand, what she is left with is not art, but
'less/ than art'. Read this way, 'property' becomes not so much an index
of wealth and prosperity, as a description of her own predicament. She
owns almost nothing but even this sacrifice isn't enough, because the art
too is insufficient. Ultimately, both ownership and dispossession seem
unsatisfactory. As her editor notes, Niedecker writes the following on
the MS: '(don't confuse this with reality – I don't have to foreclose)'.[18]
So she imagines a notional embrace of deprivation that, in one available
reading, is deprived even of the consolation of artistic production and,
in another, sets aside the vexations of her material circumstances, all of
which amount to something 'less/ than art'.

A second property poem, written in 1964, sets out the terms of foreclosure differently:

> To foreclose
> or not
> on property
> and prose
>
> or care a kite
> if the p-p
> be yellow, black
> or white
>
> (CW, p. 197)

In this poem the speaker initially presents the possibility of foreclosure as
a problem: should she or shouldn't she? Property and prose are aligned,
and opposed to poetry. Read on its own, it is unclear how the second
stanza develops this thought. However, a letter to Zukofsky indicates
that the poem draws on Horace Gregory's translation of Catullus:

> Just wrote poem on foreclosing. Venom against property, the law, etc. I
> invoked Cat. 93 (Gregory's 2 lines for 93), the second line changed enough to
> suit what *I'm* talking about.[19]

The lines from Catullus she refers to are, in the translation she uses: 'I
shall not raise my hand to please you, Caesar, / nor do I care if you are
white or black.' Niedecker thus adapts the conventional 'render-unto-
Caesar' representation of the dictator as a metonym of power and
wealth. Again, the poem offers a kind of renunciation: for the speaker,
it doesn't matter what shape property or prose take. Both are rejected
out of hand. The addition of 'yellow' to the Catullus's white and black is
mischievous: 'pee pee' in 'p-p' provides the answer. The striking phrase
'care a kite' is skilfully unidiomatic, placed as if to produce a contrived
rhyme with the closing 'white'.

Thus the poem, despite its obscurities, tracks a developing thought. The opening suggests a dilemma – to be or not to be – as if foreclosing on property and prose was a decision that she really had to make. The second half of the poem is less ambivalent: the violence of 'care a kite' and the emphatic ellipsis of 'p-p' seem to choose a complete withdrawal from all that p-p/ property-prose represents. Again, condensation is integral both to the poem's manner of arguing: the poem could hardly be less prosaic. It makes a point of refusing the consecutive movement of prose and this point is best expressed through the extreme condensation of the poem.

The rhyming first and fourth lines give the poem a sentential quality, but the oddness of Niedecker's phrasing intensifies the anger in the writing. The second stanza might be supposed to amplify or complete the first, but, in fact, as if it were itself becoming enraged, the poem manages to perform the rejection of 'p[roperty]-p[rose]', while stating nothing of the sort – it actually proposes that it might 'care a kite' about them. In just twenty words, the poem follows a jagged path in which argument and ellipsis interact to achieve something like the intense reconciliation of 'energy and unrecognizability' that she wrote of in her letter to Hoard.

The third foreclosure poem is entitled 'Foreclosure' and was written in 1970, six years after the first two and just six months before Niedecker's death.

> Foreclosure
>
> Tell em to take my bare walls down
> my cement abutments
> their parties thereof
> and clause of claws
>
> Leave me the land
> Scratch out: the land
>
> May prose and property both die out
> and leave me peace

(CW, p. 291)

The poem is presented as a piece of dictation, as if from the deathbed. Again the 'p-p' duo is rejected, this time in favour of something that might be poetry and might be silence. The term 'foreclosure' this time suggests an opposition between the imperatives of financial institutions and her own priorities. More than his, however, 'Foreclosure', in Niedecker's lexicon, becomes shorthand for technique. She takes a term that is predicated on incompletion and turns it into a celebration of insufficiency. What in the world of prose and property is a devastating poverty becomes in her hands a strength.

In this poem of thematic and formal reduction Niedecker imagines the destruction of her house by those wielding legalese ('parties thereof', 'clause'). All she will have left is the bare earth (recalling her earlier poem beginning with the line 'I rose from marsh mud' (CW, p. 170)). The line 'scratch out: the land' might suggest scratching a living out of the land, but it also suggests that even the land should be scratched off the speaker's list of possessions as enumerated on a legal document. And that she might be reduced to making marks in the earth. Yet this is not a request for death: the speaker longs for the death of prose and property so she can have some peace. What remains is necessarily insubstantial – no longer land at all, rather a space of reverie, a clearing for the action of the poem. In this late poem, Niedecker appears at last to doubt the material bedrock of her poetic output.

The word 'abutments', which normally applies to the load-bearing structures of a bridge, is taken out of context. The word 'parties' refers to both a legal contract and a party wall. The heavy pun 'clause of claws' underlines the violence behind the litigation. The final couplet uses the 'May ...' construction common to both blessings and curses.[20] The speaker in the end requires not to be left in peace but to be left peace itself. Prose and property, meanwhile, will 'die out'.

In this poem, 'foreclosure' is a violent process. Yet it cannot rob the speaker of a means of speech, even as the meagre property is taken down. The incursions of property and prose cannot destroy the poem, which has an affinity with 'peace' and which deploys a technique of foreclosure for its own ends. The instruction 'scratch out', uttered as if to a scribe, supports the fiction that the poem is a thought uttered for someone else to write down. So there is a distance between speaker and text and the writer denies herself the agency even of writing her own words. Yet the poem persists, celebrating its insufficiency as an unkillable counter to the corrosive energies of property and prose.

In all of these poems there is a Dickinsonian revolt against the thought-constricting action of prose. They all endorse the speculative potential offered by the formal constrictions of poetic speech. Yet Niedecker, despite the debt to her forebear, keeps well away from the ecstatic-spiritual intensities of Dickinson. As Blau DuPlessis notes, Niedecker conspicuously avoids 'anything high, transcendent, evoking authority, bounty, glory', instead pursuing a 'materialist sublime of consciousness and reflection'.[21] The 'piercing virtue', in Dickinson's terms, of 'Renunciation' leads, for Niedecker, to a an intense encounter with a language that, through the gesture of foreclosure, becomes rich at the very moment of its impoverishment.

Interruption is crucial to Niedecker's technique: her writing often seems to function as a ritual that needs to reclaim the aggressive cessation of credit embodied in foreclosure and redeploy it as a repeated interruption of linguistic flow. This manifests itself in different ways at different times of her career. She is, in some ways, an expansive and open-ended poet, always urging the multifarious connections between poem and world. And some of her best-known work was achieved in relatively long form poetry: 'Paean to Place', 'Lake Superior' or 'Darwin'. Yet, even in such longer texts, she places her handling of the linebreak at the centre of her technique. The 'foreclosure' poems make explicit the inhibiting/ liberating nature of the foreshortened utterance. The technique is discernible throughout this body of work, even where condensation is not the matter of the poem.

* * *

Another facet of material existence, one that emphasises Niedecker's distance from the 'marsh mud', is evident in the early 1960s writing: her acquisition, at a quite advanced age, of her first flushing indoor toilet. A trio of poems written in 1962 focuses on the event. In her correspondence with Zukofsky she conveys her attachment to the new plumbing:

> my little pressure pump is a darling, jet, hums like a fan. The toilet tinkles a bit after the flushing. The faucet shines – I have no tub or shower or water heater, no rooms, heavens it was a trick to get my clothes and dresser and hip boots and vacuum sweeper back into the bathroom as it was.[22]

Niedecker writes affectionately about the pressure pump, as if it were a bird or small animal – and she makes it clear that her living conditions are very cramped. In the poems on this theme, however, the water machinery takes on a particular significance in relation to both poetic production and the watery landscape surrounding Niedecker's home. Mary Pinard has written provokingly about the importance of flood imagery in Niedecker's work. She draws our attention to the frequency with which the territory around Niedecker's house was flooded, noting: 'Niedecker's writing often shows a surrealist's appreciation for the usurpations of the flood. She took pleasure in the upended, the strange, the mongrel made from accident.'[23] Pinard refers to a letter to Cid Corman in which Niedecker uses the vocabulary of flooding to describe her writing:

> You and Jonathan Williams have thrown off the shackles of the sentence and the wide melody. For me the sentence lies in wait – all those prepositions and connectives – like an early spring flood. A good thing my follow-up feeling has always been condense, condense.[24]

Pinard links the flood to the ungovernable, but also with the repressive force of 'grammatical threats' and 'all that is implied by narrativity, exposition, its very connection to the mainstream'.[25] It may, however, be possible to construe differently what Niedecker writes to Corman. In other words, Niedecker may mean (and her meaning is, admittedly, far from clear) that the situating work that syntax does appears to offer illimitable options for narrative development. The writer feels she may be ambushed by the spring flood into a mode of utterance that is consecutive and determinate. Yet the 'follow-up feeling' to this moment of fullness and risk is offered by the impulse to condense. This allows her to excise the situating terms of prepositions and connectives through the action of condensing. The suppression of such words leads her to the necessarily paratactic mode of writing that I have begun to discuss above. In much the same way as she deploys the legal figure of foreclosure, the technology of the toilet, rather than the natural force of the flood, provides a metaphor for discussing her methods.[26]

In the first of the plumbing poems, written 8 June 1962 (the same day as 'Property is poverty', discussed above) the newly installed apparatus is aligned with poetic production:

> Now in one year
>   a book published
>   and plumbing –
> took a lifetime
>   to weep
>   a deep
>   trickle

(CW, p. 195)

Niedecker compares her career-long struggle for publication with acquiring the basic necessity of plumbing at the age of nearly sixty.[27] The first three lines sum up the year's achievements with some urgency. Yet the wide spaces of the second half of the poem cause it to move more slowly, its slowness aided by the long vowels of the weep/ deep rhyme. The subject pronoun for 'took a lifetime' is suppressed. Initially, the phrase appears to refer to the twin achievements outlined in the first three lines, but it then becomes clear that Niedecker is referring to the 'deep/ trickle' of her writing process, which is set against the business of publication. The 'deep/ trickle' suggests a leak or a wound, or even urination, with both publication and plumbing offered as a means of channelling the flow. Rather than the vocabulary of flooding, with its sense of natural excess and the breaching of boundaries, both imagery and formal movement are restrained and hesitant. The poem's speaker seems ambivalent: does the poem address a triumph over suffering, or does it instead suggest that in publication and plumbing something both personal and ungovernable is domesticated?

The poem counterposes the public, interactive, social and technological processes of plumbing and publication with the private, and in this case melancholic, act of writing. The speaker seems almost regretful to relinquish the 'deep/ trickle' that ends the poem. Driven perhaps by what Niedecker calls 'depth of emotion condensed',[28] the movement of the poem is from the large and public to the small, hesitant and concentrated – the reverse of what one might expect from a poem that considers the subject of publication.

Another poem from this period directly addresses the water pump. The following poem was published in the first issue of *Joglars* (co-edited by Clark Coolidge and Michael Palmer) in spring 1964. It is one of three that also included the untitled poem beginning 'to foreclose' and cited above:[29]

> *To my small*
> *electric pump*
>
> To sense
> and sound
> this world
>
> look to
> your snifter
> valve
>
> take oil
> and hum

(CW, p. 197)

The dedicatory title is peculiar – Niedecker is indeed writing an occasional poem to welcome a water pump into her house. What follows, however, is both anti-metaphysical and anti-humanistic. It parodies the kind of sententious instructional poem that is designed to inculcate wisdom in a child. A snifter valve allows air to enter or leave a pump's cylinder, almost as if it were allowing it to breathe. Besides that, the pump receives oil and hums. The second and third stanzas carry out the sensing and sounding recommended in the first. The dry humour of 'snifter/ valve', with its suggestion, in combination with 'oil', of inebriation, deflates any possibility that Niedecker might be reaching for a grand statement. Humming is both musical and mechanical. The breath of inspiration arrives via the humble snifter valve and poetry becomes the mild domestic pulse of the water pump. The poem is thus quietly but firmly anti-Romantic – writing becomes a modest but intense gesture of attunement.

The lines into which the poem's single sentence are broken are extremely short. Each, with the exception of 'valve', contains just two short words. All of the poem's words, with the exception of 'snifter', are monosyllabic. The only deviation from the disyllabic pattern on each line is the couplet 'your snifter/ valve', which simply breaks four syllables into a 3/1 pattern. Two kinds of temporal flow – the even syntactical unfolding of the sentence, and the unbroken hum of the pump – are described through the repeated interruption of the linebreak. The breaks do not have a jarring or disjunctive quality, yet they do have the effect of confronting linearity with insistent breaks. The poem thus replaces the regular pulse of the metrical line with the regular pulse of interruption. Rhythm is experienced by the reader not through accents, but through the linebreak.

Humming is also a feature of the final poem in this series, which shows a more equivocal attitude towards the arrival of plumbing in the Niedecker household. As with the first poem of the three, 'Now in one year', a contrast is drawn between a 'before' and an 'after', with technology as the dividing line between the two:

> *To my pres-*
> *sure pump*

I've been free
    with less
        and clean
I plumbed for principles

Now I'm jet-bound
by faucet   shower
heater   valve
ring seal   service

cost to my little
    humming
        water
            bird

(CW, p. 201)[30]

For Jonathan Skinner, discussing this poem, 'This sensitive "pressure pump" itself becomes one fulcrum in a writing practice gauged to felt parity between words, ideas and things, a mechanism adequate to the shifting contours (and occasional flooding) of their relations.'[31] However, while Skinner is surely right to focus on the levelling effect across categories, Niedecker's attitude seems less than celebratory. Here we see an example of the anti-materialistic attitude we saw in Niedecker's poems about property. Niedecker is clearly impelled to hymn the period when she was free of the financial burden of plumbing. The phrase 'I plumbed for principles' suggests that there was a greater ethical reach to her poetic existence when living a life of more rigorous austerity, closer to the marsh that spawned her. If this asceticism seems almost impossibly unforgiving, then there is room for manoeuvre towards the end of the poem. While she regrets being 'bound' to the new facilities by her investment, she also, as in the previous poem discussed, finds joy in its humming, which becomes a lyric throb. The *mise-en-page*, with the increasing indentation in the closing lines of the poem, suggests the freedom invoked in the first line has been supplanted by a new kind of textual freedom.

Niedecker's technique of condensation is strongly felt in this poem from the first linebreak, which conspicuously splits the word 'pressure'. The first unit of sense draws the kind of parallel between lived experience and poetics that is often found in Niedecker's work. In this way her tangles with property and plumbing in the poems discussed above become indissociable from her experience of writing. Ultimately, in both life and work, Niedecker has indeed chosen to be 'free with less'. The attribute of cleanliness might as much be attributed to a spare form of poetry as to Niedecker washing herself. The suppression of the full stop that might have come after 'clean' allows the two syntactical units to merge: the speaker evokes a state of bare existence, utterly unsupported by softening comforts. The austerity here represented looks past poetics, over the shoulder of the 'hard, clear' rhetoric of imagism, towards a Thoreauvian commitment to simplicity in living.

In the remainder of the poem she imagines herself 'jet-bound': pinned by a jet of water, by the paraphernalia of plumbing, to the pressure pump and all it entails. The hummingbird analogy brings an ancient metaphor for poetic speech – birdsong – into contact with twentieth-century machinery. As in the previous poem, humming is sound, not music. The poem changes direction as it moves down the page. At first it seems sceptical about the pump, with the spacing in lines 9–10 accentuating the burdensome qualities of the list: 'heater   valve/ ring seal   service'. Then the affectionate diminutive 'little' reverses the flow of the poem, as the speaker accommodates herself to the new technology and finds delight in the new machinery. Rather than song, the poem finds the poetic in a mechanical vibration, and then endorses this through the analogy with the hummingbird. Neither nature nor technology is privileged.

Such points are reinforced by the fictionalising that Niedecker does. In the letter to Zukofsky cited above she asserts, 'I have no tub or shower or water heater'. The fictional faucet, shower and heater mentioned regretfully in the poem are too luxurious for Niedecker herself. Her privation exceeds that even of the poem's speaker. These devices are introduced, then, to emphasise the contrast between the responsibility of possessions and the untrammelled principles of asceticism.

The plumbed-in devices are scattered to obstruct the flow of the poem in the halting middle stanza until the speaker can string together the freeing clause 'little/ humming/ water/ bird', which extends towards the right margin. The conclusion of the poem appears to move from the restrictions of relative luxury to the freedom of austerity. The flow enabled by the the bird/pump is a regulated flow that is enabled by the poem's dedicatee, the water pump. Niedecker's speaker is 'bound' to the 'cost' of the pump. The poem thus finds a way of diverting the inevitable encroachments of technology – like those of law in other poems – to suit her model of poetic production, in which restraint is enabling.

In this trio of water pump poems, which resemble each other closely, Niedecker approaches the question of poetic production from slightly different angles. In each, technology might appear as a breach that may sever the poet from a virtuous austerity – a more profoundly poetic asceticism – and tie her to the inhibiting expense of worldly exchange. Yet she distances herself from such a goal. In the first poem cited, publishing and plumbing are addressed with ambivalence as encounters with the wider world that, on one hand, potentially endanger a pristine solitude but, on the other, offer a kind of liberation. The latter two poems close with what appears to be an embrace of the machine. Niedecker entertains the overburdened image of birdsong, but rejects it in favour of the undifferentiated and wordless mechanical hum of the pump, which begins to resemble a localised and undemonstrative version of the 'a nerve-sense, a vibration, a color, a rhythm' she praises in her letter to Hoard.

A self-consciousness about form is integral to Niedecker's poetry. Compression permits highly distinctive effects, as the unfolding sentence is tripped up by the repeated linebreaks, stanza breaks and breaks in syntactical coherence. The three water-pump poems embrace an extremely modest technological intervention and adopt it as a model for a form of poetic production. The three poems on foreclosure reflect on the very formal parsimony I have been discussing, claiming poetic substance for reduced means that span the speaker's own material circumstances and the formal austerity of the writing.

* * *

One influential model of short-form poetry that Niedecker explored and ultimately rejected was oriental – that of the haiku tradition. She mentions the tradition's most famous practitioner, the seventeenth-century Japanese poet Bashō, by name in her poem 'Alliance', published in 1969, and his name provides the title for a variant that remained unpublished in her lifetime (CW, p. 270). Japanese poetry – that of Bashō in particular – was associated for Niedecker not so much with Imagist *japonisme* as with the work of the poet Cid Corman. Corman translated Bashō, lived in Japan, and espoused a form of poetic minimalism that was heavily indebted to his studies of the Japanese haiku. He published Niedecker in the influential journal he edited, *Origin*, and engaged in a significant correspondence with her, visiting her in the last year of her life.[32]

Niedecker wrote little prose about poetry, but she did publish a brief text entitled 'The Poetry of Cid Corman'. In it, she identifies Corman's poem 'The Offerings' as 'perfect', and on a par with his friend Williams's 'The Red Wheelbarrow':

Too many things on the altar.
A petal would do.
Or the ant that stops for a moment at it.[33]

Corman's poem suggests a religion corrupted by ceremony. This overworldly and over-human religion is found wanting in the presence of the humble insect. A single ant, or a lone petal (to revive the poignant floral topos beloved of the Imagists), offers better access to the sacred than mere religious ceremony. The short lines give clear boundaries to the experience, magnifying it, and emphasising the weight of each word choice and linebreak. However, while early Imagism seeks to gesture at unspoken or unspeakable significance through the pathos of curtailment, Corman's 'The Offerings', shows greater reticence. Exposed to the influence of Zen, the reader is left not with a pregnant silence but with a Zen-inflected apprehension of nothingness that bypasses conceptual thinking in favour of unmediated experience.[34] The poem is the conduit to a contemplative state through which the existential is found in the everyday. Corman's poem might, indeed, might be read as a version of one of Bashō's best known haikus, in which an animal also serves as a force of disruption leading to insight:

old pond
frog leaping
splash[35]

In both poems an initially static tableau falls away. The provoking 'is-that-all-there-is?' insufficiency of the text invites the reader to reflect on time and the natural world. The jolt of the conclusion urges a reappraisal of not just of experience, but of the condition of experiencing.

Niedecker has little to say about Corman's poem. Indeed, her essay is largely composed of quoted poems, along with such terse remarks as 'short poems on large subjects: Wonder, Contentment' or 'poems precise, plain and sweet'. She describes Corman as a 'poet of quiet' and admires his phrase 'the mystery of simple seeing'.

In Niedecker's own writing, we can detect a renewed interest, partly motivated by her contact with Corman, in an oriental model of concision that had been important to Imagism but that had not provided a model for the work of Williams, Oppen or Zukofsky. Most of the short poems she wrote in this mode have five lines (rather than the haiku's three). They are grouped together in a section entitled 'In Exchange for Haiku' in both *T&G: Collected Poems* (1969) and *My Life by Water* (1970), the two near-contemporaneous *Collected*s that emerged at the end of her life. (She would also use a five-line stanza, often with rhyming third and fourth lines, in her long poems 'Paean to Place' and 'His Carpets Flowered'.) The following short poem is an example of own work in this mode:

> July, waxwings
> on the berries
> have dyed red
>   the dead
> branch
>
> (*CW*, p. 174)

This is a poem of clear-eyed observation, offering plain description of a natural scene. Yet, Niedecker, instead of offering a snapshot of natural life, presents the reader with an image redolent of death: the blood-like residue of the birds' feasting on berries as it sinks into dead wood. This nonconformism is typical of her writing in her 'In Exchange for the Haiku' five-liners. In this work, Niedecker often complicates the images she presents, whether through the obliquity of compression or by introducing a political or technological theme that disturbs the encounter between speaker and scene. While compression and precise observation are felt everywhere in her work, her writing typically looks beyond the confines of the phenomenological lyric style favoured by Corman, sometimes quite playfully, as in this example from the late 1950s:

> Van Gogh could see
> twenty-seven varieties
>   of black
>   in cap-
> italism
>
> (*CW*, p. 183)

In the first three lines, Niedecker refers to a famous remark Van Gogh made about the Dutch painter Frans Hals's use of black.[36] However, the shock comes at the end of the poem with the decapitating line-break of 'cap-/italism'. Instead of a salutary encounter with a plant or creature, Niedecker spins us away from the passively contemplative and into a more complicated position: how the economic and political circumstances of aesthetic production might impinge even on the non-conceptual experience of colour. This clipped allusion to wider circumstances is similar to that expressed, albeit less directly, in the foreclosure and water pump poems from the early 1960s. In such works, Niedecker develops her poetics beyond the momentary insight that feeds the Bashō-Corman line in her work, and into a short-form poetics in which both particular moment and general conditions have a role to play.

In much of her later writing, Niedecker wrote short-lined poems that incorporated reflections on geography, geology, American politics and natural science. Some of these poems, as with the series *North Central* and 'Paean to Place', are serial poems, combining long form with short lines. In many, moreover, citation is used. These citations are marked as such by inverted commas – a significant gesture as many poets of the modernist tradition omitted such marks, or only used them sporadically. In such work, Niedecker moves away from the intense focus of her five-liners. Even when the individual poems of a sequence appear relatively discrete, they take on new meanings in the context of the serial poem, which houses many voices. These are poems in which experience and reading interact. As Peter Quartermain observes, 'She does not place her trust in books as Authorities (with a capital A) but as companions, as direct voices in her life.'[37]

One brief mid-1960s poem points the way towards this more flexible use of both form and voice in her writing. A haiku-like description of nature is buried in the middle of a poem that has a bracingly obscure agenda:

> You see here
> the influence
> of inference
>
> Moon on rippled
> stream
>
> 'Except as
> and unless'

(CW, pp. 228–9)

To infer is to make a deduction from insufficient resources, and insufficiency is central to this poem. The mental action of inference is grounded in uncertainty. Indeed, the styles of reading that are invited by Niedecker's condensed working methods might be described as 'inference'. This brief text is almost a mini-serial poem, anticipating the shifts of register in the work of Rae Armantrout, discussed in my final chapter. The middle section might be a parody of a haiku-like moment of intensified perception. While the poem seems to recommend 'inference' – to ask the reader to interpret the play of moonlight on the water, that is – the final stanza is of Oppen-like opacity. The material in quotation marks might derive from a legal contract, but its relationship to the foregoing lines is unguessable. The reader is left with neither the expressive voids of Imagism nor the compacted experiential encounter of the haiku. The invitation to reverie contained in 'moonlight on rippled/stream' is immediately followed by four words that conduct the poem away from the visual representation of nature and into the thicket of textuality. While words such as 'except' or 'unless' might indeed belong to a process of inference, the poem will not allow any deductions to be made. The quotation marks are powerful, destroying the intimate hush – the suppression of the textual in favour of the visual – that surrounds the poet-perceiver and reader's encounter with the natural world. The unattributed citation breaks the spell of solitariness that hangs over the haiku-like poem. The bracketing gesture that isolates the momentary experience of experience – a lyric variation of the phenomenological reduction – is no longer viable.

This brief poem is one of a series of eleven poems entitled *Hear & See* that was published in Corman's *Origin* in 1967. In what follows, I will discuss how Niedecker's short lines and stanzas operate within her serial poems, which allow Niedecker to develop a distinctive blend of condensation and expansiveness.

* * *

Niedecker's book-length long poem *North Central* contains three sequences: 'Lake Superior', 'Traces of Living Things' and 'Wintergreen Ridge', as well as the short poem 'My Life by Water'. The first of these is based on material generated during a summer trip to Lake Superior that Niedecker made with her husband in 1966. While it is long by her standards, it remains remarkably condensed: her notes on the geology and history of the region run to almost 300 pages,[38] while the poem is only about thirty pages long.[39] The text is highly fragmentary and it often contains specialised geological vocabulary, as in this example:

And at the blue ice superior spot
priest-robed Marquette grazed

azoic rock, horneblende granite
basalt the common dark
in all the Earth

(CW, p. 233)

In this remarkable stanza, Niedecker pushes the five-line technique into new territory, thick with recondite vocabulary. The syntax fails in the first line, with 'blue ice superior spot'. She offers no clue why either the French Jesuit explorer Jacques Marquette or the town named after him should have 'grazed/ azoic rock'. The archaic term 'azoic' refers to the period before the appearance of life on earth. Niedecker, who paid increasing attention to geologic time in her later work, confronts the reader with a stratum of 'common dark' that predates human existence. Culture, such as that presented by the 'priest-robed' missionary, begins to appear fragile from such a perspective. That fragility becomes cryptic through the impenetrability of the text: what is this 'superior spot' on Lake Superior? How can rock be 'grazed'? Does the 'common dark' look beyond the beginning of geologic time to a scripturally inflected meaning of primal Chaos? And perhaps to the psychic region Niedecker describes as 'inchoate thought'?

'Lake Superior' comes back to the vocabulary of geology again and again, not just as a means of exploring the deep structure of a certain space, but as a resonant acoustic resource:

Ruby of corundum
lapis lazuli
from changing limestone
glow-apricot red-brown
carnelian sard

(CW, p. 234)[40]

At such moments, the poetry is driven by sound and colour, materialising the suggestive terms of Niedecker's letter to Hoard: 'a nerve-sense, a vibration, a color, a rhythm'. Yet these lines also look back to the poem's opening, in which the inorganic runs in the blood of living creatures: 'In every part of every living thing/ is stuff that once was rock// In blood the minerals/ of the rock' (CW, p. 232). These brief lines are studded with internal rhyme, which gives them a compacted quality. Hard objects are both the bedrock of the text and the basis of organic matter. Bodies emerge from the landscape, which continues to inhabit them. Like Oppen, Niedecker pursues the substantive. In drilling into the landscape around Lake Superior, Niedecker appears to reach for a foundational layer of poetic technique in which obdurate object-words form the basis of poetic expression.

The 'Traces of Living Things' section of the poem is leaner and more varied in register. This part of the series is prefaced by the phrase 'strange feeling of sequence', a remark made by the book's publisher, Stuart Montgomery. In some poems in the sequence, human and non-human life interpenetrate, such as a man who is 'part coral/ and mud/ clam' (*CW*, p. 239) or a poem in which a human spine and the spine of a leaf are simultaneously addressed (*CW*, p. 241). Several of the poems only have one or two words per line. The poem addresses not just 'life by water' but death by water: the section's final stanza contains the line 'we sink to Water death', which looks back to the line 'And his bones of such is coral' of 'Lake Superior' (with an allusion to Eliot's use of *The Tempest* in *The Waste Land*). The compression of the line in these two parts of the series emphasises the precariousness and provisionality of the processes of perception and representation, and, once again, the writing steers the reader towards the emergence of poetry from reflection on thinking and objects: 'Thoughts on things/ fold unfold/ above the river beds' (*CW*, p. 246).

The final 'Wintergreen Ridge' section of the poem, written a year after 'Lake Superior', contains the names of many of the plants Niedecker encountered during a trip to Door County, near Lake Michigan in September 1967. Niedecker uses Williams's triadic line. Instead of varieties of mineral, the vocabulary is floral. The poem celebrates the persistence of plant life: 'horsetails/ club mosses// stayed alive/ after dinosaurs/ died' (*CW*, p. 250). The poem mocks the space race and hippie culture. Both are seen as symptomatic of the excesses of the 1960s. The text, on the other hand, recommends insufficiency. The hardy plants that populate the poem are examples of 'have-nots' – a phrase derived, as Niedecker's biographer points out, from one of Niedecker's source-texts, Virgina Eifert's *Journeys in Green Places: The Shores and Woods of Wisconsin's Door Peninsula*.[41] There are plants that, in the words of Eifert, 'manage to live with too little water or with too much water, in too much sun or in too much shade, in too much acidity or with too little nitrogen, in too much heat and too much cold ... in too much wind or in too little air'. This vegetation has, like Niedecker herself, made an accommodation with very difficult circumstances. At times, a gesture of renunciation is recommended:

> Sometimes it's a pleasure
>   to grieve
>   or dump
>
> the leaves most brilliant

(*CW*, p. 253)

The final section of the poem advances a position in favour of the wild flowers found on Wintergreen Ridge. The poem argues that they were protected by women protestors who stood in front of bulldozers: 'We want it for all time/ they said' and 'Women saved/ a pretty thing: Truth' (*CW*, p. 250, p. 252). Niedecker mentions many species she encounters on her walk but devotes several stanzas to the carnivorous Dropera and the Lady's Slipper orchid, which traps insects.[42]

Plants are emblems of fortitude in this poem, which celebrates them above both mineral and human existence. The poem's most forceful moments come as it celebrates the shedding of leaves, the ability of lichen to break apart granite and lichen's potential to survive the fallout from a nuclear explosion: 'thin to nothing lichens/ grind with their acid// granite to sand/ These may survive/ the grand blow-up' (*CW*, p. 253). Niedecker, therefore, finds a resistant quality that she greatly admires in the ability of plant life to survive on the barest of means. Transposed to the poet's needs, the most valued resources are time, light and silence, 'which if intense/ makes sound' (*CW*, p. 253). The reduction to the rich impoverishment of a sounding silence captures the paradox in her writing: that it communicates most fully when its means are at their barest.

The use of quotation in Niedecker's poems is more pointed than that achieved in the voice-collages of Pound, Eliot or Zukofsky. In 'Wintergreen Ridge', some of her citations, notwithstanding the tight economy of the poem, appear to have only tangential relevance to her argument: the lines 'half of Sussex/ and almost all/ of Surrey', for example, are derived from Bertrand Russell's autobiography. Russell goes on to express his love of being outdoors but this context is suppressed in Niedecker's poem. The lines 'Every creature// better alive/ than dead,/ men and moose// and pine trees' derives from Thoreau.[43] She cites Darwin on insectivorous plants, notably the 'Bedeviled little Drosera' – a plant that reappears in her 'Darwin' poem, discussed below. The apparently trivial lines 'We have a lovely finite parentage' derive from *The Literary Remains of the Late Henry James*, where James makes an argument for spirit over and above 'things-in-themselves'.

The effect of citation in such clipped stanzas is to amplify the tension between the impulse towards simplicity, which drives towards a single voice, and the multivocal impulse that incorporates material from unidentified speakers. Where modernist innovators such as Pound, Williams, Olson and Zukofsky had focused their experiments with citation for relatively long and often long-lined poems, Niedecker forces cited material into short-lined stanzas, amplifying the effect of the linebreak as constraint. In this way, the cited material becomes another of the means by which word groups are differentiated from one another. Citations within quotation marks establish a further category of breaks within the poem, which sit alongside phrases, sentences, lines and stanzas. These contending elements subsist in 'Wintergreen Ridge' within a loose triadic-line form that provides an overall visual shape to the text.

In her later writing, Niedecker begins to make explicit the erudition that informs her writing. Rather than concentrating on a moment of intellection, the poems embed themselves, in ways that are both implicit and explicit, in ontological questions. *North Central* embraces both the pervasiveness of death and the dynamism of life, from the gnat consumed by a plant to 'the evolution of matter'. The brief poem 'My Life by Water' is an anomaly in the context of *North Central*, which might otherwise work perfectly well as a composite of its three longer parts. This anomalous clearing of space might even allude to the Bashō haiku cited above:

> My life
>   by water —
>   Hear
>
> spring's
>   first frog
>
> (CW, p. 237)

Lines run across stanza breaks until the sonorous neologisms of the penultimate stanza:

> thru birdstart
>   wingdrip
>   weed-drift
>
> (CW, p. 238)

The poem frames Niedecker's own existence by water as one of elemental simplicity. This, on one level, offers the bare conditions not only for existence but for writing. The merging of poet and environment in this poem echoes that achieved at the opening of one of her best-known early poems, conceived in 1945: 'I rose from marsh mud,/ algae, equisetum, willows,/ sweet green, noisy/ birds and frogs' (CW, p. 70).[44] There is nothing of Niedecker's life noted in 'My Life by Water', but it clearly develops ideas contained in the opening 'Lake Superior', section of the book, in which organic and inorganic matter merge. A severe curtailment of the line is evident, but in 'My Life by Water' the preponderance of monosyllables in very short lines does not lead to simplicity of prosody:

>   or board
>   out on the cold
>   ground
>   giving
>
>   Muskrats
>   gnawing
>   doors

(CW, p. 237)

In addition to the halting quality brought by uncertain syntax, the poem's language is further animated by the irregular incidence of internal rhyme. The lines are so short that sounds sometimes echo one another across stanzas: 'board'/ 'doors', 'letters'/ 'lettuce'. Rather than selecting a single object for contemplation, the poet's consciousness opens and expands to incorporate environmental sounds and animal activity. Niedecker may be dedicated, like Zukofsky, to the 'particulars', but she levels the relation between observing subject and natural world, allowing for an immersive experience of the environment in which mind and surroundings merge, at odds with the scientistic 'desire to know' that she critiques towards the end of 'Wintergreen Ridge' (CW, p. 256).

Such scepticism is not so apparent in the late sequence 'Darwin', the last in her last book, *Harpsichord and Salt Fish*, written at the very end of her life. It is composed of five sections of variable length. She uses an adaptation of Williams's stepped line, with the addition of a fourth line that is ranged left in her *Collected Works* but slightly indented in the typescript MS sent to Roub.[45] Whether indented or not, the grounding final line curbs the rightward drift of the three-line stanza, which, as we have seen in some of the poems discussed above, tends to underscore a speculative movement away from the mooring-point of the left margin. Line lengths vary in the poem, in which Niedecker seeks a new accommodation between the words of others and short-form poetry.[46]

The poem contains many brief citations from Darwin's pen: correspondence, *The Voyage of the Beagle* and other writings. This work of conceptual and textual collaging raises questions about the value accorded the cited material, the need for sources to be located, and the peculiar pressure brought to bear on citations pressed into short-form stanza shapes. Niedecker's work identifies a space for speculative thinking that uses part-statement and curtailment as a means of encountering a field of cognitive potential that is specifically poetic in kind. Reading 'Darwin', then, is very different to reading Darwin.

There are five sections to the poem. Each contains five stanzas, except the middle section, which runs to nine. In the first two sections, each stanza is discrete, and most are comprised of direct citation or description of Darwin's texts. For the remainder of the poem, sentences often run across stanzas. As with 'Wintergreen Ridge', Niedecker uses a loose but regular form to impose an overall visual matrix on a succession of suggestive word groups.

One of the phrases Niedecker cites, 'Species are not/ (it is like confessing/ a murder)/ immutable', captures the spiritual risk that Darwin thought to be attached to his theory, which, two stanzas later, presented as 'I believe Man . . . / in the same predicament/ with other animals' (*CW*, p. 295).[47] Yet other passages have no theological weight, drawing on chit-chat from family correspondence: 'I shall be ravenous for the Piano-forte', as he wrote to his sister Susan.[48] In Niedecker's hands, the surrealism of the image effected by 'ravenous' emerges, as her astringent stanza form turns the casual prose of Darwin's letters into something else entirely:

> 'Dear Susan
>   I am ravenous
>   for the sound
>   of the pianoforte'
>
>   (*CW*, p. 296)

Niedecker's collage of materials combines Darwin's personal and philosophical preoccupations with references to the physical environments he encountered as he travelled. While the poem is preoccupied with temporal scales that far exceed the human, its success lies in the way in which these thoughts, large and small, are rendered within the determinate densities of Niedecker's compact four-line stanzas.

The poem concludes with a quotation from Darwin, who thought there was 'too much misery in the world' for it to be possible to believe that the universe was the result of intelligent design, and that the whole subject was too profound for the human intellect to fathom. Rather, he concluded, in Niedecker's stanzaic reframing:

>   'Let each man hope
>   and believe
> what he can'
>
>   (*CW*, p. 299)[49]

We might align this foregoing of the ambition for a totalising vision with Zukofsky's commitment to the localised viewpoint: 'impossible to communicate anything but the particulars'.[50] However, Niedecker's poem does not embody the intellectual self-effacement of Darwin, who remarked alongside the cited passage that 'a dog might as well speculate on the mind of Newton'. She exceeds the particulars. The conclusion of the poem is more ambitious than Darwin's self-deprecating words, offering a relationship to knowledge in which poetry's associative range and scalar flexibility can test the limits of sense-making.

The poem is apocalyptic in places, referring to a catastrophic earthquake and the blasted lavascape of the Galápagos (Niedecker invokes Melville's alarmed response to this environment). While Niedecker's linebreaks have no direct relation to the persistent theme of death in the poem, the meshing of formal and thematic endings promotes an atmosphere in which curtailment is generative of thought. A severe winnowing process is applied to the vast accumulation of words to proceed from Darwin's pen. This allows for a style of textual organisation in which the breaks both between and within clauses and sentences are subject to the supervening organising principle of stanza form. Spatial order not only frames but complicates the semantic movement of the text.

In Niedecker's writing, in which reflection and direct observation combine, she sets out to present 'everything in a movement of words', dissolving the boundaries between mineral and organic, environment and self, fullness and emptiness.[51] Condensation is the process through which this movement of these poems is organised – a commitment to elision that modulates and inhibits the flow of words. The pressure of contraction in Niedecker points towards silence, but then leads away into an unusual poetic register in which the impulse to speak and the impulse to foreclose on that speech are felt simultaneously. Niedecker's 'deep/ trickle' makes a virtue of renunciation. The interruptedness of her writing re-routes narrative thought, offering instead a succession of sharply delimited textual spaces whose impededness is the motivating force of their potential for unimpeded thinking.

Notes

1. Jenny Penberthy's edition, published by California University Press in 2002 and hereafter referred to as *CW*.
2. The edited collection *Radical Vernacular: Lorine Niedecker and the Poetics of Place* (ed. Elizabeth Willis) contains various considerations of the local in Niedecker's work. See, especially, Michael Davidson's essay 'Life by Water: Lorine Niedecker and Critical Regionalism' (pp. 3–20). Peter Middleton's 'The British Niedecker' addresses the British reception of Niedecker, which tended to stress her rural isolation (pp. 247–70). See also Ross Hair's 'The Avant Folkways of Lorine Niedecker', in *Avant-Folk, Small Press Poetry Networks from 1950 to the Present*, and Gilbert Sorrentino's 'Misconstruing Lorine Niedecker'.
3. Niedecker, in a letter to Corman, 28 May 1969, in *'Between your house*

and mine': the Letters of Lorine Niedecker to Cid Corman, 1960 to 1970, ed. Lisa Faranda (p. 193).
4. Rachel BlauDuPlessis, 'Lorine Niedecker's "Paean to Place" and its Reflective Fusions'.
5. See Elizabeth Willis 'Who Was Lorine Niedecker?'
6. Niedecker, June 1969 letter to Kenneth Cox, cited in Margot Peters, *Lorine Niedecker: A Poet's Life*, p. 36.
7. Louis Zukofsky, *A Test of Poetry*, pp. 81, 65, 89. In her article 'A Little Too Little: Re-reading Lorine Niedecker', Jenny Penberthy has argued that critics have focused on the short-form work at the expense of her more surrealist impulses: 'A poetics of condensation is rigorously applied within the individual poems but also within the body of work that she puts on show. So much is excised, so much of the record is missing – lost or deliberately destroyed – that we are left with a lean and partial view of her enterprise.' Penberthy directly attributes the condensation of Niedecker's work to Zukofsky: 'An aesthetic of condensation was not, I believe, a natural or easy choice for her; it was one that she adopted under Zukofsky's sway' (n.p.). My chapter takes a very different view of Niedecker's ideas on poetic form, embedding them in a version of the poetics of Objectivism.
8. Peters, *Lorine Niedecker*, p. 196.
9. Letter to Gail Roub (20 June 1967), cited in Gail Roub, 'Getting to Know Lorine Niedecker' (p. 86). Blau DuPlessis explores the idea of reflection in 'Lorine Niedecker's "Paean to Place" and its Reflective Fusions'.
10. Elizabeth Willis, for example, remarks: 'She was acutely aware of the interconnectedness of things, masterfully mixing the universal with the regional' in her editor's introduction to *Radical Vernacular*, p. xvii.
11. Undated letter to Mary Hoard, University of Wisconsin Digital Collections.
12. Undated letter to Mary Hoard, University of Wisconsin Digital Collections.
13. Niedecker, letter of 2 July 1965, in *'Between your house and mine'*, ed. Lisa Faranda (p. 64).
14. Willis writes: 'Even in defining her own poetic process, she would localize Pound's sweeping command that the poet "condense" by translating it into the economy of Wisconsin creameries', in her editor's introduction to *Radical Vernacular*, p. xvii.
15. See Willis, 'The Poetics of Affinity: Niedecker, Morris, and the Art of Work', in Willis (ed.), *Radical Vernacular*, p. 224: 'Jefferson County, Wisconsin, was headquarters for the theory and practice of the American dairy industry. At its height, it was home to eighty-four creameries, many containing condenseries, and it continues to be home to *Hoard's Dairyman*, the industry's publication of record, for which Niedecker at one time worked as a proofreader.'
16. Peters, *Lorine Niedecker*, p. 164.
17. Letter received by Zukofsky on 1 April 1963, in Penberthy (ed.), *Niedecker and the Correspondence with Zukofsky, 1931–1970*, p. 327.
18. Penberthy, editorial note, CW, p. 424. Peters observes that Niedecker eventually foreclosed on the property in early 1963 (Peters, *Lorine Niedecker*, p. 293).
19. Letter received by Zukofsky on 1 April 1963, in Penberthy (ed.), *Niedecker and the Correspondence with Zukofsky*, p. 327.

20. For example, Christ's curse on the fig tree: 'May no one ever eat fruit from you again!' (Mark 11: 14)
21. Blau DuPlessis, 'Lorine Niedecker's "Paean to Place"', p. 166, p. 173. Blau DuPlessis goes further in rejecting Romantic/ symbolist lyric tradition than seems warranted to me.
22. Letter dated 19 September 1962, in Penberthy (ed.), *Niedecker and the Correspondence with Zukofsky*, pp. 319–20.
23. Mary Pinard, 'Niedecker's Grammar of Flooding', p. 22.
24. Niedecker, in Faranda, ed., *'Between your house and mine': the letters of Lorine Niedecker to Cid Corman*, p. 33.
25. Pinard, 'Niedecker's Grammar of Flooding', pp. 29–30.
26. For discussion of Niedecker and technology, see Jeffrey Peterson, 'Lorine Niedecker: Before Machines' and Lisa Robertson, 'In Phonographic Deep Song: Sounding Niedecker'. Peterson writes of a 'machine aesthetic' (p. 250) in Niedecker's writing, and links this both to the 'formalist "condenser"' (p. 257) of her Objectivist mode and to the 'flux of surrealism' evident in both her 1930s writing and her very late work.
27. Cf. her 1962 'Nursery Rhyme' poem, which commemorates the repair of the pump:

> The greatest plumber
>   in all the town
> from Montgomery Ward
> rode a Cadillac carriage
>   by marriage
>
> A sensitive pump
>   said he
> that has at time a proper
>   balance
>   of water, air
> and poetry
>
>   (CW, p. 285)

28. Niedecker, *'Between your house and mine': the letters of Lorine Niedecker to Cid Corman*, ed. Faranda (p. 64).
29. The third poem was '*I visit/ the graves*' (CW, 210). A facsimile of the publication is available at the Eclipse archive.
30. The poem was one of those selected for the handmade gift books that Niedecker sent to Cid Corman, Jonathan Williams and Zukofsky in 1964.
31. Jonathan Skinner, 'Particular Attention: Lorine Niedecker's Natural Histories', pp. 43–44. See also Peterson, 'Lorine Niedecker: Before Machines', pp. 269–70. Peterson suggests that the pun on 'plumbed' 'plays Niedecker's investigative freedom against the obligations of property' (p. 269).
32. Corman visited Niedecker towards the end of her life to make a brief but moving recording of her reading a number of late poems. See Cid Corman and Gregory Dunne, 'Thirty-One Poems & an Interview: A Special APR Supplement', p. 25.
33. Reproduced at the Pennsound online archive, available at <https://writing.

upenn.edu/epc/authors/niedecker/three-essays.pdf> (last accessed 14 May 2019). Originally published in *Arts in Society* 3 (1965): 558–60.
34. Tim Woods. 'Cid Corman: Editor, Translator, Poet', p. 58. Woods gives a helpful account of the relationship between French writers (Bataille, Ponge, Blanchot) influenced by phenomenology, and Zen poetics in Corman's writing.
35. This is Corman's version of a poem that has been rendered into English by dozens of translators. See Bashō, *Old Man's Moon: Poems by Bashō & Other Japanese Poets*, trans. Cid Corman, p. 18.
36. The remarks appears in a long letter on colour that Van Gogh wrote to his brother in 1885.
37. Peter Quartermain, 'Take Oil / and Hum: Niedecker/ Bunting', p. 274.
38. Penberthy, editor's note, *CW*, p. 434.
39. In the original Fulcrum edition, published in London in 1968.
40. Peters, in her biography, gives an account of Niedecker's Lake Superior trip (pp. 205–10). The documentation presented in the superb 2013 Wave Books edition of *Lake Superior* makes it clear that Niedecker collected stones throughout the journey.
41. Peters, *Lorine Niedecker*, p. 222.
42. Peters, in *Lorine Niedecker*, notes that Niedecker used a locally produced pamphlet as a source for the reference to the protest against developers (p. 224). She also observes that the Lady's Slipper lines (*CW*, p. 251) are a 'distillation' of a passage in Eifert's book (pp. 222–3).
43. Henry David Thoreau, *The Maine Woods*, p. 112.
44. In this stanza, the speaker imagines herself as part of a species that emerged from 'primordial slime', a term used by Niedecker in a 1948 letter describing her compositional method when writing this poem (cited in Penberthy's editorial note to the poem, *CW*, p. 414). 'Paean to Place' begins with a similar allusion to Creation: 'Fish/ fowl/ flood/ Water lily mud/ My life' (*CW*, p. 261).
45. Niedecker, MS of 'Darwin', University of Wisconsin Digital Collections.
46. In his book *Unending Design: The Forms of Postmodern Poetry*, Joseph Conte argues strongly against Donald Davie's essay 'Lyric Minimum and Epic Scope', which unearths the historial references in Niedecker's 'Lake Superior'. For Conte, Davie's attempt to sketch in the historical and scientific hinterland informing the poem 'teaches us how *not* to read Niedecker' (p. 157).
47. Niedecker is mining an 1844 letter to Joseph Dalton Hooker and an 1860 letter to Charles Lyell (Darwin, Darwin Correspondence Project, 'Letter no. 729' and 'Letter no. 2647').
48. Darwin, Darwin Correspondence Project, 'Letter no. 275', 23 April 1835.
49. Niedecker bases this part of the poem on an 1860 letter from Darwin to Asa Gray (Darwin, Darwin Correspondence Project, 'Letter no. 2814').
50. Zukofsky, 'An Objective', p. 17.
51. Letter of February 1949, in Penberthy, ed., *Niedecker and the Correspondence with Zukofsky, 1931–1970*, p. 157.

Chapter 5

Robert Creeley

Robert Creeley is one of the most published and discussed of twentieth-century American poets. However, while numerous critics have noted his use of short form, there has been relatively little discussion of the specific effects of that use of form or its wider implications. Creeley's characteristic clippedness is often used, sometimes with support from Creeley's remarks in interviews and the ostensible content of his most famous collection, *For Love*, to assign him to a kind of lyric space characterised by the channelling of great emotion into spare frameworks. Less sympathetic critics have attacked Creeley on the same score.[1] Notwithstanding his involvement with Black Mountain, the Beats and later generations of experimental writers, he becomes, in this analysis, a poet of essentially private concerns, with the explicit or implicit corollary that his work is ultimately of less substance than such long-form public-discourse monuments of American poetic modernism as Ezra Pound's *Cantos*, William Carlos Williams's *Paterson*, Charles Olson's *Maximus* or Louis Zukofsky's '*A*'.

Creeley, of course, had contact with all of these poets. All of them practised a version of the Poundian *condensare*, even in longer works, but Creeley pursued this impulse towards condensation to a distinctive conclusion. The result is work that engages with the world in similarly complex ways to those of the epic projects of his forebears and contemporaries in the Pound line. His writing challenges a pervasive assumption in academic poetry criticism: that short and long form tend to correspond respectively to lyric interiority and epic collectivity. Creeley's renovation of Poundian poetics cuts across private and public in a language that is characterised by refusal, negation and hesitancy. In this work's ascetic formal contours is an eloquent and sceptical encounter with the limits and risks of social being. The writing is the equal, in scope and ambition, of the more explicit visions of the interplay between *ego scriptor* and the social body offered in the modernist epic. I will make my argument through an analysis of the motif of refusal in Creeley's writing, and develop it by examining the *melos* to which Creeley attaches such weight in his short poems. The focus of my attention will be the writing of *For Love*, *Words* and *Pieces*, a series of books published in the 1960s in which Creeley probes the relationship between experience and poetic form.

* * *

In his interviews and critical prose, Creeley places himself in a line that runs back through Zukofsky and Williams to Pound. In particular, he makes many references to Poundian precepts and slogans, which he often quotes verbatim. While it is clear that Creeley's own development of short form is at a remove both from the Imagism of 1913–16 and Pound's later refinements of his own poetics, it nonetheless betrays an unmistakable debt to Poundian ideas.

Imagist theory, as I have argued in my first chapter, desired to strip away ornamentation and abstraction and to celebrate a 'direct' encounter with reality – the thing, or 'thing'. Hulme celebrates 'accurate, precise and definite description' of 'things as they really are'. This requires a 'concentrated state of mind, the grip over oneself'. Verse produced in this way will have 'nothing to with infinity, with mystery or with emotions'.[2] Often the vagueness and sensuality of symbolism is implicitly coded as feminine. In this version of Imagism, the 'myth of lucidity', noted by Altieri and discussed in my introduction, is readily discernible.

Compression is integral to Pound's poetics, which favours immediacy over abstraction. Yet Poundian immediacy implies a kind of plenitude. As well as the stripping away of the merely decorative, Pound insists on a form of writing that is stuffed to the point of bursting, 'charged with meaning'.[3]

Pound's notion of compression, then, implies not Hulme's 'dry' neoclassical vacuum, but quite the opposite: a repleteness that verges on the explosive. In this highly overdetermined model, the condensed poem must communicate a great deal more than its brevity would suggest. It is not necessarily, therefore, the vehicle for a truncated or incomplete representation of cognitive experience, at least if Poundian 'charge' is adopted over Hulme's 'accurate, precise and definite description'. Complexity is rendered through the close-packing of content. Its relation to objects, which may, of course, be internal or psychic, will necessarily be anything but lucid.

Of all the Poundian slogans, it is perhaps the definition of the image as an 'intellectual and emotional complex in an instant of time' that brings us closest to Creeley's aims. Yet it is notable that when Creeley discusses Pound he places the emphasis decisively on the emotional half of Pound's dyad.[4] What came to be known as literary high modernism was differently expressed, of course, due to the reception of the doctrine of impersonality. However, the 'intellectual' part of the 'complex' seems to lead to an incomplete version of experience for Creeley. In 'A Sense of Measure', for example, Creeley writes, 'it must be seen that no merely intellectual program can find reality, much less admit it, in a world so complexly various as ours has proved'.[5] It is striking that Creeley at various points in his interviews and essays references Pound's 'Only emotion endures' and 'Nothing matters but the quality/ of the affection' (from the *Pisan Cantos*).[6] At one such juncture, having cited both these phrases, he amplifies his point, separating his own work from a poetry guided by 'meaning':

> I feel rather it is that complex of emotion so experienced, that is the most signal characteristic of what a poem possesses. So I feel that the measure of poetry is that emotion which it offers, and that, further, the quality of the articulation of that emotion – how it is felt, the fineness of its articulation, then – is the further measure of its reality.[7]

Creeley, in short, seeks to emphasise the emotional, not the intellectual. Moreover, he wishes the poem to be judged ('measured') by its relation to reality. A poem presents, in a Poundian phrase denuded of its intellectual half, a 'complex of emotion'. Moreover, in Creeley's version of the 'direct treatment of the "thing"', he refuses to separate the object-world from the linguistic and cognitive processes that represent that world to consciousness. In his writing we see something akin to Nicholls's reading of the Poundian 'thing', discussed in my introduction: 'arrangements in social and psychic space that the poem delicately conjoins'.[8] In Creeley's complicated 'articulation' of experience in his writing of the 1950s and 1960s the boundary between internal and external objects becomes increasingly difficult to maintain. The writing's gradual immersion in a kind of anxious self-monitoring leads to work that communicates nothing if not the relation between perception and its poetic realisation. The clear desire to communicate the immediacy of emotional experience in *For Love* is complicated, in the later books *Words* and *Pieces*, by a self-reflexive habit of expression in which the mediatedness of the poetic utterance tends to become the object of contemplation.

Nicholls's expanded and notably social understanding of the object of the poem in Pound's famous formula can help us open up the latent 'charge' in Creeley's dense and compacted poems. We can begin to view the work as writing that entertains a notion of collective as well as private or domestic experience. And we can begin to complicate the relationship between poet and world from a static and representational 'image'-based mode, in which inner and outer are kept neatly apart, to a more dynamic, processual model that better accommodates the vicissitudes of perceptual experience.

A key reference point for Creeley as he thought through these ideas of form was William Carlos Williams, with whom he corresponded between 1950 and 1962 (a year before the older poet's death).[9] Williams's spare style, his commitment to vernacular speech and his conception of measure were clearly of great significance to the young Creeley.[10] Yet, the 'thing' in Williams's anti-metaphysical 'no ideas but in things' (which corresponds to Altieri's notion of objectivist lucidity) is clearly doing very different work to the 'thing', or perceptual gestalt, that Pound aspired to treat directly. A more relevant Williamsian precept for Creeley is 'the poet thinks with his poem', a formula that embraces affective and unconscious as well as intellectual processes. Writing of some lines from Williams's 'To Daphne and Virginia', Creeley remarks that what he admires in Williams is the possibility that 'mind may make evident its resources apart from the limits of intention and purpose'.[11] In other words, Creeley is presenting the poem as the best available site for a full rendering of cognitive activity as it is subtended by various combinations of emotional, social, unconscious or intellectual processes. Williams's category of 'measure' foregrounds poetic form as a constitutive feature of the poetry's communicative capacity.

The concept of 'measure' is one that, as Paul Mariani has shown, the poets discussed in several letters.[12] For both poets measure was a way of thinking the expressive implications and entailments of form (a matrix of ideas that received different emphases in the epistolary dialogue with Olson that led to the latter's 'Projective Verse' essay). For Williams, 'measure' informed a poetic language that 'will be commensurate with the social, economic world in which we are living as contrasted with the past'.[13] In his Eliot-bashing 'Letter to an Australian Editor', an essay admired by Creeley, Williams writes that 'the poet's very life *but also his forms* originate in the political, social and economic maelstrom on which he rides' (my emphasis).[14] For the younger poet, form remains similarly inseparable from the 'social, economic world'. However, Creeley places greater emphasis on the unconscious components of individual experience, the 'complex of emotion' that exceeds 'intention and purpose'. Drawing on Williams's assimilation of poetic form to social processes, Creeley developed an idea of the poem as a dynamic emotional field in which large processes – undifferentiated entanglements of psychic and social – can be explored. For Creeley, poetry was about the play of intensities: 'this field of force we call a poem'.[15]

The late 1940s, when Creeley began writing in earnest, was a time when the dissident aesthetic and social energies that early modernism had harboured were discernible at the fringes of an increasingly fragmented American culture. One hallmark of a nascent alternative that would go overground in the 1950s with the Beat phenomenon was a particular avidity for a notion of 'experience', as if life itself were, in Poundian terms, 'pregnant' and 'charged' with meaning. In his interview with John Sinclair and Robin Eichele, Creeley discusses the hipster culture of the day: 'it was a time when one wanted desperately an intensive and an absolutely full *experience* of whatever it was you were engaged with. So Charlie Parker – think of his place in Jack Kerouac's writing – became a kind of hero of this possibility.'[16] Here the Poundian rhetoric of 'energy' – 'Energy, or emotion, expresses itself in form'[17] – is refashioned as a modus vivendi. For Williams, in his introduction to *The Wedge*, a comparable fullness of experience puts intense pressure on the language of the poem, as the poet moves towards 'an intense expression of his perceptions and ardours that . . . may constitute a revelation in the speech that he uses'.[18]

Creeley, developing a compressed mode of writing in the wake of Pound and Williams, presents the poem as a full, not an empty, dry or ascetic thing. Despite the evident appetite for attenuation and ellipsis in his verbal approximations of experience – and, in later work, the painstaking self-reflexive monitoring of those verbal approximations – there is a desire to use very few words to represent complex experiential states.

The short and short-lined poem, in Creeley's hands, communicates a great deal because his handling of the Poundian *condensare* makes such full expressive use of the various kinds of boundedness that short form potentialises. Creeley plays relentlessly on the communicative potential of ellipsis, incomplete syntactical units, sonic patterning and abruptly truncated lines. Such effects, of course, are often evident in the long-form modernism of Pound or Olson. However, the unitary nature of a short poem produces an entirely different relationship between part and (implied) whole.[19]

In a 1961 interview, Creeley explicitly links his use of short form with the narration of emotional states: 'the truncated line, or the short, seemingly broken line I was using in my first poems, comes from the somewhat broken emotions that were involved in them'.[20] The abrupt concision of Creeley's writing of the 1950s and 1960s does not stem from a paucity of experience or emotion: what is left out is itself communicative, exerting pressure on the few words that are presented to the reader. In other words, the violent self-editing that is intuited in a Creeley poem renders affective states that are resistant to consecutive explication. The reader, moreover, is frequently aware of a psychic and editorial process that is the agent, variously, of suppression, excision and effacement. The operations of this self-mutilating apparatus in such constrained poetic frames makes evident the expansive range of the *condensare* gesture.

The self-editing movement of the writing is, I believe, best understood as a form of refusal: refusal to utter, refusal to narrate, refusal to admit into consciousness. I do not mean by this a subjective process of 'denial' or a drama of superegoic censure. Rather, I mean an unwillingness to engage with narrative plenitude because of its entailments: psychic integrity, on the one hand, and an accommodation with a cohesive political identity on the other. Anything but a damaged version of American vernacular speech would concede too much to the culture from which that speech arises.

* * *

How, then, do social materials that appear inimical to the claustrophobic domestic settings of many of these poems make themselves apparent in this compulsively truncated work? There are glimpses of the young Creeley's attitudes towards form in his intense early 1950s correspondence with Charles Olson, but little about his social perspectives. The ten volumes published by Black Sparrow, covering April 1950 to July 1952, run to more than 2,000 pages, not including notes. Yet, as their editor George Butterick observes in his introduction to Volume 8, 'little seeps into the exchange from the larger world – the Korean War, McCarthy's intimidation campaign, Europe still struggling to its feet'.[21]

Creeley's politics in these letters, written at a time when he saw himself as a fiction writer, is generally as visible as it is in his poetry.[22] One notable exception, however, is a vitriolic letter in which we get a peculiar and impassioned version of masculinity and its relation to Cold War ideology. The letter was written on 8 September 1950, a few months after the beginning of the Korean War and at the beginning of the ten-year period covered by the *For Love* collection.[23] In it, Creeley engages in a furious diatribe against American culture, the 'national character' as displayed in magazines and on the radio:

> My impotence. To either shake off or get beyond the sense of this current biz. It revolts me, turns my stomach, sickens altogether. I hate the whole of it, despise, loathe & feel contempt for every damn one who deals in it. The nation: fucking idiotic lying/ : perverts. Perverts in the head/ rotten, filth,

> hate hate, hate. Voices: oily, & shrewd, know, exact, how to lie attractively to each and every one. Against that, just that, we put a handful of sounds/ one feeling, two, a complex: love. Say, one woman, one feel of one way, one thing, one knowing, one day, sun, moon, fresh, rain, love, dying, as it's been done. Against a multi-form (one complete lie) put: handful of words, tentative & wistful thought. Time, perhaps for exact fierceness, for being taken apart, strip by strip, torn by such, if the body didn't break, give in, betray.[24]

And so it continues. Recalling his own experience at the end of the Second World War in Burma, he lambasts the American military – 'fucking idiots'. The Americans were hated, he writes, by their opponents and Creeley appears to sympathise with this hatred: 'Loathed them. My people. Coming from one huge leper-like lie, white and edged: blue with disease. Rotten at the heart/ rotted out.' He signs off with 'Monstrous egotism. I don't want.'[25]

Creeley's rage at 1950s America amounts to a good deal more than superficial hipster disdain for the values of the mainstream.[26] It is an extreme counter to all that the dominant culture of early 1950s America represented: both a sceptical response to America's claim to be the guardian of a new world order, and a disgusted rejection of the oppressive consensual normality of the period. What he sets up against it is both ambitious and conspicuously meagre – 'a handful of sounds/ one feeling, two, a complex: love' and a 'handful of words, tentative and wistful thought'. Small gestures are set against 'a multiform ... lie'. Is Creeley already moving towards a poetics of insufficiency? Does a kind of socially embedded refusal constitute the bedrock of this commitment to the 'small'?[27]

Creeley perhaps has such ideas in mind in the two poems entitled 'For W. C. W.', one written in the 1950s and one in the 1960s. Each tells us something of value about Creeley's use of form. Here is the first of them:

> The pleasure of the wit sustains
> a vague aroma
>
> The fox-glove (unseen) the
> wild flower
>
> To the hands come
> many things. In time of trouble
>
> a wild exultation.
>
> (CPC1, p. 126)[28]

In this poem, half-rhyme (in Creeley's habitually dispersed manner, avoiding end rhymes) and assonance play a significant part: the poem hangs on the movement from 'wit' through the two 'wilds', each compressing the first syllable of his dedicatee's first and last name. 'Unseen' in line three houses the middle initial too: W. C. W. leaves an audible stamp on the poem. The declarative statement of the first stanza is broken in stanza two. However, the syntactical collapse harbours an acoustic relation, with 'The pleasure', 'wild flower' and 'vague aroma' echoing one another. The last two sentences of the poem repeat this movement from complete syntactical unit to verbless statement, with the half-rhymes of 'come' and 'time' and the assonance of 'time and 'wild' holding them tenuously together.

This poem is notable for its witholding qualities: two short declarative phrases that might almost be sententious if their meanings were not so elusive. The Williamsian foxglove and wild flower are offered as attempts to concretise the source of the 'vague aroma' but the thread of thought is already unravelling into unpunctuated parataxis. The unexpected 'wild exultation' may be understood as one of the 'many things' that come in 'time of trouble' (a term that is redolent of superstition). In such a short poem, the repetition of 'wild' is telling: becoming in its second utterance an unsettling incursion into the cultivated precincts of the poem. The closing 'wild exultation' and the cooler 'pleasure of the wit' are the emotional poles between which the poem moves. What the poem offers, then, is a movement from formed statement to the unresolved details that exceed 'intention and purpose'. Line endings slice the sense at unexpected places: before the article in 'sustains/ a' and 'trouble// a' but after it in 'the/ wild'. The stanza break between 'In time of trouble' and 'a wild exultation' suggests that the two might be in apposition: the extreme compression of the verse disallows any linking phrase such as 'there is'. The deferral of punctuation until the penultimate line gives the poem a suspended quality by forestalling the resting point of the full stop.

All of this fine detail adds up to something substantive. The fact that the foxglove is '(unseen)' leads us, perhaps, to a crux: that the poem's ostensible objects are only accessible via the mediatedness of the poem, through the sounding of words, not visual images. In this setting, compression, syntax and rhyme render the poem's uncertainties pervasive. The repetition of 'wild' suggests both the wild propagation of meaning and the suppression of meaning through phonic excess. As Susan Stewart suggests in the context of a discussion of rhyme, '[i]ts relation to semantics remains both under- and over-determined, for rhyme can endow meaning with greater depth or empty it of its syntactical or context-bound force'.[29] Creeley often uses repetition that exhibits this doubled effect. The foxglove that is withheld from the reader's view is emblematic of the feats of elision that mark the poem – even its invisibility is parenthetical, awkwardly inserted after the noun it describes.

To summarise; sound, syntax and linebreaks combine to give the measure of this poem, as it unfolds in time – a crossflow of projected statement and its deferral. In its reluctance to add up, Creeley's poem is making a point about experience and its representation: process and incompletion are defining qualities of the timebound experience of being. He not so much orchestrates the patterning of exclusions as lays the work open to a set of linked, episodic part-utterances. The formal fact of brevity intensifies the poem's effects, accentuating the force of the linebreak and complicating the expressive range of the parcels of language that Creeley organises. Longer-form work might set its thoughts out with greater exactitude, but it is precisely the partial, hesitant, processual, patchy nature of cognition, as linguistically apprehended, that Creeley wants to communicate.

The second of Creeley's two 'For W. C. W.' poems appeared in the 1967 collection *Words*. Through its use of the present tense, the poem revives the older poet for a continuation of their exchange:

'For W.C.W.'

The rhyme is after
all the repeated
insistence.

There, you say, and
there, and there,
and *and* becomes

just so. And
what one wants is
what one wants,

yet complexly
as you
say.

Let's
let it go.
I want —

Then there is —
and,
I want.

(*CPC1*, p. 273)

The 1950s writing collected in *For Love* often offers an oblique rendition of the immediacy of an emotional situation. The work is typically reluctant to do anything more than hint at the context from which it emerges. Later work such as the poem above, however, turns in on itself, examines its own word-by-word development, and refuses to say. Creeley's second

'For W.C.W.' has drawn considerable commentary. Altieri discusses the void in the poem, suggesting that this negation can be a 'productive' element in the 'dialectic of experience'. For Michael Davidson, trauma is displaced into consonance: the 'violence of "insistence" is tempered by self-reflexivity: repetition compulsion becomes rhyme'. In Alice Entwhistle's view, the poem's 'very inarticulacy gradually becomes slyly expressive'. Less persuasive, however, is her suggestion that this is because 'Creeley surreptitiously affirms Williams's craftsmanship by putting his own inadequacies on display' – or that the linebreaks are 'apparently arbitrary' and only successful when voiced.[30] I think it is possible to make much more of the communicative range of Creeley's hesitancy.

This unrhymed poem begins with a statement about rhyme as repetition and insistence – an allusion perhaps to Stein's distinction between the terms and a signal of the internal loops of the poem itself.[31] The following stanza is almost entirely composed of various arrangements of two words: 'there' and 'and'. Desire comes to the fore in stanza three – 'what one wants'. This is articulated through another – 'as you say' – who we assume is the conventional addressee of lyric but who may, of course, also be Williams. As the poem comes to its end 'one wants' is supplanted by 'I want' – all is stripped away to leave nothing but the pulse of desire, the 'repeated/ insistence' of 'I want'.

Shuttling between pronouns – one, you and us – the poem seems to peel off all poetic artifice, any veneer of the social, or indeed of history, to leave us with the bald conclusion 'I want'. The poem is in dialogue, 'complexly', with Williams's empirical inclinations – the assent to a decipherable object-world evidenced in his recommendation that the poet should 'write particularly, as a physician works, upon a patient, upon the thing before him'.[32] In lines such as 'there, you say, and/ there, and there,/ and *and* becomes', language is presented as the medium rather than an instrument of thought. 'I believe in a poetry determined by the language of which it is made', Creeley writes.[33] To think the world, for Creeley, is also to make the world. Yet the object is plainly not adequate to the perceiver's desire, as the objectless insufficiency of 'I want' suggests. The poem remains unsatisfied.

What of the social in this poem? Creeley says in his *Paris Review* interview that 'history, as a form of experience, is truly not something I've been able to articulate with, nor finally engaged by'. Later in the interview he remarks, 'I've been given to write about that which has the most intimate presence for me, and I've always felt very, very edgy those few times when I have tried to gain a larger view. I've never felt right. I am given as a man to work with what is most intimate to me – these senses of relationship among people.'[34]

I believe that at such moments Creeley is not fully alert to either the historical meanings or the force of negation in his writing. That is where we find the 'larger view'. The second 'For W.C.W.', like many of his works, is a poem that strips itself bare, that is 'taken apart, strip by strip', to quote again the early letter cited above. Yet, as the poem edges towards a conclusion, it cannot quite fully reduce itself to the monadic 'I want'. The very word 'and', crucial to the poem, implies sociality: an I, a you, an it, an us. In the poem, Creeley – a friend of Ginsberg, writing in late 1960s America at a time of immense social and cultural upheaval – strives not to let that wider America in.[35] The refusal itself is the salient point. In the second 'For W.C.W', and in other highly reflexive poems of the period, Creeley's retreat to the syllable-by-syllable occasion of a poem's self-utterance is a means of registering and withstanding the pressure of the very reality that he so noticeably seeks to exclude. His painful attention to the nature and conditions of utterance are his way of attending to what America was living through.

Exclusions give compression its peculiarly compelling currency. Creeley makes the challenge clear in his famous poem of reduction, 'A Piece'. This dense little poem begins as simple maths and ends as the barest of narratives, almost a condensation of the 'a handful of sounds/ one feeling, two, a complex: love' of his earlier letter to Olson.

> One and
> one, two,
> three.
>
> (CPC1, p. 353)

We hear the chanting of a children's addition table: 'one and one is two'. But 'is' is omitted in that second line, replaced by the fractional pause of a comma. So one train of thought becomes another, the literal enumeration of one, two, three. Lineation is crucial: each implied mini-sequence is fulfilled across a linebreak. That faltering moment when 'one and one is two' becomes 'one, two, three' depends on subtraction, the disappearance of the word 'is'. The subtracted 'is' prevents the poem settling into a single sequence. If, on the other hand, we hear a bandleader counting in the musicians, the phrase is similarly truncated: the poem becomes the prelude for a main event that occurs off the page. Doubt and vigilant self-awareness form the atmosphere of this poem. The refusal to countenance anything other than a cognitive glitch is an attempted withdrawal from the world. Its corollary is an alert openness to the other – 'a handful of sounds/ one feeling, two, a complex: love'. This is, on the face of it, a poem that excludes history. However, I'd like to suggest that, in its 'exact fierceness', in its conspicuous refusal of the existent, this poem also invites consideration as a refusal of complicity with American 'hate hate hate'.

Stephen Fredman has written of 'negative space' in Creeley's writing, by which he means the ways in which its attention to its own unfolding gives rise to 'a heightened awareness in both the writer and the reader to appearances in the present'.[36] This negative space, I suggest, provides an atmosphere in which the sceptical alertness of the writing probes fissures in social experience. In 1967, Creeley writes: 'The American condition has much to do with place, an active spatial term which differs in that way from what has been assumed its European equivalent. Space, as physical ground, not sky, I feel to be once again politically active.'[37] This version of space implies both the space of the page and a wider social imperative. Rather than the expansive, outward Westward push of Olson's *Call Me Ishmael*, Creeley is interested in effects of spatial contraction – this is where the space of his poetry is 'active'. He looks for a new, and tacitly social, articulation of American space in an extremely impacted version of poetic form.

It was in the 1969 book *Pieces* that the challenge of 'A Piece' would be developed. One feature of this work is Creeley's adoption of serial technique: poems in short sections separated by a single indented bullet point. The segmentation of the poem that Creeley introduced in *Pieces* allowed for a fracturing of the surface of the poem, multiplying the number of available voices. In addition to the linebreak, the stanza break and irregular syntax, Creeley adds a further disruptive device to exploit the intensifying effects of short form. An example is the poem ' "Time" is some sort of hindsight':

'Time' is some sort of hindsight, or else rhythm of activity—e.g., now it's 11 days later—'also alive' like they say.
   •
Where it is
was and
will be never
only here.
   •
—fluttering as
  falling, leaves,
  knives, to
  avoid—tunnel
  down the
  vague sides . . .
      •
—it
 it—

(CPC1, p. 391)

In this poem, the movement of reduction is episodic. In the opening paragraph, the copula 'is' precedes two incommensurable descriptions of 'Time'. Is Time known retrospectively as 'hindsight', or as the animating 'rhythm' of life? The immediacy of 'activity' and 'alive' on the one hand seems to be set against the '11 days later' of 'hindsight', though the paratactic syntax makes the relations between terms undecidable. The offhandness of the 'like they say' that concludes this section places all the foregoing at an ironic distance.

The next stanza pulls apart the sententious 'is was and ever shall be' of public speech acts, concluding with a paradox – 'will be never/ only here' – that questions the very act of predication. The following stanza offers a lyrical image of fluttering, falling leaves, only to puncture this with 'knives'. And how can one 'tunnel/ down the/ vague sides' – tunnel anywhere but underneath? The poem seems to be reconciled to the forward, downward movement of words on the page but at the same time to be resisting spatial or temporal location.

The concluding pair of words is a striking image on the page, a visual effect that cannot be reproduced by the speaking voice. On one hand we can understand '—it/ it—' as a rendering of the falling of leaves, a visual miniaturisation of an old trope of passing time. Yet there is an undeniable moment of temporal arrest, as if the fixing of words on the page fixes a moment. Where 'For W. C. W.' moved towards the unadorned urge of 'I want', this poem desubjectivises Being: nothing remains but the blankest of pronouns, doubled and hovering in apposition on the page.

In the poems I have discussed, the motif of refusal cannot be separated from the formal characteristics I have described. Refusal becomes, sieved through Creeley's formal choices, a refusal of communicative plenitude. Ellipsis, compression, syntactical uncertainty, and the insistent breaking of the line make hesitancy and undecidability integral to the overall effect of the poetry. The poems become the receptacle of a kind of volatile potential for meaning that is repeatedly constrained by self-silencing gestures that reject the totalising ambitions of the complete and unequivocal statement. The shocks administered to the drive towards syntactical and semantic completion by linebreaks and stanza breaks lead to a reconfiguration of Poundian energy. In this version of the *condensare*, incompletion becomes integral to the verse's compression effects. Instead of seeking a language that is 'commensurate with the social, economic world in which we are *living*', Creeley pursues one that withdraws sceptically from it.

Compression is eloquent in this work. Subtle movements of reduction move Creeley's writing against the grain of American culture of the 1950s and 1960s: expansionist, consumerist and wealthy on the one hand, and paranoid, conformist and bellicose on the other. The complicated parsing of emotional states that resist sequential narration led Creeley into a position in which the dyadic encounter implied by lyric tradition became an analogue for the social bond. In this way, he develops Williams's suggestion that a poet's forms 'originate in the political, social and economic maelstrom on which he rides'.[38] Social being is examined as a space of dynamic, provisional communicative exchange that refuses any legislative force. It is relation per se that is tested in this writing, rather than particular human relationships. Creeley's insistent probing of the risks of communicative utterance continually played aspirations to linearity against various kinds of disjunction and repetition. Meaning is found negatively in this writing, in what the poem refuses to say as it declines to go along with a culture that Creeley can only 'despise, loathe & feel contempt' towards. Against this he offers not the campaigning countercultural alternative of a Ginsberg but the 'exact fierceness' of his manifold refusals.

* * *

I have argued thus far that Creeley amplifies the expressive power and speculative reach of his poetry through a kind of withholding. Despite their spareness and their restricted vocabulary, his poems are unwilling to state things in a simple or straightforward way. In what follows I will probe the role of the acoustic in his writing. I believe that the various compression techniques I have discussed above are both enhanced and complicated by Creeley's use of sound.

In sound, as with the drive to reduction, Pound is Creeley's point of departure. 'For my company', he remarks in an interview, 'one rule of thumb was Pound's proposal of melopoiea, phanopoeia, and logopoeia – and the *melos* or melody of poetry has occupied me much over the years.'[39] Melopoeia, for Pound, is the means through which 'the words are charged, over and above their plain meaning, with some musical property, which directs the bearing or trend of that meaning'.[40] Creeley's remarks on meaning tend to tally with this understanding of the acoustic: that it functions as a part of the overall 'articulation' of the poem.[41] Creeley is unequivocal about the weight he assigns to sound: 'I guess if I needed to choose one precept that most served my senses of poetry over the years, it would be Pound's injunction: "Listen to the sound it makes!"'[42] This is the material through which the 'arrangements in social and psychic space' of which Nicholls writes in his discussion of the Poundian 'thing' are most fully articulated. Compression is felt less as an instantaneous effect than as an unfolding sequence of suggestion, implication and withdrawal. Creeley's use of syntax and the linebreak, and his positioning of vowels and consonants allows for a particularly self-aware remodelling of the continual interweaving of the temporal flows of sense and sound in language. He uses an adaptation of Williams's theory of 'measure' to describe his experience when writing of articulation and being articulated:

> I want to give witness not to the thought of myself – that specious concept of identity – but, rather, to what I am as simple agency, a thing evidently alive by virtue of such activity. I want, as Charles Olson says, to come into the world. Measure, then, is my testament. What uses me is what I use and in that complex measure is the issue.[43]

With the phrase 'what uses me is what I use', Creeley announces himself as both receiver and maker. The speaker is 'used' by the conspicuously social medium of language. What is at issue is more than just the 'quality of the articulation of ... emotion', discussed above, but what Pound defines more amply, in a phrase cited by Creeley in his 'Poems are a Complex', as prosody: 'the articulation of the total sound of a poem'.[44] By this I understand the shifting relationships, experienced temporally, between sense, sound, rhyme, rhythm and the linebreak. All these effects are typically deployed in irregular, unpredictable ways, combining to provide the unstable *melos* activated by Creeley's poetry as he seeks to communicate the mind's 'resources apart from the limits of intention and purpose'.

An example is the poem 'The', the title of which is itself a bald gesture at incompletion:

'The'

The water
waiting far
off to the
east, the
west — the
shores of the world.

(*CPC1*, p. 422)

Here, melopoesis is driven by a conjunction of rhyme and chiasmus. The 'the' that follows the title establishes an immediate, almost ironically deadening use of echo. It is followed by the half-rhyme of 'water'/ 'waiting', which, in turn, is followed by the chiasmic half-rhyme of 'far'/ 'off' and the more emphatic double chiasmus of 'the/ east, the/ west — the'. We might understand the dash to introduce a term that restates the first half of the poem. Instead, the phrase 'the/ shores of the world' asserts the land mass, not the water itself. This opposition seems to invite reflection on the formed and the formless, with the premonition that what is finite and formed will at some point be overcome by the waiting water. However, any metaphysical speculation on the theme of Chaos and Creation, with 'the' figuring, perhaps, as a prototypical word, is deflected into the intransigence of language-as-language. The dash arrives at a point when the reader is expecting the conclusion of the opening statement but instead there is yet another definite article leading off into a new statement that is not quite equivalent to the first statement. The closing 'world' is perilously extended on the poem's only 'long' line, evidencing again Creeley's desire to 'come into the world'. Only one word in the poem – the 'to' of the third line – is not an echo or half-rhyme or visual rhyme of another word. Such reduced acoustic materials help greatly in defining the atmosphere of constriction that leads up to the concluding 'world'.

'Echo', also from *Pieces*, is another poem in which repetition and a series of small, concise gestures are used to generate intense feeling. The poem announces itself from the outset as a love lyric but even its truncated first sentence is hard to resolve. What follows the dash at the end of the second line is set up as a clarification of the opening words but, as might be expected, nothing is really clarified:

'Echo'

Yes but your sweetness
derives drunkenness —

over and over, not
your face, not your

hand — no you nor
me is real now —

Nothing here now,
nothing there now.
•
Is this fact of face and body — looking out — a *kind* of pleasure. That is, no argument stops me. Not — 'yes'—'no' — gradually? Only involved as openings, sexual also, seem to be — but is 'no' my final way of speaking? Eg, *a* 'poet' of such impossibilities 'I' makes up?

(CPC1, pp. 417–18)

Repetition begins in earnest with 'over and over' in the second stanza. Creeley sets up a rhetorically replete three-fold repetition of 'not your' but, as with the poem 'The', this barely suggested pattern is fended off. The words 'no you', a truncated variation of 'not your', feel like a typographical error on first reading, causing the reader to turn back to check on the unfolding of the sentence. The succeeding 'nor' invites the reader to replace the 'no' with 'neither'. This strange phrase 'No you' is at the heart of the poem, suggesting that the linguistic event of the poem is enough entirely to efface the addressee. The linebreak 'not/ your face' and the stanza break 'not your// hand' add to the feeling that the lover is being dismembered. Does all this brokenness stem from the 'drunkenness' at the start of the poem? The poem's opening 'yes' is followed by a cascade of negations: 'not', 'not', 'no', 'nor', even 'now'. The force of sound in the poem is sufficient to embed 'no' in the closing 'now' of the first section, giving the poem the ability to simultaneously evoke and deny the 'now' in which the speaker is made present. This no/ now is a point of temporal and logical arrest. Creeley, then, has taken the process of fragmentation to the point of dismantling individual words, the 'w' making all the difference in the world.

With the concluding prose stanza, a prose reflection on the foregoing sections, the poem continues to undermine its own apparent suppositions. Does the speaker indeed gravitate towards a final 'no' but still persist in speaking, with nothingness offered as a version of the traumatic 'hole' found in earlier poems such as 'Anger', 'The Hole' and 'The Language' – a frightening void that is both desired and desiring?[45] Scare quotes serve to place an ironic distance between the speaker and the key points at issue: affirmation, negation, poetic speech. The poem moves close to the pure performance of poetic process, words forced out of nothing and apparently leading towards nothing. Yet it cannot divest itself of its situatedness in the contemplation of erotic love and the violence of its emotion.

This is a poem, then, in which Creeley presents a possible human encounter at the same time as withholding it. There is even the possibility that 'over and over, not/ your face' might refer to an 'unreal' scene of drunken violence. The poem does not conclude with the denial of reality it imagines in its brief second section. Rather, the rhyme-driven sounding of the poem as it moves down the page works to flatten sense-making utterance at the expense of the acoustic. The poem ends in an atmosphere of apparent negation, strewn with holes that may, once again, be sexual, but also offering a 'complex articulation' that is far from a conduit to silence. Emotion endures in the poem, even as it begins to stand outside and critique the representational frame. Again, extreme compression and its concomitant refusal of conclusive statement allow Creeley a form of 'articulation' that encompasses presentness and negation, sense and non-sense, lyric address and its refusal.

The relentless foreshortening and breaking of Creeley's utterances is part of a complex and necessarily discontinuous tracking of cognitive processes. Sound is integral to the unfolding of these processes, throwing up provisional networks of association and dissonance that cut across the patterns of syntax, sense-making, and line- and stanza-breaks. Creeley's writing is certainly emotional, but his attention to the 'total sound of the poem' broadens the ambit of the acoustic to embrace a profoundly social understanding of poetic speech. As with Williams, George Oppen and Lorine Niedecker, statement and non-statement are housed within formal strictures that shape, rather than limit, the poem's intricate relation to social being. In Creeley's writing, hatred, abjection and negation are features of a generalised aesthetic of refusal that permeates the earlier writing. Yet, in these very negations lies an index of the Creeley's insight into the deep entwinement of form and feeling. The relationship between qualities of emotion and quantities of poetic measure is potentialised. The foreshortened utterance does not just intensify what is implied but unstated, it opens the poem's play of sound, meaning and syntax to a revisionary strand of contrapuntal energies that continually reframe the unfolding sequence of words. Creeley's 'resources apart from the limits of intention and purpose' are not brooked by the limits of the speaker's implied interiority, or any 'specious concept of identity'. They spill into a self-aware embrace of 'measure' as an index of the confusion and contradictions brought about by using and being used by language. Rather than a restricted intellectual range that is impoverished by its asceticism, we find a way of being in the world that is on one hand nuanced, sceptical and wary, and on the other, open to love as a profoundly social affect.

Notes

1. Marjorie Perloff's essay 'Robert Creeley's Radical Poetics', contains a brief survey of hostile reactions to short form in Creeley. Creeley's distinguished detractors include M. L. Rosenthal, Helen Vendler and Christopher Ricks.
2. Hulme, 'Romanticism and Classicism', p. 78, p. 79.
3. Pound, *ABC of Reading*, p. 28.
4. Pound, too, in places, appears to valorise the emotional above all else. In his 'Affirmations: As for Imagisme', emotion is equated with emotion: 'Energy, or emotion, expresses itself in form ... Energy expressing itself in pure sound, ie sound as distinct from articulate speech, can only be expressed in music. When an energy or emotion "presents an image", this may find adequate expression in words' (Pound, 'Affirmations', p. 376).
5. Creeley, 'A Sense of Measure', p. 487.
6. Pound, 'A Retrospect', p. 14; *The Pisan Cantos*, p. 35. Creeley at times miscites the line from the *Pisan Cantos*. He substitutes emotion for affection in his essays 'Frederick Eckman: The Epistemology of Loss' (p. 278) and 'Poems are a Complex' (p. 489) but gets it right in 'William Corbett:

Two Books' (p. 327). See also Pound's discussion of Cavalcanti for the relation of emotion to rhythm: 'The perception of the intellect is given in the word, that of the emotions in the cadence.... The rhythm of any poetic line corresponds to emotion. It is the poet's business that this correspondence be exact, i.e., that it be the emotion which surrounds the thought expressed' ('Introduction to Cavalcanti Poems', pp. 23–4). In the same piece, Pound contentiously asserts that music is 'rhythm and nothing else, for the variation in pitch is the variation in rhythms of the individual notes, and harmony the blending of these various rhythms' (p. 24).
7. Creeley, and Linda Wagner 'A Colloquy with Robert Creeley', p. 91.
8. Nicholls, 'Poetics of Modernism', p. 57.
9. Paul Mariani and Lynn Keller offer accounts of this correspondence.
10. In his essay 'After For Love', Robert Duncan remarks: 'Not only Pound, but Williams himself in *The Wedge* (1944) and *The Clouds* (1948) gives the young Creeley his challenge of what form and measure in poetry must be and defines, more certainly than Pound, the particular mode or convention of the common-speech song with a persisting convention of two, three, or four line stanzas, highly articulated to provide close interplay and variation, which Creeley is to specialize in and to develop toward his own poetic voice' (p. 234).
11. Williams's poem was published in *Desert Music* (1954). Creeley discusses it in 'I'm Given to Write Poems'. Another quotation from the Williams poem provides the epigraph to his key book *Words*.
12. Williams wrote in a letter of January 1960 that Creeley had 'the subtlest feeling for measure that I have encountered anywhere except in the verses of Ezra Pound' (cited in Mariani, 'Fire of a Very Real Order', p.187). This commendation found its way on to several of Creeley's dust jackets.
13. Williams, 'The Poem as a Field of Action', p. 283.
14. Creeley, introduction to *Collected Essays*, p. xiv; Williams, 'Letter to an Australian Editor', p. 11. Creeley was disappointed that Williams's piece was omitted from the elder poet's *Selected Essays*.
15. Creeley, 'A Note on the Objective', p. 465.
16. Creeley, John Sinclair and Robin Eichele, 'Interview with Robert Creeley', p. 47.
17. Pound, 'Affirmations', p. 376.
18. Williams, CP2, p. 54. Creeley talks of *The Wedge* as '*fire* of a very real order' ('I'm Given to Write Poems', p. 498) and cites this passage from the introduction of *The Wedge*.
19. Ben Friedlander discusses Creeley's preference for 'partiality' over totality, in his essay 'Reading in Pieces'.
20. Creeley and David Ossman. 'Interview', p. 7. In an essay on the book *Echoes*, Altieri describes Creeley's line endings as 'marks of anxiety, each expressing an urgency to see emptiness somehow filled and each frustrated by the order of things that produces the feeling of emptiness' ('What does *Echoes* Echo?', pp. 42–3).
21. George Butterick, editor's introduction to Charles Olson and Robert Creeley, *The Complete Correspondence*, vol. 8, p. vii.
22. Public positions were a different matter: Creeley's later opposition to the Vietnam War and the invasion of Iraq is well known.

23. Olson and Creeley, *The Complete Correspondence*, vol. 2, pp. 128–31.
24. Olson and Creeley, *The Complete Correspondence*, vol. 2, p. 129.
25. Olson and Creeley, *The Complete Correspondence*, vol. 2, p. 129.
26. Michael Davidson, in 'The Repeated Insistence: Creeley's Rage', discusses Creeley's anger at length. It is striking, in this regard, that Creeley considers William Carlos Williams, a key influence at this point in his development, an angry poet: 'Many of the early poems are really angry, and their emotional base is their revulsion and anger at the world he finds around him' (Creeley and Al Filreis, 'Asking Creeley about Williams', n.p.).
27. In this I am developing a suggestion made by Friedlander in his introduction to Creeley's *Selected Poems:* '[Creeley's] refusals are often as important as what he embraced' (p. 1). Michael Davidson, in *Guys Like Us*, makes much, albeit briefly, of Creeley's poetic technique in his book on Cold War gender roles. He writes of how both halting enjambement and 'lexical insecurity' challenge a construction of maleness as the sturdy and self-assured lynchpin of the American family – that key bulwark against the threat of communism (pp. 57–8).
28. References to first of the two volumes of Creeley's *Collected Poems* are henceforth given as CPC1.
29. Susan Stewart, 'Rhyme and Freedom', p. 43.
30. Charles Altieri, *Enlarging the Temple*, p. 184. Michael Davidson, 'Repeated Insistence', p. 70. Alice Entwhistle, ' "For W.C.W.", "Yet complexly": Creeley and Williams', pp. 135–6.
31. Stein, 'Portraits and Repetition', pp. 100–1.
32. Williams, *Autobiography*, p. 391.
33. Creeley, 'A Note', p. 478.
34. Creeley, Lewis MacAdams and Linda Wagner-Martin, 'The Art of Poetry X: Robert Creeley', p. 16, p. 26. This latter quote was used on the dust jacket of the 1969 Scribners edition of *Pieces*, and so it clearly carries some weight for Creeley.
35. There are exceptions. See, for example, 'The Province' from *Pieces* (CPC1, p. 415), which refers to 'tactical nuclear weapons'.
36. Stephen Fredman, *Poet's Prose*, p. 78.
37. Creeley, 'Introduction to The New Writing in the USA', p. 94.
38. Williams, 'Letter to an Australian Editor', p. 11.
39. Creeley and Daniel Kane, 'Interview', p. 61.
40. Pound, 'How to Read', p. 25.
41. As with many Poundian terms, melopoeia varies in its application in different formulations by Pound. For my purposes, the term helpfully describes an acoustic dimension to poetic speech that works hand in hand with Pound's celebrated 'dance of the intellect' (or logopoeia). In his article 'A Necessary Blindness: Ezra Pound and Rhythm', Peter Nicholls outlines the role metrical echoes play in Pound's poetry.
42. Creeley and Daniel Kane, 'Interview', p. 64. Creeley's love for bebop is well known. In the same interview Creeley describes less familiar musical enthusiasms, asserting the importance to him of repetition in Satie and condensation in Webern (p. 62). Satie appears to have shown Creeley how a substantial work could be grounded in very simple elements. Webern's

severe ellipsis may have suggested the potential resonance in an artwork of a very few intensely significant gestures.
43. Robert Creeley, 'A Sense of Measure', p. 488.
44. 'Poems are a complex, and exist by virtue of many things. First, they are a structure of sounds and rhythms which cohere to inform the reader (whether he listen aloud or in silence) with a recognition of their order. In this respect, I much agree with Louis Zukofsky's note of his own poetics, which, as he says, comprise a function having as lower limit speech, and upper limit music.' Pound's note, that 'Prosody is the articulation of the total sound of a poem,' has equal relevance (Creeley, 'Poems are a Complex', p. 489). Pound referred to the 'articulation of the total sound of a poem' in a note appended in 1940 to his 1917 review of Eliot's 'Prufrock and Other Observations', *Literary Essays*, p. 421.
45. Rachel Blau DuPlessis discusses holes in Creeley in her essay 'The Hole: Death, Sexual Difference, and Gender Contradictions in Creeley's Poetry'.

Chapter 6

Larry Eigner

Larry Eigner's extraordinary body of work extends from his early contact with the Black Mountain poets and inclusion in Don Allen's pivotal *New American Poetry* anthology to his encounters in later life with the West Coast community of Language writers. Eigner was a talismanic figure for the latter group, and, for some, his example clearly helped validate a particular reading of post-war, open-field poetics. His work was featured in the magazines *This*, edited by Barrett Watten and Robert Grenier (who later became Eigner's carer); *L=A=N=G=U=A=G=E* (edited by Bruce Andrews and Charles Bernstein); and *Tottels* (edited by Ron Silliman).[1] Ron Silliman's anthology *In the American Tree* was dedicated to Eigner and, once he had moved to Berkeley following his father's death in 1978, Eigner became a regular presence at poetry events in the area, publishing a series of books until his death in 1996. He suffered from cerebral palsy, following an injury at birth, and was confined to a wheelchair. His disability conditioned his creative output in crucial ways.[2] After hearing Cid Corman's radio show *This Is Poetry* in 1949, he initiated a correspondence with Corman. This, in turn, led to an exchange of letters with Robert Creeley, who published Eigner's first book from Mallorca through his Divers Press imprint. Olson's theory of Projective Verse had a profound impact on Eigner, and Eigner's writing, as Ben Friedlander notes, was an important influence on the later work of Robert Duncan. Duncan's jacket note to Eigner's book *Another Time in Fragments* (1967) is a helpful early description of Eigner's style: 'phrasings are not broken off in an abrupt juncture but hover, having a margin of their own – stanzaic phrases – suspended in their own time within the time of the poem'.[3]

It is the particular form of ellipsis occasioned by these 'stanzaic phrases' that is the concern of this chapter. The compression of Eigner's work does not depend on sharp disjunction. Yet, at the same time, the writing does not adhere to grammatical norms. As Duncan notes, Eigner's work derives great energy from his manipulation of the relationship between line, stanza and part-sentence. Eigner's use of 'suspended' 'stanzaic phrases', each line only loosely – if at all – tethered to its neighbour, serves Eigner's aim of representing a particular mode of apprehending the world. Some critics have turned to spatial and tensile metaphors to describe Eigner's technique: Jessica Lewis Luck writes of 'spatial syntax of word constellations', and Bernstein describes a 'reinsistent prosody of shift/ displacement/ reconstellation'.[4]

Yet this airy, dynamic body of work was produced by a writer who spent his first fifty years and nearly two decades as a writer – 1959–77 – living in one place.[5] Most of the poetry written in the first half of Eigner's writing career emerges from the perspective of someone positioned on the porch of the family home in Swampscott, Massachusetts. After his move to the West Coast, the attempt to communicate the experience of a moment in the world with a combination of radical simplicity of ostensible subject matter and formal audacity remains a defining feature of the poetry. The severe boundedness of his physical experience became one of the work's core characteristics, his writing exploring a similar fundamental setting hundreds and hundreds of times. With neither the mythical freight of Olson nor the mystical baggage of Duncan, Eigner used the space of the page to communicate the right-here-right-now of experience from countless minutely different perspectives, as if he were writing a single enormous minimalistic serial poem.

Eigner's poetry is, as Ben Friedlander argues, ultimately 'a mode of apprehending reality, a means of engaging with the world'.[6] This conceptualisation of the poem as apprehension and engagement will inform the arguments below. For Michael Davidson, there is a close link between Eigner's poetics and his disability, the 'irregular surfaces within the poem' and 'the world, as a physical set of limitations'. Eigner, he argues, 'measures an objective world full of "lines" and "broken curbs" as one which he must negotiate with difficulty'.[7] In this view, the irregular formal features of the poem are an expression of a distinctive and compromised experience of space and movement. Barrett Watten points to a different kind of irregularity, which is based on incompletion rather than obstruction. In particular, the organisation of noun phrases in the writing communicates a distinctive syntactical organisation in which the 'world' is missing because it cannot be indicated in a conventional propositional manner. For Watten, 'the noun-to-noun progression, rather than the grammatical bracketing of the phrase structure, reflects the process of thought in the poem'. He continues: 'The nouns are hinges in the process of thought; other levels of the poem (line, stanza, phrase structure, complete figure) . . . are built up from the noun, which is the basic unit of linguistic perception in Eigner.'[8]

Lytle Shaw has recently sought to complicate accounts of the mutual entwinement of life and work in Eigner's poetics by placing emphasis on other significant contexts. Among these are the temporality of broadcast media in relation to 'administered time' during the Cold War era and, much closer to home, the role of Eigner's mother Bessie, whose labour in organising Eigner's living and working space was 'a framing condition for Larry Eigner's thought'.[9] Shaw remarks on the continuities between the New American Poetry and Language Writing with regard to developing a 'contestatory time'.[10] In this view, Eigner combines the open-field potential of Olsonian poetics with the reflexivity of Language Writing.

> The project of Eigner's projectivism was at once to insist on and destabilize his literal field by testing relations between its fleeting effects – sonic, visual – and the field of the printed page, where Eigner's lexemes invariably uncouple themselves from any simple, instrumental role and begin to take on reflexive relationships only possible on this second field.[11]

Shaw makes a good case for a Projectivism shorn of its diachronic dimension and focused primarily on the 'fleeting' intensities of the unfolding moment, but conditioned by a particular, historically specific experience of temporality. Eigner himself was cautious about the relationship of his project to the many kinds of writing that flourished under the Language banner. He had had ample opportunity to reflect on the topic, as his own connection to these writers began in the early years of the movement. In a 1987 letter to the publisher of *In the American Tree*, Carroll F. Terrell, Eigner acknowledges that he does, perhaps, have affinities with the Language writers. Yet, Eigner is surprised to see no mention of Corman in Silliman's introduction, which points to himself and Creeley as significant precursors. In Eigner's view, the connection between Language Writing and his own poetry is found in the idea of the active encounter with the world:

> Hm, maybe this 'language' poetry is centered on thinking – the descendant or else the parent of speech? – rather than speech itself. Putting it up my alley. Thinking that gets man from one thing to the next. And realization, recognition or real awareness of things, may not be a different kettle of fish, much.[12]

This remark binds Eigner to a tradition running back to William Carlos Williams, a writer admired by Projectivists and Language writers alike. The implications of Williams's statement 'the poet thinks with his poem'[13] were still being felt by writers of the late twentieth century, as is evidenced by Watten's description, via Searle, of Eigner's poetics: 'The illocutionary act of the poem is the poem.'[14] Eigner (at least in the context of the informal tenor of his letter to Terrell) makes a distinction not between speech and textuality but between speech and thinking. For Eigner, 'thinking' may not be a process merely of intellect. In the state he describes as 'real awareness of things', it makes little sense to cede priority to either verbal or non-verbal aspects of cognition. The elliptical nature of his writing has more to do with the category of mobility: the movement 'from one thing to the next', which demands a self-conscious fidelity to the registering of the moment-by-moment unfolding of an experience in time.

For Eigner, 'realization' is integral to his project. The parameters of this realisation are, in material terms, those of the single sheet of typing paper. Whether or not by reason of the physical difficulty of changing a sheet of paper, Eigner typically wrote to the page. Although many of his poems lack the brevity that characterises the work discussed hitherto in this book, techniques of compression are central to their operations. Eigner clearly works within the tradition of the phenomenological short poem, transposing the Objectivist preoccupation with the nexus of thought, word and object into the mapping of consciousness through *mise-en-page* that fascinated Olson and his followers. And, in a move that recommended him to the Language writers, he shared with the Creeley of the 1960s a self-reflexive tendency. This, while it stopped short of the scrutiny of the politics of meaning-making enacted in much of the new avant-garde writing, saw language become the object as well as the instrument of poetic writing.

When Eigner writes of moving 'from one thing to the next' he may be expressing a version of Olson's vigorous suggestion that 'in any given poem always, always one perception must must must MOVE, INSTANTER, ON ANOTHER'.[15] However, as Davidson, Seth Forrest and Luck have noted, Eigner's physical circumstances greatly complicate his relationship to Projective verse. The urgency of the imperative of 'MOVE, INSTANTER' implies an uncomplicated relationship to movement in space that was not available to Eigner. His writing stands at one remove from the breath- and speech-based poetics of Projectivism. While his perceptions are often apparently rapid, the effect of his writing is generally of a slowing of attention.

Eigner's odd equivocation in his letter to Terrell, where he describes thinking as 'the descendant or else the parent of speech?' – is telling. His poetry reflects upon a dual process of attention and representation in which neither thinking nor experience has priority. As the process of writing and experiencing merge on the page, it is of no theoretical or practical benefit, so far as the production of poetry goes, to put one before the other. What Duncan describes as the 'suspended' quality of the stanzas is a way of representing poetic activity that begins in the moment but immediately commits itself to an awareness of its own operations. The provisional relationship between phrases and stanzas is a representation of the mind reflecting on its own experiencing and is thus more faithful to the doubled temporality of that writing-experiencing process than a more complete and consecutive form of utterance.

* * *

While Eigner's primary concerns are perception and representation, it is also the case that extraneous materials, often political or historical, find their way into the work. His 1968 book *Air The Trees*, for example, contains poems that reflect obliquely on the legacy of Frederick Douglass and Leopold Senghor.[16] External sources such as radio and TV programmes are sometimes referenced on the page. An example would be 'd e a d l y   e n o u g h', which contains a note referencing the documentary *Chronicle of the Warsaw Ghetto Uprising According to Marek Edelman* (CT, p. 331). Such references are typically given in a side note, prefaced by typewritten '‡' symbols to demarcate them from the poem. Other texts begin with epigraphs from novels such as *Lord Jim* or *War and Peace*. It is clear that books and radio and TV documentaries gave him a sharp awareness of the natural world. A recognition of emerging environmental catastrophe left a mark on Eigner's late work and he has, like Lorine Niedecker, recently been read as an ecopoet.[17] Yet, remarkably, he writes about nature in the generic terms of the city dweller. One revealing late prose text sheds light on his preoccupations in this area. 'Here and There', was composed in response to the question 'what keeps you interested?', posed by a little magazine in 1986. Eigner refers with concern to NPR interviews and features on global warming and says that he wants to take the 'long view' rather than the 'short run'.[18] The mini-essay is a remarkable digest of information received via the radio. It is prefaced with a poem that ends 'think think think', which is clearly intended as a parallel poetic response to the prose section, and it concludes with two lines from Keats's 'Ode to a Nightingale': 'Where but to think is to be full of sorrow/ And leaden-eyed despairs'. 'Thinking', in other words, is offered as the only way out of a crisis that humans are only just becoming aware of. In the face of questions of scale – 'distances, times' – that far exceed the human perspective, thinking becomes an imperative. He cites Ezra Pound's Δώρια – 'Be in me as the eternal mood/ of the bleak wind' – as an injunction: to turn one's attention from what Pound goes on to describe as 'transient things'[19]

Eigner appears to be giving authority, via Pound and Keats, to poetry as a means of bypassing the scalar problems inherent to representing environmental crisis. In the poem, Eigner refers to local specifics – 'gables, cloud, smoke, treetops' – but the text repeatedly looks beyond this to much larger figures that are intrinsically hard to grasp: 'everything', 'past', 'present', 'future'. In addition to the factual knowledge he describes in the accompanying prose text, he is recommending a specifically poetic 'think, think, think'. His version of open-field poetics gives his poetic thinking a temporal and spatial flexibility that exceeds the possibilities of consecutive utterance while at the same time avoiding the long-range historical and mythical specificities of Pound, Olson and Duncan.

We can get closer to what Eigner means by 'thinking' by discussing the unusual treatment of birds in his poetry. These are a persistent feature of his writing, from the early 1950s ('The midnight birds remind me of day/ though they are/ out in the night/ beyond the curtain I can't see') to the end of his career in the mid-1990s: ('to go in sleep some day/ with birdsong// out the window').[20] Along with trees and the sky, they feature in poem after poem. In my view, birds are a signal example of the kind of curiosity recommended by Eigner. Yet it is hard to situate the writing in the tradition of radical American nature writing. He is oddly reluctant to name species. No one could argue that Eigner is writing with the patient attention of Thoreau. There is a marked difference between Eigner's blank 'birds' and their presence in the work of Dickinson, say, or Niedecker.[21] And there is no parallel to Niedecker's scrupulous use of plant and mineral vocabulary in her later works or to the enjoyment of the vocabularies of plant species in Louis Zukofsky's *80 Flowers*.

When he writes of birds that 'different kinds/ streak the sky',[22] he does not seem interested in detailing differentiation. While there are occasional exceptions to this reticence about naming common species (gulls, robins, bluebirds, blackbirds, pigeons, for example), such cases only make it more puzzling that Eigner should typically favour the generic term, as in the following example, poem #237, written 15 August 1968:

```
A bird from somewhere   The wind rouses the tree
     there is only green in the sunlight

       up and
         down
       nothing
          sound ends
```

(*CT*, p. 142)

Despite decades of observation, Eigner could not be less specific about the bird. His perception narrows to the momentary movement of the tree branches in the sunlight. The bird that begins the poem turns out to be incidental to it. This willed blankness that attaches to birds is mysterious. Is he, perhaps, seeking to universalise his experience by removing geographical indicators? Is he pointedly hanging back from naming because he sees coercion in it: a spelling of animal species into human culture? Is he attributing humility or even ignorance to the speaker of the poem? Or does he seek to communicate a sensibility that is attuned primarily to sensory input?

Another poem adopts a haiku-like style to present the bird as a bare index of motion:

```
in the air   the slant snow
    the bird rising away
  from the wild and bare tree
```
(*CT*, p. 151)

The poem presents an Imagistic contrast between two elements: the downward slanting movement of the white snowflakes and the upward trajectory of the silhouetted bird. It is almost a motion-enhanced version of Pound's 'In a Station of the Metro'. Yet, Eigner's poem – like most of his work – is unpeopled. What Kit Robinson calls Eigner's 'understated registration of current, fleeting phenomena in time' requires the perception of change.[23] Eigner's speakers characteristically notice minute alterations in the surrounding environment. However, to name the bird or the tree, or to identify another human consciousness, would be to claim a very different status for the observing consciousness. The poem does not attempt to know the world, or the nuances of naming – the richly various reach of human language. It is unwilling to claim that power. Instead, Eigner opts for the barest of terms: air, snow, bird and tree. Unlike the natural world of the Stevens of 'Anecdote of the Jar', the 'wild and bare' remain wild and bare. And Eigner's 'slant', unlike Dickinson's 'tell it slant', has no metaphorical application to the business of writing. There are two diagonal vectors in the poem – downward and upward – and the tree moves in a 'wild' fashion in the wind that drives the snow. In registering the upward movement of the bird but not naming it as a swallow, a pigeon, a crow or a robin, Eigner asserts, quite carefully, a fundamental modesty about his own position as observer. Putting his considerable knowledge to one side, he confines himself to noting visual and acoustic stimuli. He is not, of course, suggesting that the human perceptual apparatus can be a neutral recording device, free of cultural positioning. However, he does seek to arrive at a very reduced representation of the intertwinement of verbal and non-verbal forms of cognition. His drive to simplify serves ultimately to foreground the density of the simple act of attending to the world.

The poem 'in the air the slant snow', discussed above, was written in 1969, at a point when Eigner's writing was becoming increasingly compressed. Like his correspondent Cid Corman and like Lorine Niedecker, Eigner was interested in haiku and the work of Bashō. Three October 1970 poems are designated 'after Bashō'. (One of these, #448, October 7 1970 (*CT*, p. 169), notably fuses a poem by Bashō with lines from Keats's 'Ode to a Nightingale'.) In poem #473, dated February 18 the following year, Eigner considers the relationship between local and general, small and large. On this occasion, he does not ground his remarks in what is visible from his porch. Indeed he considers what is not visible as he speculates on the vocabularies appropriate to immensity.

```
common sense
    experience              ‡ varieties over
                                enigma
 the milky way
   river of heaven                   - for L N ‡

            elements
   out there
   a pulsar
   intrinsically winks

           all the route
         not imagined

         the naked eye

    could not discover

                          time

         so much

                    or any thing
```
                                                    (*CT*, p. 174)

The poem is dedicated to Niedecker, but Corman is clearly in the background too. The opening lines can be read both as 'common-sense experience' and 'common sense-experience'. They appear to refer to the experience of looking up at the night sky. The lines 'the milky way/ river of heaven' allude to a famous haiku by Bashō, putting Eigner's text in dialogue both with haiku tradition and Corman's modification of that convention. Eigner adapts the ultra-minimal observational naming of the haiku mode to his own more expansive style. The poem moves from the Milky Way to the winking of a pulsar (which is not visible to the naked eye). However, in a move that is typical of Eigner's representation of perception, the winking is described as happening 'intrinsically'. The 'out there' becomes, simultaneously, internal, returning him again to his question, cited above: 'how does the extrinsic turn intrinsic at times, the extraneous become digested?' The mirror of the vastness that he witnesses, mediated by scientific knowledge, is the imaginative response of the perceiver. However, even this is not capable of comprehending the 'route' taken by the light that arrives from the stars.

The poem aims at much more than wonder at the vastness of the cosmos. At the heart of the poem is the 'naked eye', punning on 'I', that absorbs the 'sense experience' of astral light. Pulsar and eye/ I are overlaid. The poem moves through small bundles of words, some of which are connected across lines, and some of which are isolated. The greater spacing of the last three lines leaves a stronger sense of uncertainty. Human insufficiency is underlined as the limits of sense perception are contemplated. How can the eye be adequate to the apprehension of distances so great that they are measured in timescales that are many times beyond the human lifespan? As it concludes, the poem returns to the human scale, extending its spatio-temporal perplexity to the here-and-now. The uncertainty embraces not just anything, but 'any thing'. The quasi-metaphysical gesture at the start of the poem is short-circuited and reined in, as the poem plays variations on the 'enigma' of perception, installing doubt at every level of the encounter between the 'naked eye' and the world. Neither Pound's 'thing' nor the 'thing'-as-object of the subsequent tradition can be recovered or accessed. The perceiver/speaker is reduced to a cipher of experience, a 'naked eye', as blank and enigmatic as the birds that populate so many of Eigner's poems. This careful construction of provisionality is heavily dependent on Eigner's method of restricting his lines to one, two or three words, and leaving the relations between line and line uncertain.

Many of the poems from this period in his work contain only one word per line. Eigner had been reflecting on the uses of concision for some years. A decade earlier, for example, he had written to *Mica* magazine to take issue with a remark by the English poet J. H. Prynne, who had complained that American poetry had not progressed 'further than the basic Imagist resolution at the beginning of the century'. Prynne argues that too many poems open on to a space of irresolution:

> Hence perhaps the way so many poems need the pool of silent reflection that follows their close, into which the strong concerns not shaped into a final relevance by the last line can lose themselves in free contemplation. For the concern must have a fully articulated object (so I believe); the object should not be the poet's anterior experience (Eliot's fundamental error), but the poem's achieved shape. This is not only the words as isolated monads, but their ordering.[24]

Although Eigner's response is equivocal, he appears to assert the importance of an object in 'extrinsic' reality rather the poem's 'achieved shape':

> But the object he says the concern must have, if not the 'strong concerns' which he pleads be 'shaped into a final relevance,' doesn't it, or don't they, lie beyond poetry or certain poems, which are pieces of language, nodes of language risen in thought out of the general continuum to prompt or orient us? Objects beyond the action of language?[25]

At this point in his writing at least, Eigner was committed to an idea of the world outside the poem that was apprehended as a moving target, an exteriority in a state of becoming. Eigner goes on to ask 'how does the extrinsic turn intrinsic at times, the extraneous become digested?'[26] In my view, the bare facticity of the word 'bird' acts as a blocking mechanism, preventing the reader from conjuring up a clear visual image that is external to the poem. The wordness of 'bird' cannot be suppressed. It is unapologetically a generic noun, without the visual resonance of a more specific word such as 'crow', 'heron' or 'eagle'. Poems built around such nouns become wilfully provisional gestures, pointing towards a reality that they knowingly fail to evoke, and at the same time indicating that the very difficulty of such evocation is the point. The world outside the poem is the bare existence that provides the experiential trigger for Eigner's text, but the poem itself can only reproduce the complex interaction between extrinsic and intrinsic, pushing this complexity to the point where the division between the two is itself at issue.

In his introduction to the *Calligraphy Typewriters* selected edition, Charles Bernstein argues that, 'in place of a psychodrama beyond the poem, action in Eigner arrives at the level of the phrasal hinge'.[27] This 'phrasal hinge' – the ambivalent movement between phrase and phrase – is the motor for the remarkable mobility of these poems, and the justification for Duncan's remarks about suspended 'stanzaic phrases'. Both Bernstein and Duncan focus on the 'instrinsic' qualities of the poems. However, while there is clearly no 'psychodrama beyond the poem', I would argue that Eigner's poems do, as he himself argues, indeed have an extrinsic moment. This might best be described as an unardorned and undramatic encounter with experience that is knowingly communicated in a language that is aware of the difficulties of linguistic mediation. There is, moreover, as Duncan observes, sometimes a differentiation between the time of the poem – its 'now' – and the much broader timescales at which its phrases gesture. These often open on to political or ecological 'dramas' that eclipse the merely psychodramatic.

Eigner's short poems depend on his orchestration of small phrasal word-clusters into larger arrangements. The process that Bernstein describes as 'reconstellation' depends on various kinds of break. Eigner remarks that 'typographic devices, notation (the alphabet and numerals and punctuation marks and paragraph-, line-, double-, x-line-breaks, indentation and lacunae ... are typography), as in mathematics, can be means to (some of the means of) thinking, of making things out'.[28] Thought, in this view, is outlined not just in words, but in their arrangement in space and their relation to a battery of breaks, gaps and punctuation marks.

Eigner's writing is of significance because it plays a part in a long poetic trajectory of formal development. More than this, the formal contours of the work facilitate a mode of attention that is, on one hand, open-ended and associative, and, on the other, rigorous in its patterning of a style of encounter between subjectivity and world. Another way of presenting its qualities of incompletion would be to point to the care that it takes not to draw conclusions. The poets I discuss in this book all, one way or another, use – in Williams's terms – the 'pinhole' of reduced form as a means of allowing the poem to acknowledge the 'dialectical necessities of its day'.[29] Eigner uses page-space in such a way that the blunt fact of interruptedness occasioned by the short line simultaneously opens, through syntactical and visual means, new vectors of meaning. As Duncan argued very early in the reception of Eigner, meaning emerges in the interrelation between the phrases that float on the page.

Other poems of this period, such as #427 (August 21 1970), also explore temporal and spatial scale, exploiting the gaps between word and word, line and line. In this case, a phrase is counterposed with three nouns:

```
You ride for some hours
                stalagmites
         clouds    cities
```

(*CT*, p. 166)

The poem begins with what is probably a car journey. The present simple tense makes it unclear whether this is a habitual action or a mental projection of fantasied travel. In a characteristically audacious shift, the poem moves from the parameters of a few hours to geologic time. It is hard to disentangle object and dream. There are implied visual associations. Clouds and cities are both large, unstable masses. Stalagmites suggest skyscrapers. There is minimal half-rhyme: 'hours'/ 'clouds'; '-mites'/ 'cities'. The extreme elision gives the reader just three apparently unrelated nouns to set against the grammatically intact clause that opens the poem. While the first line suggests a landscape, the remaining nouns gesture at three categorically distinct spaces: underground caverns, the sky and urban experience. The poem's energy derives from the disparity between the easy movement of the first line and the decontextualised objects that complete the poem. This is poetry as a resource for mental time travel, opening a matrix of possibilities for cognitive leaps. One such leap might be literary. The poem might be alluding to *The Tempest* and the 'cloud-capp'd towers and gorgeous palaces', and 'insubstantial pageant' of Prospero's hymn to the transporting power of artifice.[30]

Read this way, Eigner's poem is exploring the reach of imagination motivated by the barest of prompts. Whether or not the clouds resemble stalagmites and cities, the text moves seamlessly from earthbound travel to a fantastical virtual space. Characteristically, Eigner draws on the intensifying potential of ellipsis. The 'you' in Eigner's poem might be Eigner himself, a notional speaker, the reader or an undefined collective. The experience described might be a single incident. Even if so, its narration in this reduced form compels the reader to consider the hallucinatory potential of a few disarranged words. The clouds in Eigner's writing, here and elsewhere, stand on the boundary, as for Prospero, between the substantial and the insubstantial.

In his prose text 'not/ forever/ serious' Eigner argues that pausing is related to paying attention over time. Scale, once again, becomes a question at this point: how is a 'moment' or 'attention' to be understood? At such moments, Eigner seems at once to be recommending curtailment, and suggesting that what a poem 'realizes' might extend into both past and future.

> If you're willing enough to stop anywhere, anytime, hindsight says, a poem can be like walking down a street and noticing things, extending itself without obscurity or too much effort. . . . While the future is inescapable, near or far in the background or over the horizon, maybe the most a poem can be is a realization of things come to [*sic*] or that come together. At moments. (Nothing lasts forever, sure thing, or for ages, and it's a question how much can or should anything last or occupy attention. A single line can register as a poem, monostich, the line 'break' take effect from the practice of poetry.)[31]

In this formulation, Eigner is concerned with how attention rests. There are 'moments' of rest, or pauses, when the walking stops and 'things . . . come together'. These moments of rest are of great importance to his early 1970s writing. They are found not only in linebreaks or intra-lineal spacing, but in Eigner's most common typographical gesture: indentation. A great many of his poems use gradual increments of indentation to give the impression of rightward drift as the poem moves down the page. As Eigner explains in interview, the indentations initially stood for missing words, but increasingly became a way of emphasising the open-endedness of his writing:

at first, indentations and distances between words came mostly from skipping over prepositions et al., to keep the immediacy and force, leaving the spaces where they were. But soon the indents got to be mainly a matter of not going all the way back leftwards to another pretty full or not-partial renewal. If you start a poem or a line with an upper-case letter it's like the big beginning of all speech, not just a piece of language. In general, the indents and other spacings became distancings, not in a derived way, but directly realized.[32]

This helps us understand how important the desire to avoid fullness was to Eigner. Rather than part of a closed system, the indented line can be apprehended as a 'piece of language' – he uses the same phrase in the retort to Prynne cited above and in his 'not/ forever/ serious' statement. A 'piece of language' is necessarily partial. Eigner had a distinctive use for brevity. His version of the short poem is quite unlike the haiku, which aspires to a kind of minimal integrity. For Eigner, the act of foreshortening is a means of unmooring parcels or 'pieces' of language to allow them to come into new relationships with one another. The suspended temporality of his syntax allowed his poems to be anchored in the moment but open to extension into larger timescales. Whether Eigner uses progressive indentation or a more varied and ragged presentation, each line emerges as an autonomous unit. Eigner, as his editors note, was careful about the spacing of each letter on the page. The recent *Collected* and *Selected* editions of his work have, as the latter's introduction specifies, 'replicated the typewriter's equivalent spacing, to reproduce and preserve Eigner's meticulous and horizontal settings of letters, words and lines of various lengths and shifting (potential) positions on the space of the page'.[33]

Most of his poems begin on a dated page, but their journal-like, documentary qualities are undermined by the provisionality of the relations between each piece of language. Eigner thus both exploits and explodes the left-to-right, top-to-bottom linearity imposed by the typewriter. However, unlike Olson and some of his followers, his open-field practice does not extend to quasi-pictorial textual arrangements. There is a vestigial narrative moment, however contested or disrupted, to most of the poems. One extremely condensed version of Eigner's style of incremental indentation can be seen in poem #371, from January 27 1970:

```
          co-op

            wind

          ows a

            door
```

(*CT*, p. 157)

The first word has no evident relation to what follows: it is a bare, lower-case noun, itself an abbreviation for co-operative, which might imply a co-operative store or housing development, with all the loose connotations of collectivity that that entails.[34] However, the word also suggests the constraint of 'coop': a place of confinement or restricted movement. The next line brings the possibility of freedom or even inspiration, though this is immediately bound to the following line, and 'wind' retrospectively becomes a part-word. The 'ows' syllable echoes the two 'o's of co-op, with three potential 'o' sounds tested by the poem: long, short and the 'oo' digraph. The momentum established by lines two and three pushes the poem on to the concluding noun, a point of entry or exit. The poem offers the barest outline of a building, though it is unclear whether the speaker is describing an interior or an exterior. Although there are only four or five words across the four lines (depending on the status of 'wind') the poem is as unstable as the 'wind' it refers to. The words 'co-op' and wind/ows' are both split, and the variations on 'o' explore the implications of blankness and openness that attach to the figure 'o'. The poem is relatively unusual for this period in Eigner's writing in that the space invoked is not viewed from a domestic vantage point. The intense compression reduces the encounter with the environment to the barest enumeration of substantives, and this list is itself guided by the minimal patterning of the poem: two iterations of a trochaic pairing followed by a stressed monosyllable. Such details are 'intrinsic' to Eigner's poetry.[35] This door, like any door, is both an opening towards the future and a boundary between present and past. It might be read as a figure for a point of rest, the 'phrasal hinge' Bernstein describes. We cannot be sure if this door is open or closed. The poem brilliantly evokes and withholds at the same time, offering the sparest of visual cues. It looks outwards, inviting the reader to constellate a world from meagre materials, at the same time as looking inwards, scrutinising the world-making capacities of the words it depends upon.

As we have seen, scale is an important issue for Eigner. His attention to the physical world immediately around him often gives way to broader perspectives, despite the apparent simplicity of the language and ostensible focus on the phenomenal. This process can be implicit, as in #423 (8 August 1970):

```
rain

    curtain

        birds and

            thunder
```
(*CT*, p.166)

In this five-word poem, the viewpoint appears to be located inside a house. Three of the four objects described are outside the house, while the 'curtain' is inside. Had the poem merely alluded to rain, birds and thunder it would have been very different. As it is, the curtain functions as one of the points of rest, or hinges, that define the space of the poem, implying a house, a room and a perceiver. The curtain must be drawn aside to reveal the rain and birds, so it acts as a condition of possibility for what the speaker experiences. This screen can disclose or withhold the world outside the room. The poem invokes the sounds of rain and thunder, and each line is bound to the next with acoustic echoes: 'curtain' half-rhymes with 'rain' and 'birds and'; and 'and' half-rhymes with 'thund-'. The birds are, once again, generic, their blankness refusing any metaphorical freight. The poem seems to revolve around several figures of mobility: the raindrops that strike the ground and vanish; the temporarily drawn curtain; the birds in flight or about to fly; the volatility of thunder. As ever with Eigner, the only human present in the text is the implied perceiver whose consciousness shapes the poem. The poem might simply offer a thumbnail of an unremarkable moment: an individual sits by a window looking at the rain and birds, and hearing thunder. However, of course, it does more than this. The suppression of articles, pronouns and adjectives promotes a generalisable horizon within the poem. We might be paying attention to the rain in the barely sketched scene, or to rain per se. Ditto the featureless curtain, the generic birds and the characterless thunder. Again, the parameters of the moment are at issue. Are we attending to a thunder clap? To a thunderstorm? Or, beyond this instance, to thunder in itself? I would argue that the erosion of particulars broadens the communicative range of the text, allowing it to function at all three of these levels simultaneously. There is none of the luminosity typically attached to the haiku, no gentle nudging of the reader towards insight. The poem speaks of an encounter with the world that is at once facilitated by and mediated by the words that it uses. At the same time, it implicitly reflects on these facts with its confrontational use of brevity.

Poem #478, dated March 24 1971 (*CT*, p. 175) similarly brings a relativising perspective to bear on human sense experience. In this case, Eigner's attention is attuned to listening rather than seeing. Many of the lines are a single word, sometimes a monosyllable:

```
            motor
                some process
            simulates the sea
                                's

                 sound


                a result


             cross
             winds


             salt
                 is harsh

         indoors the refrigerator
                         once in a while
             hums    a wall


                    and voice
                            mechanism


                 the earth is
                    how
                 lost in space
```

(CT, p. 175)

The ostensible setting of the poem is hearing a passing vehicle from the Swampscott porch. This is placed in parallel with nature: Eigner refers to the sound of the sea, which was very close to his home. Tyres on tarmac heard from a distance do indeed sound similar to the white-noise-like sounds of the sea or the wind, which enters the poem a couple of lines after the sea. The floating ''s', isolated on a line, mimics the hiss both of surf and machine at the same time as turning itself into a dramatic bridge between 'sea' and 'sound'. The 'cross/ winds' are apprehended acoustically too. The sound of wind in leaves also resembles surf. The opening 'motor' is now bound to three kinds of motion: machine, tides and wind. The sonic qualities of 'salt/ is harsh' embed the words in the rushing sounds previously evoked, but hold at arm's length the possibility of an uncritically romanticised version of nature. Indeed, all but two of the poem's eighteen short lines contain an 's' sound.

All this unfolds while Eigner, whose 'motor ... process[es]' were so affected by his disability, pays close attention. Once again, the speaker/ perceiver is a blank receptor rather than a psychologised actor. The poem moves from hiss to hum as the poet's attention moves indoors, and the hum is compared to the vibration of a 'voice mechanism'. The sound, made by artificial and natural phenomena, is now placed alongside with Eigner's embattled physical condition – speech was extremely difficult for him, and the Swampscott house was very quiet.[36] Having laid out a very bare presentation of existence – a voice, shelter – Eigner moves to a concluding stanza that relativises the entire scene. Rather than say simply that the earth is lost in space, Eigner inserts the word 'how', disrupting the flow of the sentence. The word appears, after the various hisses and hums, as the first articulate intervention from outside the acoustic texture of the poem, and the first line not to contain an 's' sound since the opening 'motor'. The unfolding meditation is interrupted by a sound from within the scene that provides its setting, positioning the poet as an inquirer. What might have been a rather banal concluding gesture is complicated by the insertion of the monosyllabic question word. The concluding 'Space' is an important word for Eigner, and here it seems to refer all at once to the cosmos, to his own domestic environment and to the space of the page. Neither artificial nor natural processes are compared to poetic production (unlike Niedecker's method in her water pump poems). On the contrary, Eigner seems to use space to indicate reception rather than production. The severe restriction of the poetic line enhances the quality of careful acoustic attention, as the poem moves from word to word. If the refrigerator hums 'once in a while' then the speaker must be listening for more than a moment. The poem once again suggests attention over both the span of a moment, and of 'a while', concluding with a thought that places his attentiveness within a cosmic timespan.

One of the poems, #769, from 30 March 1973, is of exemplary simplicity. It consists of just four words:

    i

       mean

      at

       moments

(*CT*, p. 218)

Eigner is careful and rigorous in his unwillingness to allow his poems to resolve into statements. As far as it says anything at all, this poem announces that it speaks in time and that sense-making is intermittent. It may be that each poem captures or represents a moment in time, or that each poem makes sense – in the conventional reception of that word – only occasionally. The layout suggests an on-off pulsing of sense. How long is a moment? Is the moment inside or outside the poem? Is it an hour spent on a Massachusetts porch, or the line-by-line flashing of meaning in a poem? The echo of 'meant' in mo*ment* installs the past tense of the main verb, and thus another temporal dimension, at the end of the poem. The words 'mean/ at' and the suggestion of 'meant' are only a single letter apart, and 'mean/ at' forms a half-rhyme with 'moment'. Thus the acoustic and the temporal effects of the poem are intertwined. The absence of an object or a transitive verb leaves a gap at the centre of the poem. Instead of meaning this or that, the question of how meaning is conveyed in the poem is left pointedly open. Like many of Eigner's poems, it suggests both compression and expansion, as indentation and syntax combine to produce effects of contingency with the most restricted of means.

Eigner's poetry combines the push to condensation of the post-Poundian lineage discussed throughout this book with the more expansive gestures of Projectivism. For all the ellipsis in the writing, linearity is integral to its movement. If one line does not appear to follow another easily, a clustering effect complicates but does not impede the overall momentum of the poem. The objects of Williams's poems of observation are held in structuring frames that are unavailable to the bare, unsituated objects in Eigner's writing, which are suspended in the line-by-line stanzaic phrases identified by Duncan. As with George Oppen and Creeley, Eigner's world is inseparable from his attempt to parse it into language. His perceptual experience comes into being in the utterance, which captures moments of attention, both local and imaginative, near and far. While the spatial circumscription occasioned by Eigner's disability is, as Davidson and others have argued, integral to the writing, figures of freedom and imaginative transformation place mobility at its heart. Eigner's use of disjunction helps him articulate a poetic thinking in which incompleteness and implication serve to intensify the range of meanings made in moments.

Notes

1. Eigner was featured in the first five issues of *This*, beginning in 1971. The first issue of L=A=N=G=U=A=G=E magazine appeared in February 1978 and contained a brief feature on Eigner's work. He subsequently was a regular contributor. Eigner's writing featured in several issues of Tottels from 1971, and no. 15 was a special issue dedicated to his work.
2. Michael Davidson's chapter 'Missing Larry: The Poetics of Disability in Larry Eigner' in his *Concerto for the Left Hand* is a key essay on this topic, as is Seth Forrest's article 'The Body of the Text: Cerebral Palsy, Projective Verse and Prosthetics in Larry Eigner's Poetry'. Forrest discusses the auditory dimension of the poetry, and Eigner's relationship to radio. Also very helpful is Jessica Lewis Luck's 'Larry Eigner and the Phenomenology of Projected Verse'.
3. Cited in Ben Friedlander, 'Larry Eigner'.

4. Luck, 'Larry Eigner and the Phenomenology of Projected Verse', p. 474. Charles Bernstein, 'Introduction' to *Calligraphy Typewriters: the Selected Poems of Larry Eigner*, ed. Curtis Faville and Robert Grenier, p. xi). Faville and Grenier edited the monumental four-volume *Collected Poems* of Larry Eigner. In this chapter, I have taken most of my examples of poems by Eigner from the very generous selection the editors made for *Calligraphy Typewriters*, henceforth referenced parenthetically as *CT*.
5. The first *Selected* edition of his poems (ed. Samuel Charteris and Andrea Wyatt, Berkeley: Oyez, 1972) groups his poetic output into three sections: 1959–77; a two-month period in early 1978, when Eigner was living in a group home; and his subsequent years in Berkeley.
6. Friedlander, 'Larry Eigner', n.p.
7. Davidson, *Concerto for the Left Hand*, p. 133. The terms in citation marks are from Eigner's poem 'Back to It'.
8. Barrett Watten, 'Missing "X": Formal Meaning in Crane and Eigner', n.p.
9. Lytle Shaw, *Narrowcast: Poetry and Audio Research*, p. 79.
10. Shaw, *Narrowcast*, p. 86.
11. Shaw, *Narrowcast*, p. 85.
12. Larry Eigner, letter dated 4 January 1987, *Areas Lights Heights*, n.p.
13. Williams, *Autobiography*, pp. 390–1.
14. Watten, 'Missing "X"', n.p. Watten quotes Williams's famous dictum earlier in his essay, as he compares Eigner to Hart Crane: 'The poet thinks with his poem. Manner and matter, separate in Crane, are identical in Eigner.'
15. Charles Olson, 'Projective Verse', p. 240.
16. Eigner, *Air the Trees*, p. 33, p. 48.
17. George Hart, ' "Enough Defined": Disability, Ecopoetics and Larry Eigner'.
18. Eigner, 'Here and There', *Areas Lights Heights*, n.p.
19. Also referenced in my introduction.
20. Eigner *CT*, p. 6, p. 334.
21. In his essay 'Birds in Dickinson's Words' Jonathan Skinner writes: 'According to my last count, nearly 15 percent of Dickinson's poems contain birds (264 of 1789 poems), with twenty-four species named; about one third of these are specifically bird poems', p. 107. The poet Susan Tichy has compiled an online listing of birds in Niedecker, available at <http://mason.gmu.edu/~stichy/Niedecker%27s%20Birds.html> (last accessed 12 August 2019).
22. Eigner, 'Three Poems', p. 20.
23. Kit Robinson, 'What do you Know: A Read on Larry Eigner', n.p.
24. J. H. Prynne, in *Mica*, no. 5, cited in the editor's notes to Eigner's *Areas Lights Heights*, n.p.
25. Eigner, 'Like a Dog Bark in Music', *Areas Lights Heights*, n.p.
26. The phrase recalls Pound's stated aim, in 'In a Station of the Metro', of recording, the 'precise instant when a thing outward and objective transforms itself, or darts into a thing inward and subjective'. See Pound, 'Vorticism', p. 89, in *Gaudier-Brzeska*.
27. Bernstein, 'Introduction' to *Calligraphy Typewriters*, p. xi.

28. Eigner, 'OF THE SPONTANEOUS/OR/ WHAT WILL MAY BE/ COME' *Areas Lights Heights*, n.p.
29. Williams, 'The New Poetical Economy', pp. 223–4.
30. *The Tempest*, IV, i.
31. Eigner, 'not/ forever/ serious', *Areas Lights Heights*, n.p.
32. Eigner, 'Qs & As (?) Large and Small Parts of a Collaborate: The *Stony Hills* Interview', n.p.
33. Faville and Grenier, 'Note on the Text', *Calligraphy Typewriters*, p. xiii.
34. See 'Among various hills', 6 August 1966 (*CT*, 109) for another poem that appears to be grounded in Swampscott retail spaces.
35. Eigner, in 'Qs & As (?)' writes: 'Distances between words are not negligible elements of a piece: pauses or silences. Punctuation can be intrinsic, as a title or heading can be, lacunae too can be, times when you (can) come up with such, ditto a parascript, and even a footnote has seemed nondistracting at least once', n.p.
36. Eigner remarked on the quietness of the Swampscott house. Cited in Grenier, 'Larry Eigner Biography', n.p.

Chapter 7

Robert Grenier

The short-form tradition in twentieth-century American poetry that I have been describing is marked by certain lines of descent. These are usually acknowledged by the poets concerned, whether in essays, interviews or correspondence. Some of the poets I discuss, moreover, corresponded with each other over many years. The bond between Eigner and Grenier, however, is almost familial. In 1978, Eigner moved to the West Coast. A few months later he moved in to the household of Grenier and his partner, who became his carers. The younger poet helped induct Eigner into a West Coast literary environment that was dominated by the Language writers: Ron Silliman, Barrett Watten, Carla Harryman, Lyn Hejinian and many others. Grenier was active in conversations and publications that led to a shift from the open-field poetics that had prevailed among avant-garde poets since the publication in 1960 of Donald Allen's *New American Poetry* anthology (in which Eigner appeared), towards a mode of writing that placed language itself at the heart of its enquiry.

Grenier's early 1970s thinking on poetics did not amount to the radical proposal that has sometimes been described in narratives of American avant-garde writing. This account of a rupture that ushered in the era of Language writing is often grounded in accounts of Grenier's essay 'On Speech'. This is one of five Grenier prose texts published in issue 1 of *This* in 1971.[1] The text's enduring influence, however, is owed to its presence in the 1986 anthology *In the American Tree* and its prominent place in the editor Ron Silliman's introduction. This introduction begins with 'I HATE SPEECH', an aggressively capitalised phrase that became Grenier's best-known utterance on poetics. Silliman argues that the phrase 'announced a breach – and a new moment in American writing', and it has often been taken, notwithstanding Silliman's careful caveats, to inaugurate a decisive break from Black Mountain models of breath-based composition.[2]

It is certainly true that Grenier shared none of the mythopoeic interests of Robert Duncan or Charles Olson, and that neither Allen Ginsberg nor Olson's attitudes towards the page as the record of the embodied utterance were important to his own writing. However, Olson's typographical innovations, which dramatically expanded the visual potential of page-space, were clearly an enabling model for Grenier. And Robert Creeley's poetry, of course, even in this period, never relinquished the close tie between the linebreak and the voicing of the poem. Eigner, as I have argued, was family, and his preoccupation with the vicissitudes of the perceptual process clearly had a profound impact on Grenier's poetry. As Silliman concedes when he describes 'On Speech' as 'a break from tradition in the name of its own higher values', Grenier's work can best be understood as an evolution of ideas already present in post-Black Mountain writing, not as the embodiment of a revolutionary new paradigm. Grenier's early 1970s writing, both creative and critical, is also an early indication of the rehabilitation of the techniques of Gertrude Stein undertaken by writers of the Language generation ('On Speech' concludes with a minimal text from Stein's *Tender Buttons*), and it has significant affinities, as I will argue below, with the way some 1960s artists used text.

In this chapter, I will discuss Grenier's most significant piece of the 1970s, *Sentences*, a tour de force in short-form poetics. Grenier's early 1970s writing is strikingly minimal in its methods, and Silliman was very active in promoting the work and defining its value. The first issue of Silliman's mimeo journal *Tottel's* contained five very brief Grenier texts on its final page. The collection of twenty texts published in Silliman's *Tottels 5*, which was dedicated to Grenier's work, is a further, and fuller, case in point.[3] Most of the poems are only one or two lines long. One reads simply 'good good', another 'choppers'. In 1975 Silliman edited a mini-anthology of nine poets representing the emerging Language scene for an issue of Jerome Rothenberg's *Alcheringa* entitled 'The Dwelling Place'.[4] The 25-page selection includes work by Watten, Silliman, Coolidge, David Melnick and others. Silliman uses various terms to describe the poetry: 'language centered', 'minimal', 'non-referential formalism', 'diminished referentiality', 'structuralist'. The Grenier selection mostly comprises one-line poems. Silliman's note on Grenier at the end of the journal, which begins with a reference to 'On Speech', is revealing:

> 'In the process of writing what does not then occur in the head is a distraction.' Equivalent to Merleau-Ponty's 'We write in perceived space.' 'Words are words,' WCW said, but Grenier has been the first to make literal use of this. Not minimalism but gigantism: the terms are so reduced that each facet is magnified, one hears every letter, one hears the spaces between every letter.

The clarity of formal process possible when the elements are reduced as radically as in his poems becomes in his work not a tone or aridness but elegance by the fact of such precision as 'of life days like'.⁵

In Silliman's reading, Grenier calls for a new writing grounded in a formalistic attention to language *as* language. Yet, while Grenier self-consciously presents his position in 'On Speech' as a polemic ('why not exaggerate, as Williams did'), he is certainly not calling for a poetry devoted primarily to exploring its own textuality. In his essay, Grenier seeks access to an originary process through which experience is transubstantiated into language:

> what now I want, at least, is the word way back in the head that is the thought or feeling forming out of the 'vast' silence/ noise of consciousness experiencing world all the time, as waking/dreaming, words occurring and these are the words of the poems.⁶

Grenier goes on to pose a question of originary verbal authenticity: 'Where are the words most themselves?' His conclusion is that he wants 'writing what is thought/where feeling is/words are born'. He is in pursuit, then, of a moment of primal linguistic intensity at which the flux of experience forms itself into words.

This attention to 'birth' of verbal meaning, is examined through a different prism in the 'drawing poems' that Grenier has been producing since the late 1980s. This work dispenses with conventional typography altogether. The drawing poems fuse verbal and visual in compositions that use four ink colours: red, green, blue and black. In these striking works, verbal and visual are in tense counterpoint: words are abstracted into coloured lines, exploded to a point of near-illegibility.

This later visual work grows out of the anti-metaphysical positioning of writers of the Language generation. As the critic Brian Reed observes, it demonstrates 'the deconstructive potential of an improper (or perverse, untimely, inexplicable, inconvenient, deviant, etc.) emphasis on writing's materiality'.⁷ Yet, these works might also be read as a means of emphasising language's visual aspect as communicative immediacy, not mediatedness. Grenier may be pursuing the nexus of visual and verbal with the same energy he once brought to the nexus of language and experience. This would be congruent with Grenier's description of language as an active bodily event 'way back in the head' rather than a script system exterior to the body. As he remarks when discussing Creeley's book *Pieces* in issue 1 of *This*, 'all words are acts as it happens in the head, not signs/"about" something primarily but energy in time, along with all the other simultaneous goings on/in/of the organism'. Such positioning suggests a greater commitment to the kinetic alignments of Projectivism than to the variously 'deconstructive' ambitions of Language writing. Indeed, at times in his early poetics, Grenier is strongly corporeal in his representation of textual production, as in the following, which espouses a gendered model of poetic creativity that underscores the persistence (albeit comically, from this distance) of 1960s tropes in the emergent years of Language writing: 'words just like sex – both energy of organism – even better, can keep on coming, "auto-erotic" yes/no just giving energy to universe (as sperm to woman/ words to books) but that's afterward, valuation, the man in the mind in the words just go on'.[8]

Grenier's signal contribution to the reductionist tendency that I have been describing in this book occurs with his collection *Sentences*. This work extends the polemical line on short-form writing found in 1960s Creeley. It can be read as poetry by virtue of the fact that it emerged from debates on poetics, but most of the texts lack most or all of the defining features of poetry, offering instead small decontextualised parcels of colloquial language. *Sentences* is comprised of 500 short texts printed in the centre of standard 5" x 8" Oxford index cards. Grenier used an IBM Selectric typewriter[9] with a Courier 72 (10 point) ball.[10] The cards were published in a limited edition inside a handsome folding box by Whalecloth Press in 1978. The work was long unavailable but French press Editions de l'Attente issued a dual-language edition of 100 of the cards in 2005. The use of the index card format and the typewriter lends *Sentences* an impersonal, bureaucratic quality that is itself generative because so generic. The poems were effectively published as MS facsimiles, without being parsed into the formal arrangement of the book. Most contemporary readers encounter the text online. (Whalecloth published the entire text on its website in a format that delivers a new card in random order with every click of the 'next' button until all 500 cards have been viewed.) This version of the text is well suited to enforcing Grenier's preference for a non-linear path through the cards, but, of course, it cannot replicate either the physical interaction with materials that the original boxed publication demands, or the potential for arranging multiple cards alongside one another to produce spatial juxtapositions of particular texts.

The motivation for *Sentences* lay in Grenier's belief that in Creeley's 1960s work, seriality had exhausted itself. Creeley had broken the basic unit of poetic utterance down to the barest sequence: 1, 2, 3. With *Sentences*, Grenier moved towards a more open-ended concept of 'continuum':

I thought that *Pieces* had so much accomplished the serial form, opened up the one-one-one, things-following-after-each-other in the enactment of the occasion, that somehow the only thing to do was to 'stop it' and look at separate pieces . . . So out of that came the desire to reassemble things in sentences for other persons with a tolerance of the difference between one sentence and another. They wouldn't have to 'follow,' but you could build up some kind of continuum which wasn't a series but was some kind of made juxtaposition of separate elements.[11]

Grenier's innovation proved influential. Silliman's 'New Sentence' essay, first published in 1977, identified Grenier as a significant forerunner. Silliman argued for a mode of writing composed of paragraphs of grammatically intact sentences. Instead of the ruptured syntax and dispersed typographical arrangements of the modernist line, the new sentence would draw its disruptive energies from the paratactic gap between sentences that had no obvious relationship to one another. Meanings emerge from the collage-like juxtaposition of numerous disparate elements. For Silliman, 'Sentence length is the unit of measure.'[12] Grenier was, Silliman argued, an important influence, but had not fully conceived the 'sentence' as distinct from the 'utterance'. His work was thus still beholden to a speech-based poetics:

Bob Grenier's *Sentences* directly anticipates the new sentence. By removal of context, Grenier prevents most leaps beyond the level of grammatic integration. This is the extreme case for the new sentence. However, most of Grenier's 'sentences' are more properly utterances, and in that sense follow Olson, Pound and a significant portion of Creeley's work.[13]

Read from our contemporary perspective, Silliman's implicit valorisation of written 'sentence' over spoken 'utterance' is less persuasive than his alignment of Grenier's innovation with precedents in the work of Ezra Pound, Olson and Creeley. The card-index formatting and the non-sequential occurence of the given phrases serves to distance the work from anything resembling a score for spoken performance. Although the register of the writing is typically colloquial, the physical qualities of Grenier's *Sentences* serve to dislocate utterance from its physical origins. Moreover, one immediately striking feature of *Sentences* is that many of the constituent poems are not sentences at all. The forms are varied. Some have capitalised titles (or words that appear to fulfil the function of titles); some have linebreaks; some are just a single line; some are isolated phrases ('corroborative mountainous panorama'). There are neither commas nor full stops.

If the New Sentence thrived on the paratactic relationship between one sentence and another, Grenier's *Sentences* makes the isolated 'page', or index card, its basic unit. The cards can be shuffled, placed alongside one another on a table and read in any order chosen by the reader.[14] A sequence might emerge but only through the chance juxtaposition of elements. Every reading of *Sentences* is a new arrangement of the text. Grenier actively looked for new ways of presenting poetry outside the context of the book: some of the poems in *Sentences* were presented as slides at Perelman's Writing/ Talks series; others were incorporated into his 'Cambridge, M'ass' poster, published in 1979 by Lyn Hejinian's Tuumba Press.

While Grenier's later work would problematise the relationship between verbal and visual, *Sentences* is both acoustic and visual in nature. In his 2006 *Close Listening* interview with Charles Bernstein, Grenier remarks that, like Pound, Creeley was sculpting in sound.[15] A number of the poems begin with a capitalised 'BIRD' and seek to replicate the cadence of birdsong.[16] In his *Linebreak* interview, Grenier seeks to read, and then to whistle a poem that reads 'BIRD// I wonder if I do' to Bernstein, but his efforts at pitching the words are halting and not entirely persuasive. Moreover, Grenier indicates – surprisingly – that the layout of the poems of *Sentences* has a representational axis: that the blank space replicates the empty spaces, white in winter and blue in summer, of the New Hampshire site of the poems' composition. It is clear that Grenier's writing, early and late, displays an interest in acoustic and visual effects that are quite distinct in character from the specifically textual orientation of the New Sentence.

Even though he seeks to replicate the qualities of a specific song in the text cited above, Grenier – like Eigner – alludes to a generic 'bird'. The general noun serves as a means of approaching a quality of thusness in his representations of the things of the world. Grenier appears to find an expressive intensity in the simplest nouns, which seem to access a more profound encounter with the nexus of word and experience in his work. He attributes this quality to Eigner's example: 'Larry Eigner used to say that he had x-ray vision, that was because he wanted to know more than the outside of something. He wanted to look into something and see what defined it as its formal fact of itself.'[17]

The extreme compression of each of the cards and the decision to work with 500 discrete units means that Grenier presents us with slivers of information that fall far short of the pictorial faithfulness often ascribed to short-form poetry, and described in terms such as 'snapshot' or 'vignette', or even 'imagism'. The focal point for the reader is the equivocal relation between one card and those around it. This is where the originality of the work's version of modernist discontinuity is found. Grenier replaces the linebreak, the totemic formal feature of free verse, with the break between one card and the next. The linebreak, in other words, is physicalised.

For Grenier, the poem proceeds from a phenomenal understanding of the moment, offering readers the opportunity to replicate aspects of an experience captured through the eyes and body of the author. Yet his manner of working in *Sentences* works directly against any possibility of constructing the contextual information and narrative setting that descriptive realism depends upon. There is simply not enough information. Speaking of 'walking down Washington Avenue' (the card contains nothing but these words) he remarks:

> If you inhabit the poem, you might imagine yourself into existence, into real life, and be a person with mobility moving along, and be alive, and recognise that you're living in that moment of existence, without any content except existence. Many of the poems have to do with that recognition of just being there.[18]

Grenier is, in an unobtrusive way, making quite a claim: he is suggesting that the barest thumbnail can conjure lived experience. The irrepressibly referential qualities of language facilitate the movement from an event through verbal representation in the artifice of the poem to the readerly reconstruction, not only of that specific experience but (to co-opt a phrase associated with John Ashbery's work), of the experience of experiencing. The salient point lies in Grenier's assertion that his *Sentences* poems are 'without any content' beyond experience per se. This process of translation may lead to something that it very far removed from the minimal sketch of determinate experience offered in Grenier's text:

> I like to attend to phenomena and then recreate them in a form that is not themselves, which is entirely made of language phenomena. And then juxtapose that with the initial event and imagine beyond it some 'future' event which a reader might create by reading the poem. Going out from the poem back toward an experience of something which is beyond the poem.[19]

Grenier is interested in the possibility that a minimal utterance may give rise to an imaginary experience that is entirely different, by very virtue of the parsimony with which it is sketched, from the motivating experience of the poem. If a defining feature of the short-form poem is the limit that it bumps up against, then Grenier's innovation with *Sentences* is to accentuate that limit. There is no identifiable sequence with which to order the cards, which are not constrained by the sequential pagination of a journal or a book. Texts can be read singly or in sequences that emerge by happenstance. While it is commonplace to view Language writing as inviting the active participation of the reader,

Grenier's *Sentences* insists upon it. The transaction between author and readerly experience is more important than the content of the utterance. The poems thus become a species of score for reading: launch pads for imaginative experience that bear only the most tenuous relationship to the events that provoked them. Short form potentialises the texts. The extreme brevity of the formulations, rather than the somewhat unremarkable quotidian specifics narrated, is what enables them to function in this way.

* * *

Grenier was not alone in exploring the communicative potential of index cards or, indeed, of boxed collections of material. As Paul Stephens notes, various conceptual artists of the 1960s and early 1970s used index cards: Robert Morris, Lucy Lippard, Michael Harvey and the Art & Language group.[20] But there is another strong art-world precedent for *Sentences*: the Fluxus box, in particular *Water Yam*, George Brecht's pioneering collection of 'event scores' (1963). Brecht's scores were also published as a series of cards in a nondescript font, with text typically printed in the centre of the card. It would be remarkable if Grenier had not been aware of this 1960s experiment, as the thought and techniques of John Cage were an important influence on both Fluxus and, a decade or so later, Language writing.[21]

Brecht's *Water Yam* scores were compiled and issued by George Maciunas in a box of sixty-nine index cards (the number of cards varied in subsequent editions). While the Brecht texts are notionally intended as instructions for performance, he pushed the text score into abstract and conceptual territory. Not only did it no longer have any necessary relation to actual performative realisations, it had a questionable relationship to performance itself. Many of the scores are so oblique that they have a parapoetic quality. One example reads simply:

ANOTHER WEAVING

    fingers between fingers

What is most striking about the score is its status as a textual object. One can easily imagine a performance involving one or more performers linking fingers together, but such a realisation seems almost beside the point. Is there a primary 'weaving' that precedes this 'other' weaving? Do performers interlock fingers with one another? What encounter is imaged by the word 'between' and what relation does it have to weaving? Ultimately, the questions provoked by considering the potential realisation of the score are of greater interest than an actual realisation. The chiasmic phrase 'fingers between fingers' is more suggestive and compelling as language per se than as instruction.

Another score, even more obliquely, reads:

FOX TROT

  • underground metal, or coal

Here the immediate question is the relationship between the early twentieth-century dance and underground deposits of metal and coal, pleasure and the exploitation of subterranean resources. It is possible to draw a parallel between an underground foxhole and mining, yet such a reading gives the reader little interpretative traction. Of course, all manner of performance works involving reflection on nature, mineral extraction, dance and so on might develop from the score, but, again, the power of the score seems to lie more in its undecidable relationship to potential performance than in any actual realisation. (Another text, entitled 'DANCE MUSIC' and containing the sole instruction 'gunshot', is an even more condensed – and wittier – conjunction of irreconcilable categories.)

The similarities in both presentation and textual abstraction between *Sentences* and *Water Yam* are great. Grenier's series is rooted in the documentation of a phenomenal encounter with the world. He, like Robert Creeley, Lorine Niedecker, George Oppen and William Carlos Williams, is initially concerned to ground his text in the object-world in which he finds himself. Unlike his predecessors, however, his priority in *Sentences* is experience per se rather than textual parsing of experience. The world outside the poem is present as motivating detail rather than a scene to be represented. As with Brecht's event scores, Grenier's miniature texts look beyond themselves to what he calls 'some "future" event'. Some of these details might almost be pared-back versions of Eigner's already minimal experiential thumbnails:

    POPLARS

    facing away

In this poem, which appears to evoke a scene, it is immediately unclear how a tree can face away. Indeed, the very term 'facing' is obviously anthropomorphic. The object contemplated can only be seen in relation to the onlooking poet. The bare encounter between poet and object inevitably, even at this level of reduction, becomes caught up in the semantic and syntactical bindings that situate cognition and its representation as human activities. Deprived of even minimal contextual markers, the reader has no option but to construct rather than reconstruct.

A similar obligation is experienced by the reader of an event score. Traditional music manuscripts were essentially recording devices designed to facilitate a realisation that was as close as possible to the intentions of the composer. The text scores of Cage and his contemporaries gave greater – sometimes limitless – interpretative latitude to performers: certain parameters would be precisely defined, but others (such as pitch, duration, instrumentation, number of performers) might be left open. Several Fluxus artists, including Brecht, Jackson Mac Low, La Monte Young and Dick Higgins, attended Cage's classes in composition at the New School for Social Research in the late 1950s, and his influence on what became an international art movement is generally acknowledged. From our contemporary perspective, Fluxus text scores are best conceived as conceptual objects. Real-world enactment with actions and objects seems a curiously retrograde homage to a now-distant historical avant-garde that was responding to quite different set of cultural and political imperatives. Grenier's poems and Brecht's scores share an orientation towards a future realisation prompted by very few words. Both projects require an independent constructive effort from the interpreter. There is no prospect – unlike the response to a conventional music manuscript score, or a more straightforward text score, or a confessional poem – of gaining access to the determinate parameters of aesthetic experience designed by the author/ composer.

Both Grenier's *Sentences* poems and Brecht's scores often work with the simple juxtaposition of two elements, as if they were minimal verbal collages. And both Brecht and Grenier sometimes narrowed their texts to the repetition of a single element. The following score by Brecht is a case in point:

TABLE

- table

The self-ironising dynamism in the piece lies the friction between 'title' and 'score'. Read as a performance score, the two words might suggest a possible action of indeterminate duration and location, featuring an unknown number of performers, but, in some undefined way, also a table. The table might be the sole object on a stage, or it might feature in some other way. Yet the text is almost entirely uncommunicative. It is a projection of a possible future that depends on the relationship between title and instruction, which mean differently in their different contexts. The fascination of the piece ultimately consists in this relation, and not (at least not any longer) in the myriad potential realisations. The bullet point, a characteristic feature of Brecht's scores, in this case reads like a full stop before the text. In other words, this minimal text is, at a fundamental level, asking questions about interpretation that far exceed its apparent orientation towards the performative. Similarly, but from within a different aesthetic tradition, Grenier's *Sentences* contains three cards that contain the same word twice – examples of the barest exercise of repetition. The most striking of these (the others are 'close close' and 'good good') is the following:

JOE

JOE

The reference to a real individual may be imagined by the reader, or it may be received as a possible future encounter. Or the reader might take account of the possibility of word-play – a cup of 'Joe'; two cups of 'Joe'. Grenier's sentences are re-made in the act of reading. Is Grenier faced with a pair of coffee cups? Drinking coffee? Watching the approach of a friend? The simple iterative act of the poem places it in the Creeley lineage.[22] Grenier takes the reduced narrative logic of Creeley's 'A Piece' – 'one and/ one, two,/ three' – to a point where narrative only survives in the friction between 'one' and 'one'. The differential play between a word and its reiteration is the motor of the text. The reader's interpretative response is as likely to be on the relation between word and word, sound and sound, word-image and word-image, as in any attempt at constituting a scene conforming to a particular understanding of 'Joe'.

Both Brecht's table score and Grenier's 'JOE' poem, then, are far more concerned with querying the interpretative conventions within which they operate than with either actual or imaginative staging of an event.

While the two series of boxed cards have clear affinities, each is a polemical contribution to a different aesthetic debate. The 'outside' to the Fluxus event score is performance. Often such works have a parodic humour that undoes the conditions of their own performance: texts such as 'strange issue of sovereign state' and 'a port to a green' are events in language that are detached from any performative construal. As with Grenier's *Sentences*, the 'outside' to the text – performance – collapses into the linguistic texture of the score. Grenier's *Sentences* sits in a tradition in which linguistic self-awareness increasingly drives the poem. The poem becomes a verbal matrix in which neither subject nor object can sustain a secure identity. There is a notional 'outside' to the poem, but it is continually absorbed into the fabric of the text.

In both Brecht's and Grenier's card projects, the ostensible function of the text is quite consciously forestalled. In Grenier's *Sentences*, the extra-poetic material, the world to which the poem refers, dissolves into its readerly reconstruction. In Brecht's *Water Yam*, on the other hand, the performative dimension of the text is subsumed by the textual. Grenier's cards knowingly fail to depict experience, and Brecht's cards fail to outline a future action. Each is oriented towards a future construction that each simultaneously undermines.

For George Maciunas, Brecht's scores achieved a status in which performance, and indeed art itself, rendered itself unnecessary – a reading of the Duchampian readymade that aspires to the merging of art and life. Writing of a score entited 'Word Event' and containing the single word 'Exit', Maciunas said:

> The best Fluxus 'Composition' is a most non-personal, 'readymade' one like Brecht's 'Exit' – it does not require any of us to perform it since it happens daily without any 'special' performance of it. Thus our festivals will eliminate themselves (and our need to participate) when they become total readymades (like Brecht's exit).[23]

Grenier's writing in *Sentences* does not lose sight of itself as writing, but the offhand snippets of domestic conversation and daydreaming are conspicuously hostile to any separation between literature and everyday experience.

I do not wish to elide the clear differences in the context and reception of each of these series. Brecht's was part of an international movement that deployed humour and group actions to pursue its goals in relation to art, institutions and power. The Fluxus artists were playfully subversive with the handling of terms such as creativity, originality and intention, placing themselves in a tradition running through Duchamp and Cage. Brecht's cards are descriptive, using verbs in the present tense or as imperatives, whereas Grenier's often imply an interlocutor and sometimes use the past tense. Grenier's *Sentences* emerge from a reflection on the relationship between author, text and world, and their focus is on the implications of communicating private experience. While Grenier was clearly an active member of an ambitious literary grouping, these texts, read together, never lose sight of the rural and domestic setting from which they emerge. Their ambition is no less radical than that of Brecht's works, but the zone of conflict is quite different. As with Eigner's texts, each new poem emerges from a reflection on the moment that generates it. In Grenier's case, the movement is from experience to the words that collect around it 'way back in the head'. The minimal text offered to the reader leads outwards to speculative reconstruction. It is the realisation in the barest terms of Williams's 'perfect economy'.[24]

* * *

In the remainder of this chapter I will describe the range of poems in *Sentences*, and look closely at how particular instances work. The *Sentences* poems can be divided into a number of categories. The following is one way of sorting the poems:

- Single-line poems [192]
- Poems with titles (given in capitals) and one or more lines [86]
- Untitled poems of two or more lines [81]
- Poems made from family dialogue with named speakers [60]
- Two-word poems [36]
- Single-word poems [11]
- Poems made from two elements in apposition [19]
- Poems concerning birds [5]
- Typographical experiments [5]
- Repetition poems [5]

We can draw a number of conclusions from the above taxonomy. The *Sentences* poems, first of all, are far from homogeneous. Within the shared format of the index card containing centred Courier text, a number of quite different experiments are performed. Most of the poems are not sentences. About 40 per cent of the poems in *Sentences* are single lower-case lines, and just over 30 per cent are either titled poems of one or more lines, or untitled poems of two or more lines.[25] A significant minority are conceptually driven: the apposition poems; those involving multiple repetitions; the poems based on visual experimentation; and the poems comprising just one or two words. Many of the poems are based on domestic found speech: usually exchanges between Grenier and his daughter Amy and/or his partner Emily. Many poems resemble snatches of inner speech, such as 'time to go to the laundry again soon' or 'thought/ living in/ Davis would/ be ok'. Even where family members are not mentioned, a good many of the one-liners appear to be fragments of household conversation: 'I think their dog always barks when coming back from the woods', for example, or 'who are you talking on the telephone to'.

Some of the poems in *Sentences*, therefore, are undoubtedly, in Silliman's terms, 'utterances' (though I would question his suggestion that 'most' are). However, many are conspicuously textual in nature, and distant from colloquial language use. The poem 'leaf and the ants as latterly', to take one example, has no verb. There is no available context for this bundle of words. The temporal adverb 'latterly' is not attached to any imaginable situation, with or without leaf or ants. Similarly, 'mosquitos nigh in old age reflexes chip' is far removed from a viable 'utterance'. The short and ungrammatical phrase seems to be collaged from even smaller elements. The phrase 'branches are then moved by negligible quantity the' is, likewise, both syntactically and semantically awry. Indeed, this is one of the many phrases in *Sentences* to contest the very idea of the sentence. While this could, differently arranged on the page, almost be an Eigner poem, it is notable how rarely Grenier experiments with *mise-en-page* on his index cards. The single-line poems, in particular, are resolutely undemonstrative in visual terms. Such examples as these are distant both from the everyday utterance and from the typographical notation of spoken utterance practised by post-Olsonian poets. Grenier works with anti-literary methods. The flat, neutral, impersonal assocations of the uniform index card serve to reinforce the poems' status as text, at a distance from speech, from the notated rhythms of the poet's body and from any consideration of poetic language as a privileged form of language use.

Yet *Sentences* seeks, in neo-Williamsian fashion, to expand the remit of the poetic rather than to reject it. Many of the texts in *Sentences* are recognisable as poems, even though many run to only two lines. The following counting-poem evidences Grenier's interest in both acknowledging and moving beyond Creeley:

```
FIREFLIES

mostly three

often two

occasionally one

rarely four
```

Instead of 'One and/ one, two,/ three', the poem shuffles the sequence. The title is significant, anchoring a poetic abstraction in a specific night-time observation. This observation plays economically with the adverbs of frequency which begin each line. There is an abstract tension in the poem between adverbs of progressively declining frequency and the number sequence, which changes direction, moving upwards with the final word of the poem. The poem, then, plays two sequences against each other, enjoying the non-alignment. Creeley's poem opens with the shift in direction between what might have been 'one and one makes two' but is actually a number sequence. Grenier's, on the other hand, leaves the shift until the end. While Creeley's poem is devoid of external referents, Grenier's uses his title to ground the poem in the tension between the specific observation of mobile points of light, and the longer time span necessary to calculate frequency and number. Of course, the poem is wilfully absurd in its claim to log the incidence of fireflies in a particular location, ridiculing the observational ambitions of the tradition in which it participates.

Another poem is conventionally Imagistic in its observation of the world:

```
BLACK & WHITE RAIN

clear water grey drops

on windshields in a line

of cars progressing slowly

with windshield wipers wiping
```

In this rather Williamsian text, title and poem are at odds. The rain is clear and then grey, not either black or white. Water is presented first as a clear liquid and then as discrete droplets. These fall on glass, a solid but transparent screen. Each of these transparencies takes shape in the black-on-white of text. There is a marked contrast between the fluidity of water and the machines it falls on, which are trapped in a slow-moving line. It is hard not to hear the echo of 'typing' in 'wipers wiping', but the wiping-away gesture in the scene depicted in the poem stands in contrast to the material fact of the printed poem. The rainwater that gives Williams's wheelbarrow a painting-like glaze seems to be in mind, though here the relationship between natural world and human artefact is different, with rain wiped relentlessly away. The quadruple alliteration that closes the poem assimilates, with some amusement, the artifice of the poem with the machines it depicts – the human measure of the poetic foot replaced by a technological pattern. The poem draws on a haiku-like juxtaposition of two elements. The final line does not lead implicitly towards any kind of insight. Rather, driven by wilfully exaggerated succession of 'w's, it stoically observes the meaninglessness of the parade of machines. While some of the poems of *Sentences* are concerned to broaden the ambit of poetic speech, this poem is an example of those that conspicuously write themselves into the short-form tradition discussed by this book.

The poem 'INSPIRE EXPIRE' also considers driving, but this time alongside the rhythm of breath. After its two-word title, each line consists of a single word:

```
            INSPIRE EXPIRE

            more

            miles

            yes

            gas

            a

            bush
```

The poem, from the title on, begins with a set of pairings, emphasised either by rhyme (INSIRE EXPIRE; yes/ gas) or alliteration ('more/ miles'). The context appears to be a long-distance drive. However, the poem runs aground with the final two words, 'a/ bush'. Any suggestion that the 'inspiration' might be poetic or even divine in nature, revealed by means of a burning bush, is quashed with the deadpan 'EXPIRE' and the latent threat in the missing 'm' of 'ambush'. Despite the appearance of motion, the poem leads nowhere. There is nothing to be learnt from the inconsequential bush. The poem's severe curtailment allows it to restrict itself to three salient nouns. It permits itself the enlivenment of breath and motion, but neither celebrates nor derides any of its terms. While it invites a minimal enactment of beginning, middle and end, it remains impassively anti-metaphorical, anti-narrative and anti-expressive. The sole gesture it permits itself is that of bringing three discontinuous slivers of intellection into alignment with one another.

Often, Grenier's *Sentences* poems exploit the relationship between a title and the words that follow it:

```
                    YESTERDAY


            I saw no one today
```

The poem is an example of the gnomic humour found in *Sentences*. There is an obstinate opposition between the heading and its enactment. Instead of narrating an action, the poem, which reads like a diary entry, narrates a negative. There is a self-cancelling quality to the relation between 'YESTERDAY' and 'today', much like the play between 'inspire' and 'expire', or that between 'BLACK' and 'WHITE'. The text exemplifies a point Grenier subsequently made about the arrested temporality of *Sentences*, describing the works as 'attempts to stop time, prosodically'.[26] Given this temporal self-cancellation, in tandem with the negation 'no one', all one is left with is bare predication, 'I saw'. And that action relates not to a specific instance of seeing but to a day-long experience of isolation. Indeed, 'I saw' might almost be 'I was'. This brief poem is a fascinating example of poetic withholding, generating through its very paucity of means a narrative that erases itself. It brilliantly and quietly says nothing about anything but saying itself.

Sentences achieves monumental results with minimal means. The work is a significant advance in the poetics of its day, outsourcing the linebreak by introducing a 'card-break' and thus an aleatory component to poetic unfolding. This innovation might be called, following Husárová and Montfort, a 'shuffle-poetics'.[27] Decades later, it found a resonance in non-linear modes of reading introduced by e-poetry. However, the online version's perfect randomness is rigorous to the point of falling out of step with the hard-copy original. No one, after all, could shuffle a pack of 500 cards with equal rigour. Grenier's achievement lies in bringing the serial progress of reading to a halt, as the 'continuum' replaces the sequence.[28]

Although *Sentences* owes a debt to Stein, it does not present itself as the 'irritating annoying stimulating' challenge that some Language-era writers took from the Steinian model.[29] There is an easy, colloquial and approachable quality to the fragments of domestic language that Grenier presents. The paucity of detail about the settings of the poems lends the work an atmosphere of circumscription. Where poets such as Niedecker or Eigner fuse an investigation of a particular place with other bodies of knowledge, Grenier scrupulously excludes such material. There is no reference to history, science, philosophy or literature. Natural objects are presented in isolation – the ant or leaf – and not part of a broader ecological continuum. The reductionist trajectory of *Sentences* is to make intellectually engaging literature out of minute slivers of attention. The typewritten index-card binds the work into a bureaucratic environment – one that implies an administered and monetised version of temporality – that the texts themselves will have nothing to do with. There is no workplace in *Sentences*. The only form of human solidarity is that of familial love. If he is to 'stop time' Grenier needs to focus on the ephemerality of the moment as it congeals into words 'way back in the head'.

However, all these points about diction, presentation and content notwithstanding, I consider that the formal methods that Grenier uses to bracket off the micro-worlds that he narrates succeed in gaining purchase on the very contexts that they appear to deny. In presenting a varied succession of 'takes' on the short-form poem, from the single word to the compressed lyric, Grenier reconceives the potential of poetry with the barest linguistic resources. The structurally embedded qualities of interruptedness and discontinuity that obstruct any larger-scale vision in the writing do not, of themselves, foreclose the possibility of such vision. Viewed another way, Grenier's miniatures are a means of blocking the world-making or world-shaping narratives that lurk, more or less explicitly, within more fully developed literary and social forms. As such, their pointed formal insufficiency gestures at a broadly conceived imagination of social being that has to take account of the singular, the exceptional, the obdurately material and the non-discursive.

Notes

1. The issue is available at the Eclipse online archive. Grenier was living in Gloucester, Massachusetts, when this issue was co-edited.
2. Ron Silliman, *In the American Tree*, p. xv. Silliman places work by Grenier at the head of the 'East' section of *In the American Tree* because he considers him as a 'point of origin' for the younger writers in the anthology (Clark Coolidge occupies this position for the 'West' part of the book). See also a January 2019 post on Silliman's blog: 'Grenier's epic overstatement, "I HATE SPEECH," had the concentrated effect of an announcement every bit as much as Allen Ginsberg's first reading of Howl in the Six Gallery, October 7, 1955, had announced the New American Poetry, no matter that it came five years after Olson's essay on Projective Verse and even after Black Mountain College itself had closed down.'
3. Facsimiles of these undated early 1970s publications can be found at the

Eclipse archive, available at <http://eclipsearchive.org/projects/TOTTELS/> (last accessed 14 August 2019).
4. Silliman (ed.), 'The Dwelling Place' (Special Issue), *Alcheringa* 1.2 is available at the Eclipse archive.
5. Silliman, 'The Dwelling Place', pp. 119–20. Silliman cites Merleau-Ponty's essay 'Indirect Language and the Voices of Silence'. However, his remarks are at one remove from Merleau-Ponty's insistence on finding the origins of writing and painting in embodied experience. Indeed, there are clear parallels between Merleau-Ponty's argument and Projectivist proprioception.
6. Grenier, 'On Speech', *This* 1, n.p.
7. Brian Reed, *Phenomenal Reading: Essays on Modern and Contemporary Poetics*, p. 82.
8. Grenier, 'Robert Creeley, Pieces, Scribners 1969', *This* 1, n.p.
9. In response to an interview question about the 'integrity of the object' in his work, Grenier remarks: 'in *Sentences* and stuff like that, it was in the design of the letters produced by that machine. The machine produced such and such an image, and that image existed in space. It was quite a creature, the IBM Selectric typewriter. It created objects that weren't there before, in that way, and people could do it at home. It was an elephant of a heavy thing, but it made its own kind of mark, and the mark had this kind of structural integrity that allowed it to exist as an object' (Ivy Johnson, 'An Interview with Robert Grenier').
10. In his editing of Eigner's four-volume *Collected Poems* (2010), Grenier was scrupulous in his attention to page space and the equivalent (as opposed to proportional) spacing of the typewriter.
11. Grenier et al., *Farming the Words: Talking with Robert Grenier*, p. 38.
12. Silliman, 'The New Sentence', p. 91.
13. Silliman, 'The New Sentence', p. 87. This seems a fairer account of Grenier's connection to his forerunners than the announcement of a 'breach' in the introduction to *In the American Tree*.
14. Zuzana Husárová and Nick Montfort's article 'Shuffle Literature and the Hand of Fate,' presents *Sentences* as an example of 'Shuffle Literature'. The authors discuss *Sentences* alongside works by Marc Saporta, Robert Coover, B. S. Johnson and Herta Müller.
15. Grenier and Charles Bernstein, *Close Listening*, 20 October 2006.
16. Three of the BIRD poems in *Sentences* appear in 1975's *Sentences Toward Birds*, along with various other poems from *Sentences*. *Sentences Toward Birds* comprised forty-one cards that were published in an envelope by Curtis Faville's L Press in 1975. A facsimile is available at the Eclipse archive <http://eclipsearchive.org/projects/BIRDS/birds.html> (last accessed 1 September 2019). Some of the *Sentences* poems appeared, with different layout (i.e. non-Courier) in *Hills* magazine, issue 2, 1973. Thirty cards from *Sentences* were published with issue 5 of *This* (Winter 1974). Other poems appeared in *Alcheringa, Roof, Big Deal, Tottels, Boundary 2, Franconia Review, L Magazine* and *Gum*. The book *Oakland*, published much later (1980), featured many ultra-minimal poems, some similar to those in *Sentences*. *In the American Tree* contains a 'sequence' of twenty poems from *Sentences*. For further discussion of the background to *Sentences*, see Paul Stephens, 'Really "Reading In": A Media-Archival History of Robert

Grenier's Sentences' and Daniel Scott Snelson, '*Alcheringa*, "The Dwelling Place" and Structuralist Tendencies'.
17. Grenier and Ivy Johnson 'Interview', n.p.
18. Grenier and Bernstein, *Close Listening* Interview, n.p.
19. Grenier and Bernstein, *Close Listening* interview, n.p.
20. Stephens, 'Really "Reading In"', p. 299.
21. Jackson Mac Low, a former student of John Cage and a pioneer of the use of chance techniques in writing, was an important figure in the pre-history of Language writing.
22. In his 'Revisiting Seriality in Creeley's Poetry', Alan Golding compares JOE/ JOE to Creeley's lines '—it/ it—' in '"Time" is some sort of hindsight' (p. 52). The Creeley poem is discussed in my Chapter 5. Craig Dworkin, in his essay 'Klatsch', draws a parallel with the aforementioned Creeley poem, as well as work by Stein and, in particular, Grenier's friend Aram Saroyan, with whom he worked closely (even to the point of sharing a notebook) at the time the poem was composed.
23. Cited in Jon Hendricks, *Fluxus Codex*, p. 193.
24. Williams, 'Introduction to *The Wedge*', CP2, p. 54.
25. The above divisions come with certain provisos: some of the poems with titles have only a single line, for example, and some of the two-word poems might be read as poems made from two elements in apposition. The latter category contains texts such as 'JOE/ JOE' or 'whistle/ whiten', in which the same or similar elements is repeated once. Longer sequences of repeated lines come, for the purposes of this provisional ordering, under the category of repetition poems.
26. Grenier, *Attention: Seven Narratives*, p. 11. Grenier draws a parallel between *Sentences* and Stein's 'Composition As Explanation'. Grenier writes of Stein alongside Creeley in 'On Speech', which closes with the citation of a miniature poem from Stein's *Tender Buttons*. This short poem closely resembles some of the titled poems in *Sentences*, including the one just discussed:

> ROAST POTATOES.
> Roast potatoes for.

27. Zuzana Husárová and Nick Montfort, 'Shuffle Literature and the Hand of Fate', n.p.
28. Grenier et al., *Farming the Words: Talking with Robert Grenier*, p 38.
29. Stein, 'Composition as Explanation', p. 23.

Chapter 8

Rae Armantrout

Rae Armantrout's brief, downbeat memoir *True* contains some indications of the fault lines between speech and identity that open up in her poetry. They show her as a small child encouraged by both parents to see herself as ' "male-identified" and an outlaw – little Jesse James'.[1] And they show her as an adolescent infatuated with the myth of the Old West, saving up money to fund an escape across the border to Mexico, where life was, allegedly, closer to what it had been in the heroic days of the cowboys. Armantrout writes of her childhood adoration of Billy the Kid, who assumed the central position in a pantheon of rebellious male idols. This figure was consciously chosen to rival her mother's admiration for various conformist males, mainly ministers. Billy the Kid was a 'fetish figure' for the young Armantrout. It was unclear, she remarks, whether she identified with such rebellious males or was 'romantically attracted' to them (*True*, p. 34). What *is* clear, however, is that putting popular myths to her own uses provided Armantrout with a little leverage on an oppressive familial environment that she gradually realised was representative of the culture as a whole. The first sentence of *True* stakes a claim for the importance of such questioning of her own experience: 'Many people must see their lives as somehow exemplary. I tend to see my early life as an example of the pathology of "Middle America" at mid-century.'[2]

In self-deprecating low-key prose, Armantrout's memoir makes it clear that the 'pathology of "Middle America"', as exemplified by the Armantrout household, was a pathology of religious conservatism, racism and sexism. Armantrout's poetry can be read as a highly oblique attempt to expose the hidden linguistic wiring of that culture's contemporary manifestations. Disney, also an 'exemplary' aspect of mid-century American cultural life, is another part of the picture for the young Armantrout.[3] *Fantasia* inducts her into the world of Stravinsky. And, later on, Disney's presence stands over an early date with her future husband, Chuck Korkegian:

> I kept asking where he was going, but he wouldn't say. We ended up at the Tiki Room in Disneyland. That evening was symbolic for me. It seemed that Chuck would open up the Unknown. It seems ironic now that the Great Unknown was represented by Disneyland. But I romanticised his unpredictability, his unconventionality, even his poverty. (*True*, p. 50)

The Enchanted Tiki Room, in the Disneyland resort in California, in the 1960s evidently featured a Hawaiian-themed animatronic spectacle dominated by four robot macaws. The ironic perception that the 'Unknown' might be represented by Disney phantasmagoria seems especially pertinent here. The friction generated between large ideas – the Great Unknown – and popular culture is one of the motors of Armantrout's poetry throughout her long career. Her 2020 book *Conjure* contains an example in the poem 'Pinocchio':

> Strand. String.
> In this dream,
>
> the paths cross
> and cross again.
>
> They are spelling
> a real boy
>
> out of repetition.
>
> *
>
> Each one
> is the one
>
> real boy.
>
> Each knows
> he must be
>
> wrong
> about this, but
>
> he can't feel
> how
>
> *
>
> The fish
> and the fisherman,
>
> the pilot,
> the princess,
>
> the fireman and
> the ones on fire.[4]

The poem's first two sections in this recent work are relatively consecutive. 'Strand', 'string' and 'paths' come together to bring the marionette into being as a 'real boy'. But this is not an allegory of poetic facture. Armantrout is concerned with the illusionary experience of singularity felt by the boy, who is anything but real. The phrase 'Each one/ is the one/ real boy' cannot be resolved unless one acknowledges the contingency of each singular experience of selfhood. There is a direct contradiction between the repetition of the same, and the production of a singular sentient self. The poem's third section references what sound like more stories for children (references to a Russian tale by Pushkin and a Japanese anime) or the kinds of career children dream of, but the final couplet swerves out of this world and into a snapshot of suffering that bears no relation to the reflections of inauthenticity and repetition in the foregoing poem. Pinocchio's falsehoods and the fact that his finger catches fire in the film, giving the lie to his humanity, play in the background of the text's consideration of the 'real'. The combination of the austere formal features of the text and its open-ended speculative potential is characteristic of Armantrout's writing. As I will argue, her work with the short line is intrinsic to a highly distinctive patterning of recursive thought.

Armantrout is associated with West Coast Language writers such as Lyn Hejinian, Bob Perelman, Barrett Watten and Carla Harryman, although the short-lined, abstract lyric mode that she has favoured throughout her career is very different to the various kinds of experimentation practised by these writers. Since the 1970s, she has been close to one of the preeminent theorists and practitioners of Language writing, Ron Silliman (*True*, p. 59). Her writing is collected in key anthologies of the era such as Silliman's influential *In the American Tree* and Douglas Messerli's *'Language' Poetries: an Anthology*. Her first book, *Extremities*, was published in 1978. While many of her peers have used a broad range of formal techniques and procedures in the course of their writing careers, the consistency of Armantrout's formal commitments is remarkable: she has been working with short form for more than four decades. Her work shows a clear debt to such short-line forerunners as William Carlos Williams, George Oppen, Lorine Niedecker, Robert Creeley and Larry Eigner. She shares Williams's ear for vernacular,[5] Creeley's fine judgement with the linebreak, an Objectivist instinct for compression,[6] and Eigner's observational alertness and interest in science. As a student, she was taught by Denise Levertov, who encouraged her to pay close attention to linebreaks (*True*, p. 59). For many years she worked in relative obscurity, employed as a Creative Writing adjunct at University of California San Diego. Her momentum as a writer gradually increased:

she published two books in the 1980s, three in the 1990s, five in the 2000s and five in the 2010s. Armantrout won the Pulitzer Prize in 2010, an event that served as a marker of the prominence achieved by the Language-writing generation of poets. Although once a relatively peripheral figure, she has since achieved a level of recognition that is matched by few of her peers.

In her *Collected Prose* (2007), Armantrout published for the first time a short essay entitled 'The Short Poem'. In this piece, she discusses her own work alongside that of Emily Dickinson, Williams, Robert Grenier and Graham Foust, concluding that 'The short poem may be the perfect site for the presentation of transience, failure, impossibility.'[7] These three terms might misleadlingly suggest a commitment to a melancholic form of unsayability. However, Armantrout has different imperatives, finding a resilient humour in the magnified twists and turns of her texts. While she once spoke of her desire to monitor the 'interventions of capitalism into consciousness',[8] her writing's oppositional orientation is more apparent in the wary but amused attention she gives to the intermeshing imperatives of the private and public axes of language use. Her adroit handling of cliché, found speech, and diverse discursive modes, within consistently compressed forms, has the effect of holding a sceptical poetic mirror up to the narratives that define us.

The short poem, she argues, is a kind of 'magic trick': 'How did that rabbit, that train, that truck, that tree, that Arctic get into that hat anyway? And what happens to them now that they've been pulled out? They disappear into the sudden silence.'[9] For Armantrout, the compression and ellipsis of the short poem allow for very particular effects, flashing objects and concepts in front of the eyes of the reader and then abruptly whisking them away. Yet the short poem is also always partial and unachieved. Its success lies in its failure. Its very brevity is closely tied to its ability to render aspects of experience that are resistant to narrative explanation – contradiction and impermanence, for example, might be facets of the 'failure' and 'impossibility' that Armantrout describes. The short poem is an analogue of these characteristics of cognitive experience because ellipsis itself, in this writing, is communicative.

In another short essay, 'Cheshire Poetics', Armantrout writes of her enthusiasm for Dickinson and Williams when a teenager:

> I discovered Williams (and the other Imagists) early on and was very much moved by them. By what, though? I would say now that it was by their attempt to make the object speak, to put things in dialogue with mind and somehow make them hold up their end of the conversation. This is both an important project and a doomed one. The world enters the poem only through a kind of ventriloquy. *Thing* and *idea* don't really merge, as the poets

themselves knew. That red wheelbarrow is essentially separate from the 'so much' that depends upon it. But there is so much poignancy in that gap![10]

Armantrout's point about ventriloquy is significant, as it marks the distance between her work and various positions outlined in this book (even as it claims an affinity with such writing): the poem is not itself an object; the thing does not enter the poem; neither is Ezra Pound's 'thing' in scare quotes – his merging of subjective and objective – viable. Instead, there is a failure of integration between the world and its ventriloquised representation. The gaps between the two are what capture Armantrout's attention. Putting the object 'in dialogue with mind' can lead, very quickly in the intense atmosphere of the short poem, to a proliferation of communicative potential. Ventriloquising the object, or making it speak, is to claim a special kind of agency for poetic speech. The poem brings a temporary order to the world, but its brevity and insufficiency show this order to be necessarily contingent. Doubt, irony and paradox become powerful tools in Armantrout's hands.

While Armantrout places her writing in the modernist short-form tradition discussed in this book, she also outdistances it. Like Creeley and those who followed him, she shows an intense awareness of the mutual implication of language, world and consciousness. Moreover, language, for Armantrout more than for any writer discussed thus far, is shot through with the imperatives of commerce, as encountered in newspapers, radio, television and social media. Creeley, Eigner and Grenier observe, in different ways, their engagement with the world, clearing a private space for the process of reflection. Armantrout, on the other hand, knows that privacy to be invaded at every level by a collective experience of language – regressive forms of subjectivity, the delights and depredations of a banalising popular culture and the impoverishment of public discourse.

Like any short-form poetry, Armantrout's writing concerns itself with the relationship between part and whole.[11] In many of her poems, this finds formal articulation in the division of her poems into discrete sections that have an equivocal relationship with one another. Silliman has written of this segmentation in Armantrout's writing, particularly in the post-1985 poetry. For Silliman, the shifts between segments are forward-looking, as they open up a space of anticipation:

> Often . . . each section will arrive at threshold only to have the segment stop right there as the poem shifts to an entirely new scene and discourse. Connotation seems about to break into denotation *and yet* . . . To accomplish this requires a certain degree of holding meaning back . . . What is being 'depicted' in such gaps is not the leap from segment to segment, but rather the

moment before, the condition of readiness and anticipation ... Armantrout repeatedly holds us right at the point before the leap, forcing the reader to pay attention to the impulse within, that 'place/ within silence'.[12]

The sections into which many of Armantrout's poems are divided are sometimes numbered and sometimes separated by a single centred asterisk or another typographical mark. An early example of this technique can be found in her first book, 1978's *Extremities*. It is the poem 'Grace':

1
a spring there
where his entry must be made

signals him on

2
the sentence
           flies

Isn't turned to salt
no stuttering

3
l am walking

covey in sudden flight[13]

The first stanza seems explicitly to reference Williams's ['By the road to the contagious hospital']' (later titled 'Spring and All'). In Williams's poem, it is 'they' who 'enter', but Armantrout's figure is male and the entry is purely conjectural. The poem is composed of isolated fragments, though there are acoustic continuities: the 's's of 'spring' and 'signals' are echoed in 'sentence', 'salt' and 'stuttering' in the second stanza, for example. It is unclear what is not 'turned to salt'. This uncertainty about an act that is *not* performed is characteristic of the provisional atmosphere that Armantrout's writing inhabits. If it is the sentence that is *not* turned into salt, it may be that in escaping the punitive judgement suffered by Lot's wife it contrives a model of freedom. The stanza appears to gesture at fluidity, a state that 'flies' and is not subject to the quality of arrestedness that applies to the pillar of salt or stuttering. Yet the stanza itself is highly fragmented, even at the level of the line. Any surface thematic continuity on the theme of fluidity is countered by the severe breaks in both lines and syntax. The third stanza develops the concept of mobility advanced in the second. In addition to the 'he' who is to move 'on', and the sentence that 'flies', now there is an 'I' who is walking and a 'covey' of game birds 'in sudden flight'. Where the sentence had once flown, now there are birds. The lines suggest a model of being-in-language that is both atomised and agitated – and one that can only be captured, through the ventriloquising gesture of the poet, in the fixity of print.

The unusual word 'covey' draws attention to itself, capturing the compacted meanings inherent in 'flight', whether understood as airborne escape or – perhaps – as cultural or political resistance. Whatever actual real-world prompts might have steered the composition of the poem, the air that it breathes is textual and fictive. While Eigner and Grenier's poems retain a toehold in the documentation of a world that is 'out there', however glancingly this occurs, in this early Armantrout poem the reader's attention is directed towards the shaping of experience in words.

Other of the poems in *Extremities* combine extreme compression with flip endings that have no truck with the notion that the short poem might be the vehicle, haiku-style, of wisdom. In these examples, the final lines act as gateways to another style of speech, disrupting idioms that had barely had time to get established in the preceding lines. Such shifts became a central feature of a writing style that Hank Lazer would describe – citing Eigner, Creeley and Ashbery as antecedents – as the 'lyricism of the swerve'.[14] The following poems exemplify these breaks:

'View'

Not the city lights. We want

— the moon —

       The Moon
none of our own doing!

(*Veil*, p. 8)

And:

'Anti-short Story'

A girl is running. *Don't* tell me
'She's running for her bus.'

All that aside!

(*Veil*, p. 12)

Armantrout's division of her poems into sections is integral to the quality of provisionality they project. Speaking to Lynn Keller, she remarks:

> I am very much interested in pieces – I like the Creeley book, but I'm not referring to that. I'm interested in parts, sections and how they can come together in different ways: what is a unity? what is a unit? how is a unit formed provisionally, and how could it be reformed? Those are some questions I deal with.

As Silliman has argued, this breaking-down of Armantrout's poems into sub-sequences allows for a means of registering experience that is grounded in a new understanding of parataxis:

> in her divisions between sections she identifies a place within meaning – a suspension – that seems not to be capable of articulation in any other way. It is that moment when, during any experience that is new and undigested, details flood in, awaiting the gestalt organisation of data into something recognised and subject to being categorised, an instant that is privileged by parataxis.[15]

This 'moment' in the poems offers an encounter with the strangeness of the new that is at the very fringes of contemporary idiomatic utterance. The segmentation of the writing implies the exploration of social horizons. Silliman's word 'gestalt' points to a comprehended whole that is only encountered in anticipation. Armantrout's scepticism makes a positive value out of the differential between part and whole, thereby enacting a resistance to totalising forms of utterance.

This equivocation about the nature of a unit, and an accompanying preoccupation with insufficiency, rather than any number of social, national, economic, ethnic, cultural or religious fictions of community, is pervasive in this writing. A particular vision of the relation between singularity and collective being emerges. This, as I will argue below, is where Armantrout's commitment to the wary poetics of Oppen is most apparent. The politics of number is crucial to Armantrout's writing, as can be seen in 'Back', a poem from *Up to Speed* (2004), her first full collection for Wesleyan:[16]

'Back'

The teacher said
two mirror images

could come into being
by borrowing

from zero – but only
if they agreed

to cancel one another out.

We followed
from inert matter

by offering
to eat each other up.

*

What sort of place is
existence
since we can 'come into' it?

A point coincides;
it has no dimension.

Some say
matter's really energy

and energy is force of law

and law is just tautology.

*

We were taught

to have faces
by a face

looking 'back'

(*Up to Speed*, p. 68)

The poem is one of several in *Up to Speed* to explore scientific and mathematical concepts: matter, energy, geometry, the origins of life.[17] (Her 2017 book *Entanglements* collects many of her poems on science.) 'Back' thinks about the phenomenon of dividedness – how two differs from one – but it continually risks collapsing into inconclusive non sequiturs, every gesture subsiding into nothingness. 'Borrowing// from zero' implies maths, but the entities under discussion are also 'mirror images' that are capable of agreeing 'to cancel one another out' (a play on agreeing to differ). The pronoun 'we', which might apply to collectivities ranging in scale up to humanity itself, is deflated with the humour of 'offering/ to eat each other up', a different form of mutual cancellation. In the first section of the poem, two self-negating dyads are proposed. In the next section, or segment, the poem questions itself, and the phrase 'come into being' is put under pressure. What does it mean for being to emerge from 'inert matter'? In geometry, coincident points are identical: one superimposed on the other. A tautology, whether in logic or law, is another instance of doubling, the repetition of the same thought or thing in different words. Superfluous repetition is generally considered to be poor style, but in the world of Armantrout's poem it only leads to a greater nuancing of the differential energies of language. For Einstein (the 'some' of 'some say') energy and matter can be converted into one another. But the narrative crumbles as the thought moves into the assertion that 'law is just tautology'. It is unclear whether the 'tautology' referred to belongs to the legal domain or that of propositional logic –

and that lack of clarity is the point. The third section of the poem returns to the classroom, where it began. Is the poem, with 'We were taught// to have faces', addressing the constitution of identity in the contemplation of the mirror image, which grounds subjective singularity in an apprehension of doubleness? Do the scare quotes around 'back' lead us to question the capacity of the mirror image to look at all, or to think of 'back' in its temporal as well as its spatial sense?

The poem is a neat, self-consuming machine that seems to posit both singularity and duality as impossible alternatives. Terms from distinct discourses are superimposed to generate a halting, speculative conceptual foray that enacts paradox. Figuration in the poem is always on the point of self-erasure through a playfully self-cancelling movement of regress. The title word installs the idea of repetition ('back' again) in the glance towards the past. Such delicate sleights of thought derive their energy from the privileged status of interruptedness of Armantrout's thought. In 'Poetic Silence', Armantrout argues that 'Words no longer come directly from silence, but directly from other words. One finds oneself speaking, involved perhaps in a debate the terms of which are already set. And there is the impulse to call a halt, the impulse to silence.'[18] In view of many decades of poetic production, 'silence' per se seems beside the point, and, as I have suggested, the work resists any assimilation of silence to ineffability. But the drive to 'call a halt' remains intact throughout this body of writing: a powerful impulse that consistently puts a brake on the forward movement of the poem.

Armantrout often makes use of commercial forms of compressed langauge use: tabloid-style headlines, say, or TV listings (examples of the latter extend from 1978's 'Footnote to the Television Notes' to 2010's 'Previews'). In the poem 'Visualizations', from *Up to Speed* for example, the line 'Boy Wins Love With Tall Tale' sits in inverted commas at the top, its isolation intensifying the oddness of the decontextualised phrase. Moving through several darkly humorous shifts, including some acerbic material on 9/11 as a media event, the poem concludes with another headline, 'Umbilical Stump Still Pulses' (*Up to Speed*, pp. 48–9). This combines horror-film schlockiness with an echo of the tale [t-a-l-e] or tail [t-a-i-l] that opened the poem. The revolting pulsing stump might even be an expression of the amorousness announced in the first line. In a poem that discusses the recursive quality of cognition – 'We double back/ to form thoughts' – the repetitive messages of contemporary American culture are scrambled and re-directed by Armantrout's rapid edits.

In 'Entanglements', another poem from *Up to Speed*, a telegraphic snippet of re-wired sci-fi uses this doubling motif to monitor her culture's self-absorption:

In the shorter version,

tentacled
stomach swallows stomach.

(*Up to Speed*, p. 17)

The tendency of print, broadcast and online media to summarise, to reduce complex plots and arguments to stark outlines that barely make sense, is satirised in both poems through figures of doubling. Doubling is a figure of number, and number is a *social* question in Armantrout's work, taking a cue from 'Visualizations' when it asks: '... frequency/ is a matter// of counting up to what?' Ones, twos and threes – the terms of Creeley's 'A Piece' – are basic figures around which Armantrout's poetry unfolds, particularly in the early Wesleyan books. Armantrout, an only child, seems equivocal, at best, about solitude. Two is an unworkable proposition. Three, needless to say, feels like a crowd – and it often represents the larger group in her writing. Her writing hosts three communicative *im*possibilities: the singular 'I' of the speaking subject that appears to enunciate the poem; the dyad, arguably proper to lyric; and the trio that stands for the collective. Armantrout's writing invites us to contemplate and to reject all of these positions but ends up with a sceptical embrace of communicative potential in all three arenas.

The book *Next Life* contains several poems that consider, explicitly or implicitly, the figure of Echo – the mythical figure condemned first to repeat the end of people's sentences and then, spurned by Narcissus, reduced to nothing but voice. Echo and Narcissus offer us two models of captivated doubling: the merely imitative and narcissistic delusion. As Armantrout suggests in an interview with Tom Beckett, couples are not in a happy situation. Rejecting love as mutual misrecognition, she concludes that 'there is no reciprocity or simultaneity. I think a lot of my work says that.'[19] In the same interview she talks about the solitary activity of the writer as an 'autoerotic' experience that the writer desires – and fails – to duplicate for the reader.[20]

The singular comes to grief, a failed auto-eroticism that can't help looking outside itself for duplication. Couples come to grief too, through a failure to find a mutually sustaining fantasy. Where does this leave the trio? Many of Armantrout's poems ask this question in various ways. The poem 'Two, Three', from *Next Life*, puts it at the centre of its enquiry:

'Two, Three'

Sad, fat boy in pirate hat.
Long, old, dented,
copper-colored Ford.

> How many traits
> must a thing have
> in order to be singular?
>
> (Echo persuades us
> everything we say
> has been said at least once
>   before.)
>
> Two plump, bald men
> in gray tee-shirts
> and tan shorts
>
> are walking a small bulldog —
> followed by the eyes
> of an invisible third person.
>
> The Trinity was born
> from what we know
> of the bitter
>
> symbiosis of couples.
> Can we reduce echo's sadness
> by synchronising our speeches?
>
> Is it the beginning or the end
> of *real* love
> when we pity a person
>
> because, in him,
> we see ourselves?[21]

The poem starts with a 'found' image of a boy in a pirate hat and quickly moves to the key conundrum: 'How many traits/ must a thing have/ in order to be singular?' The poem asks, in other words, whether plurality can be the guarantor of singularity. Folded into this is the instablity associated with the mathematical or geometrical understanding of 'singularity'. In the poem, the notion of the single is dismissed with the figure of Echo: there is no originary utterance; we are all caught in an echoic or Narcissistic loop. Armantrout then broadens the picture: there are two men – a gay couple, perhaps? However, they are not a self-contained unit. They are observed by the 'invisible third person', a playful invocation both of the Holy Spirit and *The Waste Land* – and also the third term that stands for the larger groups that couples inevitably belong to.

Couples cannot isolate themselves and they do not coincide: would we be happier if desire was co-extensive, if we could synchronise what the poem calls 'our speeches'? Is finding oneself in another an act of narcissistic absorption or a failure of love? The reader is implicated as the singular origin of the text and, as observer, with the 'invisible third person'. The three first-person subject positions, 'I', 'you', and 'she/ he' are rehearsed in condensed fashion in this poem. All are found 'wanting', in both the lacking and desiring senses of the word.

Armantrout's poems reflect an uneasiness with various kinds of identification. A position of solipsistic self-containment is rejected. The speaker cannot speak, the writer cannot write, in a vacuum. The dyadic encounter of love or the archetypal love lyric fails too: the 'bitter // symbiosis of couples' is rejected as a failed endeavour – an ambivalent narcissistic overspill always contaminates the relationship with the desired object. It fails also because there are never simply two – the implicit privacy of the duo folds into the public life of the collective. Any attempt to assign the group a singular identity – 'humanity', perhaps, or 'America' – will necessarily compromise the fundamental fact of difference.

Despite this description of various kinds of 'failure', I want to suggest that Armantrout's writing is sceptical rather than pessimistic. She is writing about the difficulty of reconciling private experience with the experience of the collective – of, in other words, 'being numerous'. As for George Oppen, this is a genuine dilemma. In Armantrout's writing the preoccupation with number is felt through a close attention to the dimensions of the poem: there is a linguistic parsimony at work that finds greater resources for both political and speculative reflection in the moments of halting, or 'palpable stoppage', that her poetry offers.[22]

One of the poems in *Next Life*, 'Us', contains the line 'Car called Echo',[23] which is itself an echo of Oppen's perplexity about the collective in 'Of Being Numerous':

> . . . How talk
> Distantly of 'The People'
>
> Who are that force
> Within the walls
> Of cities
>
> Wherein their cars
>
> Echo like history
> Down walled avenues
> In which one cannot speak.[24]

With Oppen, the question is poised between, on one hand, the fantasy of a fully realised, finite and bounded subjectivity and, on the other, the difficulty of imagining a collective. So 'the shipwreck/ Of the singular' is held up against the 'madness in the number/ of the living'.[25] Perhaps, worries Oppen, the poet's utterance amounts to little more than 'A ferocious mumbling, in public/ Of rootless speech'.²⁶ Or perhaps there is a saving perception of connectedness between disparate singular perceptions:

> Or sees motes, an iron mesh, links
>
> Of consequence
>
> Still, at the mind's end
> Relevant²⁷

In Armantrout's case, this contemplation of the one and the many becomes a contemplation of the one, *the two* and the many. In other words, she imagines a dyadic encounter, possibly erotic, that is neither a perfect interiority nor a plausible collective. One version of this might be the possibility of lyric. Armantrout's writing implies a negative co-option of Oppen's 'links// of consequence'. It is often built on the *détournement* of the over-familiar. The space of non-compliance carved out by the writing depends not on the words themselves but on the play of context and register. This allows Armantrout's writing to suggest a kind of negative affirmation of community, even as it rejects monadic, dyadic or collective solutions to the predicament she finds us to be in.

The poem 'Upper World' (the phrase is taken from Oppen), from *Up to Speed*, is a good example of the way in which Armantrout's poems twin an examination of the echoic with temporal doubling, looking back at their own unfolding.²⁸ The sombre opening – 'If sadness/ is akin to patience' – slips into cheery bathos with the sudden tonal shift of 'we're back!' The play of registers becomes clearer in the second part of the poem, as it moves from the lines 'every name's Eurydice,/ briefly returned from blankness' to 'High voices/ over rapid-pulsing synthesisers/ intone, 'without you' –// which is soothing.' As motifs of absence and mythic loss accumulate in the poem, the virtue of patience, announced in the first line, is stranded somewhere between a Penelope-like fortitude and the commodification of feeling in pop music.²⁹ The reference to Eurydice, moreover, hints at the perils of looking back – of seeing again, of doubling or Echo. The entire poem grows out of the significance that the change of direction in the first three lines retrospectively accumulates.

When Armantrout writes in 'Upper World': 'Here and there were *like*/ one place// But we need to triangulate,/ find someone to show' we find the movement from the single ('here') to a dissimilar dyad ('here and there'), followed by the impulse to establish a trio: the 'need to triangulate'. 'Triangulate' is Clinton-era jargon for distinguishing one's position from both poles of an established debate: Republican and Democrat; or in the UK context of the late 1990s, Conservative and Old Labour. So a presentational trick of numbers exists in the poem at the same time as a more abstract shifting up the gears from single speech act through dialogue to witnessed dialogue. The language of political dissimulation undercuts this potentially utopian movement.

Yet, the halting and hesitation in this middle period of Armantrout's writing paradoxically enables a curiously affirmative communicative ethics. In these poems, in other words, the one, the two and the many are endowed with communicative potential through the endorsement of a mutual dependence that is guaranteed by shared conditions of difference and insufficiency, not similarity. Armantrout invokes a notion of community that is based on the denial of 'commonality'.

In Armantrout's poetics of condensation, Oppen's 'test of sincerity'[30] meets sceptical revision. Her awareness of the invasively social nature of language is too great to permit the truthfulness and simplicity valued by Oppen. In Armantrout's work, a vigilant and self-aware irony offers a point of purchase for the political, not an abdication of responsibility. This ironic sensibility serves to qualify and complicate every utterance. For Oppen, the world is made present in a language that is sincerely spoken. Armantrout finds herself spoken at every turn. That she can only reflect on her spokenness in the language that speaks her is a central paradox of this highly self-aware writing. The fastidious preoccupation with number and recursiveness finds formal expression in her use of short form, where every syllable is felt to count. When the line breaks, a few words into one of Armantrout's sentences, there is a miniature glitch in its movement. In such short-line work, these momentary suspensions of sequence have a cumulative effect, strewing her paths of thought with potholes. Armantrout uses these moments of arrest to caution against the ways in which we unthinkingly allow the forward-moving sentence to dictate the plot through the force of its own momentum. Similar glitches in progress emerge between stanzas and sections of the poems. These breaks in sequence cause the writing to observe its own progress and they work against the accumulation of a conclusive statement. A voice in another poem from *Up to Speed*, 'En Route', worries that 'we're always/ "about to" or/ "have just"' (*Up to Speed*, p. 57). Another, 'Box', speculates about: 'A time when we agree// the present does not exist,// has never existed' (*Up to Speed*, p. 63). A layered parataxis – working across line, stanza and section – is a means of building these equivocal temporal perceptions into the formal texture of the writing. The breaks on the page cause thought to turn back on itself, confronting the reader with the nagging intrusion of a present moment that is past as soon as soon as it becomes the object of thought.

Armantrout's short poems consistently transgress the intimate space of lyric utterance, forcing an acknowledgement of collective discourses that invade every level of linguistic being. The always-imminent glitch of the linebreak; the uncertain space between stanza and sections of the poems; the pervasive pressure of condensation: all of these factors serve to intensify the work's ability to reflect on and complicate its own unfolding. The awareness that one is not saying but saying again – that we're all slaves to Echo – is for Armantrout a source of consolation.

* * *

In Armantrout's poetry, the speaking subject is a point of confluence for numerous styles of speech, including the voice of the speaker. The strongly identifiable 'voice' that marks the writing is located in the dry, amused sensibility that appeared to be organising the fragments from which the poems were made. Slivers of apparently autobiographical material are rarely incorporated into a self-revealing narrative of any kind, whether emotional or speculative. There was, however, a shift in tone when the poet was diagnosed with adrenal cortical cancer in 2006 while writing her book *Versed* (2009). When published, the collection won Armantrout the Pulitzer Prize. The book also won the National Book Critics Circle Award and was a finalist for the National Book Award. *Versed* is divided into two sections, 'Versed' and the more personal 'Dark Matter'. The poems in the latter section were written after her diagnosis. The title 'Dark Matter', while referencing Armantrout's affection for cosmology, clearly points to a reflection on Last Things. The first poem of 'Dark Matter', 'Around', muses 'Chuck and I are pleased/ to have found a spot/ where my ashes can be scattered./ It looks like a construction site/ now/ but it's adjacent to a breath-taking rocky coast' (*Versed*, p. 67). At such moments, this poetry, which grounds itself in language's collectivity, turn its attention to the self.

Yet the book combines Armantrout's responses both to life-threatening illness and the war in Iraq. 'You could say there are things happening in your body that you can't control and you don't want them to be happening', remarks Armantrout, 'and there are things in your society that you can't control and you don't want them to be happening.'[31] The language of war occurs in both parts of the book. The last poem of the earlier 'Versed' subsection, 'Translation', points us towards the phosphorus flashes of bombing raids: 'The cumulus/ and the white flash/ from under/ the mocking-bird's wing/ make what?' (*Versed*, p. 64). And the armchair tourism of atrocity is lampooned: 'Since Fallujah/ is the new Antigua// sunlight nibbles/ on pre/-charred// terrain/ in the electric fireplace' (*Versed*, p. 45). The cremated body, then, is a figure that looks beyond the poet's own concerns about her illness. Broadening the context, laissez-faire capitalism is aligned with disease: 'In the present// cancer sets up/ a free market/ in your gut' (*Versed*, p. 85).

In her later work, Armantrout monitors the changing qualities of collective experience as mass media gives way to the online versions of social identity. The writing characterises the polarisation of the political landscape several years before the 'echo-chamber' effects of social media had received the attention they received in the wake of Donald Trump's 2016 election victory. Such dangers are predicated on imitative behaviour. This form of likeness is ironically alinged with the 'call to mimesis' – the imitation of Christ advocated by St Paul – made available in 'Translation':

> The thing that makes us human
>
> monkey-see, monkey-do, speed-up,
>
> a 'call to mimesis,'
>
> now comes from everywhere at once.
>
> (*Versed*, p. 64)

'Translation''s play with imitation becomes a collective acquiescence to an unpalatable social order. The question of identification is also addressed in more oblique ways in Armantrout's recent work, as it is in the poem 'Like':

> 1
>
> She never said, 'Look at that bush' or 'Look at the sea; that's a beautiful bruise-blue perpetually subsiding.' She drew my attention to only a few things: Xmas lights, The Last Days, Frontier Land.
>
> 2
>
> 'What it's like
> to be me.'
>
> Where watch out
> and report back
> cross —
>
> a stubborn eddy.
>
> A tendency
> to take exception?
>
> How much of me
> could be lost
> while like remained?
>
> Could like stand alone?
>
> Does it?
>
> (*Versed*, p. 82)

At one level, this poem seems to reflect on apocalyptic American expansionism – the Last Days, the Frontier, the American exception. In this context, the burning bush and the parting of the Red Sea (not the bruise-blue one) are typological forerunners of the present, a rerun of the old American narrative of the Promised Land, a biblical shadow of the doctrine of Manifest Destiny, even if bush/ Bush is certainly not another Moses. The phrases 'watch out/ and report back' suggest an activity of guarding, perhaps, or espionage. Certainly, the climate is fearful, invaded by the imperatives of post-9/11 surveillance enabled by the Patriot Act. But the watching out and reporting back might also apply to the consciousness of one's own subjectivity. The mysterious 'it's' of 'what it's like' places a question mark over agency. It may be unsurprising for a poet such as Armantrout to query the relationship between the poem's 'me' and the experiencing self that the word refers to. But, more than this, the poem seems to bracket off and question the process of identification: 'Could like stand alone?' Can, in other words, a pure notion of relation exist? Might it sustain both the workings of poetic language and the relationship between self, other and the collective? What remains of Armantrout when her poems are there but she is not? Is something like 'her' perceptible in the work? In identifying with another or with a group, what persists of the self that chooses to identify in that way? The provisional 'Could like stand alone?' gives way to 'Does it?', might refer to the word 'like' (i.e. does *like* stand alone?). In this case a question about a hypothetical possibility ('could') becomes a question about the real, 'Does it?' However, this final question is the last in a series, and can also stand as a question that is without both subject and answer. The dummy subject (the 'it' doesn't refer to anything) that opens this section of the poem in 'What it's like' returns with the baffling question that concludes the poem.

Money Shot, the successor to *Versed*, was written in the context of a collective, rather than personal crisis, the financial crash of 2008–9. Its title suggests a mingling of two kinds of thrill-seeking: the reckless corporate gambling that led to economic collapse, and the monetised desire that oils the wheels of the porn industry. One of the book's strongest themes, accordingly, is virtuality, a poetic encounter with the data-flows that organise our cultural and economic being. This attention to the virtual finds voice in airy spaces, the intangible, and the inaudible: a vanishing into 'this / patina of shadow, / flicker, whisper', as she puts it in 'With' (p. 46). Yet, as in the earlier work, her silences have no theological underpinning, and religious vocabularies are as vulnerable as anything else to comic puncturing: 'For I so loved the world // that I set up / my only son // to be arrested' (*Money Shot*, p. 26).

A playfulness with religious tropes is also evident in 'Homer'. The title might imply the homecoming after the odyssey but the poem actually figures a hellish eternal return in which good and evil are presented as an opposition between forward movement and the continuous present. A devilish figure ('Wily one') enters the poem in disguise, but the closing words leave the reader undecided as to whether the devil-Messiah is desired or not: ' "If only he would come again / as he once was," / they say.' The point seems to be that neither the stasis of self-identity nor the ruse of disguise will do. The recursive sentiment captured by 'If only he would come again', enacts a self-scrutiny that seems to foreclose any possibility of forward passage (*Money Shot*, p. 17).

The gap between the present as it happens and the present as it appears in contemplation, a lapse that is both temporal and cognitive, produces a differential friction that drives many of Armantrout's poems, as in 'The Vescicle' where 'The time travel paradox: / each passing thought / is the thinker' and 'Monks / mimed one another's / squiggles // carefully / by candlelight // as if they thought / creation trailed something.' The 'swerve' in Armantrout's poetry remains crucial – the glitch in the 'smooth passage' ('Homer', *Money Shot*, p. 17) of the poem, the hiccup of the linebreak, the suggestive lacunae that arise between discrete sections of the poems. As Armantrout makes clear in interview, she remains preoccupied, at both the formal and conceptual levels, by the differential energies generated between one thing and another:

> The first poem in [*Money Shot*], 'Staging', is indirect. It doesn't appear to have anything to do with sex or money, but it does raise the question of what constitutes an entity or unit. At first it evokes, perhaps, biological processes in which new entities are created by the reshuffling of parts. The second section turns the bits to be reshuffled into experiential units: things seen and heard in a lobby or waiting room. These experiential bits are arbitrarily paired and paired again to create hypothetical entities.[32]

Such 'reshuffling' of lived 'bits', enabled by the textural density offered by the short poem, allows a sceptical resistance to the data-flows that engulf our eternally online experience.

Environmental concerns shadow Armantrout's 2018 book *Wobble*, along with further reflections on social being, contemporary science and the concept of the future. The book is also notable for a number of explicit dedications or references to other major poets. The poem 'Old Woman's Lament in Autumn' has the dedication 'for WCW' and it takes Williams's 'Widow's Lament in Springtime' as the point of departure for a rejection of conventions surrounding ageing. 'Moment to Moment', written 'for Wallace Stevens', begins with a description of an orange glass vase, and alludes playfully to Steven's 'Anecdote of the Jar' with the bathetic 'like nothing else/ in this guest room' (*Wobble*, p. 87).[33] 'Vessels' is dedicated to H.D., and it is based on H.D.'s 'Sea Poppies' (one of several sea-flower poems contained in her first collection *Sea Garden*, published in 1916):

> Hopeful vessels:
> a few petals,
>
> thrown up overnight,
> fragile
>
> amber flutes,
> the sun's
>
> grail cups
> were not meant
>
> ~
>
> Beauty,
> you've sexted me
> too often.
>
> Your pert leaves,
> coming to a fine point
> at the glass
>
> stop at nothing
>
> ~
>
> If we hear
> the same sequence
>
> twice
>
> then someone's flaunting
> 'inner logic'
>
> but the wind loose
> in copper chimes
>
> is now far
> more[34]

(*Wobble*, pp. 104–5)

H.D.'s lines from 'Sea Poppies', 'Amber husk/ fluted with gold' provide the seed for the poem's first lines. But the poem alludes more broadly to H.D.'s early style. The harsh, wind-blown seascapes of H.D.'s imagined Greek shorelines, strewn with battered but resilient flowers, lie in the background of Armantrout's poem. H.D.'s question in 'Sea Lily' – 'what meadow yields/ so fragrant a leaf/ as your bright leaf?' – echoes the concluding question of its companion poem 'Sea Rose': 'Can the spice-rose/ drip such acrid fragrance/ hardened in a leaf?' The latter poem's play with hardness is taken up by Armantrout's 'amber flutes' and 'glass'. As I argued in the first chapter, H.D. rejects the post-symbolist investment in flowers as figures of pathos. Armantrout, 'obdurate' in 'Old Woman's Lament in Autumn', shares this desire to reappraise modernist austerity. Having followed H.D.'s severe precedent in the opening section, she opens the next with a joke: 'Beauty,/ you've sexted me/ too often'. The absurdity of 'pert leaves' gives way to the cliché of 'stop at nothing', with 'Beauty' far removed from H.D.'s neo-Hellenic reverie. In Armantrout's poem, Beauty cannot transcend the directness of the erotic transactions of digital text. The final section of the poem exemplifies Armantrout's recent style, with a thought extending over several lines and bucking the logic of 'if . . . then'. The non-completion of the 'if' condition leaves the reader speculating about the meaning of the repetition described at the opening of the section. The amber petals modulate into 'copper chimes', with the suggestion of the random sounding of wind chimes. Where H.D. had ended with a rhetorical question, Armantrout ends abruptly with 'far more', which implies an elided comparison. It may be that the asystemic music of wind chimes is endorsed over 'sequence'. The concluding section is structured around the small words 'if', 'then' and 'but'. However, the sentence that might be organised by such a syntactical arrangement simply does not follow the sense suggested by the conjunctions. While, somewhere, an 'inner logic' is being flaunted, the poem refuses the narrative structure required by logical argumentation.

In her interview with Ben Lerner, Armantrout observes: 'As we know from physics, and from neuroscience, any single object we will ever see is, in fact, a buzzing multiplicity which we have found it practical to identify as a single entity.'[35] This fascination with the non-fixity of the unit permeates the formal arrangement of her poetry. The relations between foundational units – word, line, clause, sentence, stanza, section, poem and book – are always contingent. In Armantrout's hands, brevity is a tool that neither locates beauty in the exquisite miniature, nor gestures at some extra-linguistic profundity that words alone cannot reach. There is nothing metaphysical in her project, even if religious vocabularies are among those that she explores. Short form for Armantrout communicates a style of thinking. The halts and pauses built into the writing at every level communicate an in-the-moment awareness of the risks and adventures available to the contemporary speaking subject. While she is clearly drawn to the sequential exposition of ideas in a range of disciplines, her own project is to caution against the surrender to plausible narratives. Her style of poetic thinking enacts the cognitive feints and swerves set in motion in the act of seeking to grasp an object of thought. When she says that the 'world enters the poem only through a kind of ventriloquy' she is alerting us to both to the pleasures and pitfalls that proliferate as, for better or worse, we speak our world into being.

Notes

1. Armantrout, *True*, p. 17.
2. Armantrout, *True*, p. 13.
3. In an interview with Lyn Hejinian, Armantrout remarks: 'I find cartoons more frightening than cute. They're often a shorthand way of embodying subjectivity and its contradictions' ('An Interview with Rae Armantrout', p. 25).
4. Armantrout, *Conjure*, p. 4. It seems likely that Armantrout was thinking of the Disney version of the fairy tale.
5. Marjorie Perloff notes that 'unlike Williams (or Levertov), Armantrout was never a poet of concrete particulars: from the first, her minimalist lyrics were breaking the Williams mold' ('Afterword for Rae', n.p.).
6. In her essay on Niedecker, 'Darkinfested', Armantrout reads Niedecker as both melancholic and misanthropic: 'She focuses, in many of her poems, on the way living creatures, human and non-human, dominate, exploit or infest one another . . . Systems produce their own contradictions. Niedecker is resigned, bemused, suffering witness but also active participant. She is able to use her minimalist poetics to heighten these contradictions by reducing background noise. Conflicts of interest and conundrums are starkly visible against her white page' (p. 72).
7. Armantrout, 'The Short Poem', p. 85.
8. Armantrout and Hejinian 'An Interview with Rae Armantrout', p. 26.
9. Armantrout, 'The Short Poem', p. 85.
10. Armantrout, 'Cheshire Poetics', p. 55.
11. In her interview with Ben Lerner she begins her discussion of the role of the unit in her writing with a scientific observation: 'As we know from physics, and from neuroscience, any single object we will ever see is, in fact, a buzzing multiplicity which we have found it practical to identify as a single entity' ('Rae Armantrout by Ben Lerner', n.p.).
12. Silliman, 'Asterisk: Separation at the Threshold of Meaning in the Poetry of Rae Armantrout' (p. 174). The concluding citation is from her poem 'A Pulse', from *Made to Seem* (and collected in *Veil*), and should read 'place/ in silence'.
13. Rae Armantrout, 'Grace', *Veil: New and Selected Poems*, p. 4. In the same volume, *Extremities*, 'Winter' (three sections); 'Xenophobia' (five sections) and 'Tone' (six sections) are similarly broken into sections. A facsimile of the 1978 edition is available at the Eclipse website.
14. Hank Lazer, 'The Lyricism of the Swerve: The Poetry of Rae Armantrout'.
15. Silliman, 'Asterisk', p. 174.

16. Armantrout, *Up to Speed*, p. 68.
17. For discussion of Armantrout's use of articles in *Scientific American*, see Peter Middleton's *Physics Envy: American Poetry and Science in the Cold War and After*, pp. 201–4). Larry Eigner's writing shares Armantrout's enthusiasm for parsing scientific vocabulary into poetry of lyric concision.
18. Armantrout, 'Poetic Silence', p. 21.
19. Armantrout and Tom Beckett, '"My Poetry isn't Built on Hope": An Interview with Rae Armantrout', p. 106.
20. Beckett, Tom and Rae Armantrout. '"My Poetry isn't Built on Hope"', p. 104.
21. 'Two, Three', *Next Life*, pp. 7–8. 'Units', from the same book, p. 19, is also organised around ones, twos and threes:

> Being a threesome
>
> of young palms,
> a triangle
> containing dusk,
>
> a doubled
> reflection which might yet
> be redoubled,
>
> is a way of being
> one
> by being numbered
>
> so as to have not
> begun again
>
> oblivious,
>
> in excess

22. Armantrout, 'Poetic Silence', p. 21.
23. Armantrout, 'Us', *Next Life*, p. 35.
24. George Oppen, 'Of Being Numerous', *NCP*, p. 171.
25. Oppen, *NCP*, p. 166, p. 172.
26. Oppen, 'Of Being Numerous', p. 173.
27. Oppen, 'Of Being Numerous', p. 187.
28. 'Upper World', *Up to Speed*, pp. 35–6. The title derives from the closing lines of another Oppen poem, 'A Narrative'.
29. In her interview with Hejinian, Armantrout remarks: 'I keep asking what happens to the subject – the "cogito?" – in a society where perceptions are commodities, already shrink-wrapped. The Information Age seems to be a place where The-White-House-Under-Fire competes with Russia-on-the-Brink for the slot on the nightly news half hour. Don't those topics sound like the names of race horses or cartoon super-heroes? Sometimes I wonder whether the powers behind the government are really trying to destroy the pre-conditions for thought' ('An Interview with Rae Armantrout', p. 25).
30. George Oppen and L. S. Dembo, 'Interview', p. 161.

31. Anon., '2010 Pulitzer Prizes for Letters, Drama and Music', *New York Times*, 12 April 2010, n.p.
32. Lerner, 'Rae Armantrout by Ben Lerner', n.p.
33. The book also contains a poem dedicated to the contemporary poet Ish Klein.
34. I have used a tilde between sections of the poem. The original uses a slightly different symbol, which is printed in light face.
35. Lerner, 'Rae Armantrout by Ben Lerner', n.p.

Coda

This book is primarily intended as a historical study of a tendency in twentieth-century American poetry. (Armantrout's writing, if not all of the poems by her that I discuss, begins in the last century too, though her works speaks forcefully to the present.) I have made an argument about one of the ways in which poets of the modernist line thought with their poems. The particular kind of thinking I have been describing is embedded in habits of circumscription. The trajectory that this book has narrated begins more than a hundred years ago with a polemical desire to strip out rhetorical excess and return poetry to a more authentic version of itself. That version was characterised as having qualities of simplicity and directness, and the appeal to this new writing was underwritten by the authority of non-anglophone models: French, classical and oriental. This project of restitution was developed by Williams, a poet enamoured of both the French avant-garde and the polyglot energies lying beneath the surface of American vernacular speech. In Williams's poetry, a form of writing emerges that aspires to self-sufficiency. If the poet thinks with their poem, the thinking the poem does is not external to the poem. Poetic form both shadows and gives shape to movements of thought.

The tradition discussed in this book has evolved in various ways, but the poets concerned have been quite explicit about their investment in the work of those before them in the post-Imagist lineage. Oppen and Niedecker developed distinct ways of relating form and knowledge in their writing, each evolving a practice of concision that served within serial forms as well as on the single page. Creeley's work with compression and the linebreak in the 1950s enabled a quality of hesitancy to complicate the elaboration of powerful conflicting emotions. In the 1960s, his work increasingly began to circle around the phenomenon of enunciation as an unfolding process. Eigner made spectacular use of page-space, achieving his effects by combining syntactical incompletion with careful modulations of the conventional rightward and downward drift of the poem. Grenier's innovation with his box of index cards, which, like Eigner's work, used monospaced typewritten text, was to introduce new ways of breaking, sequencing and combining his brief poems. Armantrout's witty use of the short line with both found and original text allows her to scrutinise the textures of discrete discursive modes with the briefest of gestures.

There are a number of younger writers working with short form. Joseph Lease and Joseph Massey have, in very different ways, produced work that is informed by the tradition I have been describing, as have Graham Foust and Pam Rehm. Craig Dworkin's 2011 book *Motes* is a collection of brief poems based on the model developed in Grenier's *Sentences* (and the later *A Day at the Beach*), complete with a comic afterword by Grenier. The Canadian poet Mark Truscott's books *Said Like Reeds or Things* and *Nature* are profoundly committed to a poetry of ellipsis, and each contains variations on Creeley's totemic 'A Piece'. The British poet Stephen Emmerson recently published a 480-page volume of Oulippean variations on 'A Piece'. I am unsure whether the seam of poetic technique explored in this book is on the point of exhaustion, or whether new means of exploiting its resources are on the point of opening.

I began the book with the suggestion that we can understand something about form per se from a better understanding of the tradition I discuss. Clearly the relationship between literary form and the culture from which it emerges is enormously variable, both horizontally and vertically. Poetry is, moreover, informed in the work of particular poets by considerations of voice that have their origins in inaccessible layers of psychic and somatic experience. All the same, the quality of incompletion that I discuss inevitably has a relationship to wider narratives, some of them social in nature (just as the novel, for example, has always had a formative as well as a reflective relationship to the cultures in which it subsists). Evolving considerations about the status of knowledge, the nature of experimentation and what constitutes poetic utterance have coloured the tradition I describe in various ways, not least its situation with regard to historically variable understandings of form.

Incompletion clearly played a very different role in early twentieth-century life to that which it plays in a contemporary culture in which, as has been widely observed, techniques once considered avant-garde are everywhere apparent in our media. Scattergun discontinuities proliferate. Rather than reviving arguments for the revelatory energies of modernist formal techniques, I have made an argument about the kind of thinking that short-form poetry does, suggesting that a critical foothold on our contemporary moment may be facilitated by writing that draws on incompletion as a productive resource. Central to this is an understanding of short-form poetry as both symptom and diagnosis of wider questions about the limitations of narrative. In other words, I suggest that the poets in this book have each, in their idiom, been attentive to the ways in which a literary line meshes with larger cultural transformations. One might think, for example, of the formal concomitants of different kinds of self-awareness in the poetry of Oppen in the 1930s and Creeley in the 1950s. Oppen's equivocal syntax and Creeley's handling of the linebreak lead to very different relations between phrasal units and line units, and each, therefore, produces distinctive figures of thought, different ways of figuring impasse. Similarly, the use of citation from non-poetic sources in Niedecker's late short-lined serial poetry works in a very different way to Grenier's 1970s work, which makes vanishingly brief poetic utterances with a determinedly vernacular voicing. Armantrout's cheerfully abrupt summoning of Eurydice ('Now we all know/ every name's Eurydice') in her poem 'Upper World', using the linebreak to separate two unsustainably hyperbolic phrases, could not be more different to H.D.'s austere invocation of a deeply alien pre-Homeric world.

The style of poetic thinking modelled by the poets in this book is not sustained by claims that poetry belongs ultimately to the non-discursive or the non-cognitive, or to silence, or to various tropes of inexpressibility, whether aligned with theology, trauma, ecstasy or love. Rather, the writing I have discussed shows how a variety of formal treatments of brevity can function as a critical counter to the regime of the whole: self-sealed fictions of gender or nation, for example. Poetic foreclosure – ellipsis, compression or interruptedness – can, in the work of its best practitioners, open up an experience of contingency that is not available in other modes of writing.

Pound and Bunting's Germano-Italian dictionary-borrowing *Dichten = condensare*, however awkward, remains a valid utterance, as it leads us towards, not away from, the particular density and strangeness of poetic speech. Condensation may, of course, be a feature of long-lined and long poems – visible in the use of multiple compact allusions, for example, as it is in the *Cantos* or "*A*". However, short-form writing offers a distinct readerly experience: the insistent quality of curtailment installs an insistent mini-blockage in the reading process.

Short-form poetry of the modernist line offers a particular way in which the overdetermined and unreadable densities generated by the encounter between world, word and subject can be approached. In this respect, another of Pound's injunctions – 'go in fear of abstractions' – is conspicuously not met. Indeed, I have argued that the formal imperatives of the post-Imagist line are at odds with the representation of the concrete. The writing I have been discussing invites immersion in a space of abstraction: a speculative space from which provisional lines of thought open. These always lie outside the generative structure of the poem. Such poetry does not lead the reader down an abstract pathway of narrative argumentation. The magnified impact of small syntactical shifts in the context of short-form verse leads thought away from the existent. For all its writers' claims of directness and clarity, such writing depends on abstraction. This open-ended space of non-resolution is hospitable to singularity, difference and the non-identical.

Short-form poems are always ending: phrase, line, stanza and poem itself all bump up repeatedly against an experience of limitation. Yet endings do not need to be conclusive. For the writing I have discussed, the limit is a point of departure. The strictures of the condensery are productive. In this project, Robert Creeley's example has been central to my arguments. His handling of the linebreak brings an exemplary expressivity to the fact of poetic interruption. To conclude, it seems sensible to return to one of his most beautiful and open conclusions, from one of the poems in *Pieces* (CPC1, p. 391):

—it
 it—

Bibliography

Agamben, Giorgio and Daniel Heller-Roazen (trans.), *The End of the Poem* (Stanford: Stanford University Press, 1999).
Aldington, Richard and H.D. (eds), *Some Imagist Poets: An Anthology* (Boston, MA: Houghton Mifflin, 1915).
Altieri, Charles, *Enlarging the Temple: New Directions in American Poetry during the 1960s* (Lewisburg, PA: Bucknell University Press, 1979)
— *Self and Sensibility in Contemporary American Poetry* (Cambridge: Cambridge University Press, 2009).
— 'What does *Echoes* Echo?', in *Form, Power, and Person in Robert Creeley's Life and Work*, ed. Stephen Fredman and Steve McCaffery, pp. 36–49.
Anon., '2010 Pulitzer Prizes for Letters, Drama and Music', *New York Times* (12 April 2010) <https://www.nytimes.com/2010/04/13/business/media/2010-Arts-Pulitzers.html> (last accessed 1 August 2019).
Armantrout, Rae, 'Cheshire Poetics', in *Collected Prose*, pp. 55–62.
— *Collected Prose* (San Diego: Singing Horse Press, 2007).
— *Conjure* (Middletown, CT: Wesleyan University Press, 2020).
— 'Darkinfested', in *Collected Prose*, pp. 63–72.
— *Money Shot* (Middletown, CT: Wesleyan University Press, 2011).
— *Next Life* (Middletown, CT: Wesleyan University Press, 2008).
— 'Poetic Silence', in *Collected Prose*, pp. 21–37.
— 'The Short Poem', in *Collected Prose*, pp. 80–5.
— *True* (Berkeley: Atelos, 2010).
— *Up to Speed* (Middletown, CT: Wesleyan University Press, 2004).
— *Veil: New and Selected Poems* (Middletown, CT: Wesleyan University Press, 2001).
— *Versed* (Middletown, CT: Wesleyan University Press, 2010).
— *Wobble* (Middletown, CT: Wesleyan University Press, 2019).
Armantrout, Rae and Tom Beckett, ' "My Poetry Isn't Built on Hope": An Interview with Rae Armantrout', in *A Wild Salience: The Writing of Rae Armantrout*, ed. Tom Beckett, Bobbie West and Robert Drake, pp. 104–14
Armantrout, Rae and Lyn Hejinian, 'An Interview with Rae Armantrout', in *A Wild Salience: The Writing of Rae Armantrout*, ed. Tom Beckett, Bobbie West and Robert Drake, pp. 12–26.
Balso, Judith, *Affirmation of Poetry* (Minneapolis: Univocal, 2014).

Bashō, trans. Cid Corman, *One Man's Moon: Poems by Basho & Other Japanese Poets / Versions by Cid Corman*, expanded edn (Frankfort, KT: Gnomon, 2003).

Beckett, Tom, Bobbie West and Robert Drake (eds), *A Wild Salience: The Writing of Rae Armantrout*, ed. Tom Beckett, Bobbie West and Robert Drake (Cleveland: Burning Press, 2000).

Bernstein, Charles, 'Hero of the Local: Robert Creeley and the Persistence of American Poetry', *Textual Practice* 19.3 (2005): 373–7.

— 'Introduction' to *Calligraphy Typewriters: the Selected Poems of Larry Eigner*, ed. Curtis Faville and Robert Grenier, pp. ix–xi.

Best, Stephen and Sharon Marcus, 'Surface Reading: An Introduction', *Representations* 108 (2009): 1–21.

Blasing, Mutlu Konuk, *Lyric Poetry: the Pain and the Pleasure of Words* (Princeton: Princeton University Press, 2008).

Blau DuPlessis, Rachel, *H.D.: The Career of that Struggle* (Brighton: Harvester, 1986).

— 'The Hole: Death, Sexual Difference, and Gender Contradictions in Creeley's Poetry', in *Form, Power, and Person in Robert Creeley's Life and Work*, ed. Stephen Fredman and Steve McCaffery, pp. 89–119.

— 'Lorine Niedecker's "Paean to Place" and its Reflective Fusions', in *Radical Vernacular*, ed. Elizabeth Willis, pp. 151–79.

— 'Objectivist Poetry and Poetics', in *The Cambridge Companion to Modern American Poetry*, ed. Walter Kalaidjian, pp. 89–101.

Blau DuPlessis, Rachel and Peter Quartermain (eds), *The Objectivist Nexus: Essays in Cultural Poetics* (Tuscaloosa: University of Alabama Press, 1999).

Blau DuPlessis, Rachel and Susan Stanford Friedman (eds), *Signets: Reading H.D.* (Madison: University of Wisconsin Press, 1990).

Butler, Christopher, *Early Modernism: Literature, Music, and Painting in Europe, 1900–1916* (Oxford: Oxford University Press, 2007).

Carbery, Matthew, *Phenomenology and the Late Twentieth-Century American Long Poem* (London, New York: Palgrave, 2019).

Carr, Helen, *The Verse Revolutionaries: Ezra Pound, H.D. and the Imagists* (London: Cape, 2009).

Collecott, Diana, *H.D. and Sapphic Modernism, 1910–1950* (Cambridge: Cambridge University Press, 2008).

Conte, Joseph M., *Unending Design: The Forms of Postmodern Poetry* (Ithaca, NY: Cornell University Press, 1991).

Coolidge, Clark and Michael Palmer (eds), *Joglars* 1, <http://eclipsearchive.org/projects/JOGLARS1/Joglars1.pdf> (last accessed 27 May 2019).

Corman, Cid and Gregory Dunne, 'Thirty-One Poems & an Interview: A Special APR Supplement', *The American Poetry Review* 29 (2000): 21–8.

Creeley, Robert, *The Collected Essays of Robert Creeley* (Berkeley: University of California Press, 1989).

— *The Collected Poems of Robert Creeley, 1945–1975*. (Berkeley: University of California Press, 1982).

— *Contexts of Poetry: Interviews, 1961–1971* (Bolinas, CA: Four Seasons Foundation, 1973).

— 'Frederick Eckman: The Epistemology of Loss', in *Collected Essays* (Berkeley: University of California Press, pp. 277–8.

— 'I'm Given to Write Poems', in *Collected Essays*, pp. 499–500.

— 'Introduction to the New Writing in the USA', in *Collected Essays*, pp. 89–97.
— 'A Note', in *Collected Essays*, pp. 478–9.
— 'A Note on the Objective', in *Collected Essays*, pp. 464–5.
— 'Poems are a Complex', in *Collected Essays*, pp. 490–1.
— *Selected Poems*, 1945–2005, ed. Benjamin Friedlander (Berkeley: University of California Press, 2008).
— 'A Sense of Measure', in *Collected Essays*, pp. 486–8.
— 'William Corbett: Two Books', in *Collected Essays*, pp. 326–8.
Creeley, Robert and Al Filreis, 'Asking Creeley about Williams', *Jacket 2*, n.d., <http://jacket2.org/commentary/asking-creeley-about-williams> (last accessed 12 August 2019).
Creeley, Robert and Daniel Kane, 'Interview', in *What is Poetry: Conversations with the American Avant-Garde*, pp. 50–65.
Creeley, Robert, Lewis MacAdams and Linda Wagner-Martin, 'The Art of Poetry X: Robert Creeley', *Paris Review* 44 (1968): 155–87.
Creeley, Robert and David Ossman, 'Interview', in *Contexts of Poetry: Interviews 1961–1971*, pp. 3–12.
Creeley, Robert, John Sinclair and Robin Eichele, 'An Interview with Robert Creeley', in *Contexts of Poetry*, pp. 45–69.
Creeley, Robert and Linda Wagner 'A Colloquy with Robert Creeley', in *Contexts of Poetry: Interviews 1961–1971*, pp. 71–124.
Crozier, Andrew, 'Inaugural and Valedictory: the Early Poetry of George Oppen', in *An Andrew Crozier Reader*, ed. Ian Brinton (Manchester: Carcanet, 2012), pp. 196–208.
Culler, Jonathan, *Theory of the Lyric* (Cambridge, MA and London: Harvard University Press, 2017).
Davidson, Michael, *Concerto for the Left Hand: Disability and the Defamiliar Body* (Ann Arbor and London: University of Michigan Press, 2011).
— 'Dismantling "Mantis": Reification and Objectivist Poetics', *American Literary History* 3 (1991): 521–41.
— *Ghostlier Demarcations: Modern Poetry and the Material Word* (Berkeley: University of California Press, 1997).
— *Guys Like Us: Citing Masculinity in Cold War Poetics* (Chicago: University of Chicago Press, 2004).
— 'Life by Water: Lorine Niedecker and Critical Regionalism', in *Radical Vernacular*, ed. Elizabeth Willis, pp. 3–20.
— 'The Repeated Insistence: Creeley's Rage', in Fredman and McCaffery (eds), *Form, Power, and Person*, pp. 69–88
Davidson, Michael (ed.), 'An Adequate Vision: A George Oppen Daybook', *Ironwood* 26 (Fall 1985): 5–31.
Davie, Donald, 'Lyric Minimum and Epic Scope: Lorine Niedecker', in *The Full Note: Lorine Niedecker*, ed. Peter Dent (Budleigh Salterton: Interim Press, 1983), pp. 64–73.
Davis, Alex and Lee M. Jenkins (eds), *The Cambridge Companion to Modernist Poetry* (Cambridge: Cambridge University Press, 2007).
Darwin, Charles, Letter nos 275, 729, 2647 and 2814, archived at the Darwin Correspondence Project, <https://www.darwinproject.ac.uk> (last accessed 19 September 2019).
Duncan, Robert, 'After for Love', *Boundary 2* 6–7 (1978): 233–40.

Dworkin, Craig, *Motes* (New York: Roof, 2011).
— 'Klatsch', *Convolution* 4 (2016): 8–17.
Eigner, Larry, *Air: The Trees* (Los Angeles: Black Sparrow, 1968).
— *Areas Lights Heights: Writings, 1954–1989*, ed. Ben Friedlander (New York: Roof Books (Kindle edn), 1989).
— *Calligraphy Typewriters: The Selected Poems of Larry Eigner*, ed. Curtis Faville and Robert Grenier (Tuscaloosa: University of Alabama Press, 2017).
— *The Collected Poems of Larry Eigner*, four vols, ed. Curtis Faville and Robert Grenier (Stanford: Stanford University Press, 2010).
— 'Like a Dog Bark in Music', in *Areas Lights Heights: Writings, 1954–1989*, n.p.
— 'not/ forever/ serious', in *Areas Lights Heights: Writings, 1954–1989*, n.p.
— 'Qs & As (?) Large and Small Parts of a Collaborate: The *Stony Hills* Interview', in *Areas Lights Heights: Writings, 1954–1989*, n.p.
— 'Three Poems', *Poetry* 110.1 (April 1967): 20, <https://www.jstor.org/stable/20598232> (last accessed 7 July 2019).
— *Selected Poems*, ed. Samuel Charters and Andrea Wyatt (Berkeley: Oyez, 1972).
Entwistle, Alice, ' "For W.C.W.", "Yet Complexly": Creeley and Williams', *English* 50 (2001): 127–48.
Eyers, Tom, *Speculative Formalism: Literature, Theory, and the Critical Present* (Evanston: Northwestern University Press, 2017).
Felski, Rita, *The Limits of Critique* (Chicago: University of Chicago Press, 2017).
Fitch, Noel Riley, 'Voyage to Ithaca: William Carlos Williams in Paris', *The Princeton University Library Chronicle* 40 (1979): 193–214.
Flint, F. S., 'The History of Imagism', *The Egoist* 2: 5 (May 1915), pp. 70–1.
— *In the Net of the Stars* (London: E. Mathews, 1909).
— 'The Poetry of H.D.', *The Egoist* 2:5 (May 1915): 72–3, <http://modjourn.org/journals.html> (last accessed 14 August 2019).
— 'Recent Verse', *New Age* (1908): 212–13, <http://modjourn.org/journals.html> (last accessed 14 August 2019).
Forrest, Seth, 'The Body of the Text: Cerebral Palsy, Projective Verse and Prosthetics in Larry Eigner's Poetry', *Jacket* 36 (2008), <http://jacketmagazine.com/36/forrest-eigner.shtml> (last accessed 11 May 2019).
Fredman, Stephen, *Poet's Prose: The Crisis in American Verse* (Cambridge and New York: Cambridge University Press, 1983).
Friedlander, Ben, 'Larry Eigner', in *American Poets since World War II*, ed. Joseph M. Conte (Detroit: Gale, 1998), archived at <http://writing.upenn.edu/epc/authors/eigner/Friedlander-Ben_Larry-Eigner.pdf> (last accessed 30 August 2019).
— 'Reading in Pieces', *Jacket* 31 (2006), <https://jacket2.org/commentary/ben-friedlander-robert-creeley-reading-pieces> (last accessed 1 September 2019).
Giles, Herbert, *A History of Chinese Literature* (Rutland, VT: Tuttle, 1973 [1901]).
Golding, Alan, 'Revisiting Seriality in Creeley's Poetry', in *Form, Power, and Person in Robert Creeley's Life and Work*, ed. Stephen Fredman and Steve McCaffery, pp. 50–65.
Grenier, Robert, *100 Sentences = 100 Phrases*, trans. Martin Richet (Bordeaux: Éditions de l'Attente, 2005).

— *Attention: Seven Narratives* (Canton, NY: Institute of Further Studies, 1985).
— 'Larry Eigner Biography', <http://writing.upenn.edu/epc/authors/eigner/bio_grenier.html> (last accessed 14 July 2019).
— 'On Speech', *This* 1 (1971), <http://eclipsearchive.org/projects/SPEECH/speech.html> (last accessed 12 September 2019).
— 'Robert Creeley: Pieces, Scribners 1969', *This*, 1 (1971), <http://eclipsearchive.org/projects/SPEECH/speech.html> (last accessed 8 January 2020).
— *Sentences* (online edn), <http://www.whalecloth.org/grenier/sentences_.htm> (last accessed 30 September 2019).
— *Sentences Toward Birds* (Kensington, CA: L Press, 1975), <http://eclipsearchive.org/projects/BIRDS/birds.html> (last accessed 1 September 2019).
Grenier, Robert, Timothy Shaner, Jonathan Skinner and Isabelle Pelissier, *Farming the Words: Talking with Robert Grenier* (Bowdoinham, ME: Field Books, 2009).
Grenier, Robert and Charles Bernstein, *Close Listening* Interview, 20 October 2006 (audio), <http://writing.upenn.edu/pennsound/x/Grenier.php> (last accessed 7 September 2019).
Grenier, Robert and Ivy Johnson, 'An Interview with Robert Grenier', <http://s3.amazonaws.com/fca-website-production/system/comfy/cms/files/24/files/original/10._Interview_with_IJ.pdf> (originally published in *580 Split* 15, 2013) (last accessed 25 June 2019).
Guest, Barbara, *Herself Defined: The Poet H.D. and Her World* (Tucson: Schaffner Press, 2003).
H.D., *Collected Poems, 1912–1944*, ed. Louis L. Martz (New York: New Directions, 1986).
— *End to Torment: A Memoir of Ezra Pound* (New York: New Directions, 1979).
— 'Goblins and Pagodas', *Egoist* 3 (1916): 183–4.
— *Sea Garden* (London: Constable, 1916).
Hair, Ross, *Avant-Folk: Small Press Poetry Networks from 1950 to the Present* (Liverpool: Liverpool University Press, 2017).
Hart, George L., ' "Enough Defined": Disability, Ecopoetics, and Larry Eigner', *Contemporary Literature* 51 (2010): 152–79.
Hendricks, Jon, *Fluxus Codex* (New York: Abrams, 1995).
Hulme, T. E., 'Lecture on Modern Poetry,' in *Selected Writings*, pp. 59–67.
— 'Romanticism and Classicism', in *Selected Writings*, pp. 68–83.
— *Selected Writings* (New York: Routledge, 2003).
Husárová, Zuzana and Nick Montfort, 'Shuffle Literature and the Hand of Fate', *Electronic Book Review* (August, 2012), <https://electronicbookreview.com/essay/shuffle-literature-and-the-hand-of-fate/> (last accessed 13 August 2019).
Joyce, James, *Portrait of the Artist as a Young Man* (New York: Penguin, 1964 [1916]).
Kalaidjian, Walter B. (ed.), *The Cambridge Companion to Modern American Poetry* (Cambridge: Cambridge University Press, 2015).
Kane, Daniel, *What is Poetry: Conversations with the American Avant-Garde* (New York: Teachers & Writers Books, 2003).
Keller, Lynn, 'Lessons from William Carlos Williams: Robert Creeley's Early Poetry', *Modern Language Quarterly* 43 (1982): 369–94.
Kenner, Hugh, *The Pound Era* (London: Pimlico, 1991 [1971]).

Kermode, Frank, *Romantic Image* (London: Routledge, 2016 [1957]).
Kern, Robert, *Orientalism, Modernism, and the American Poem* (Cambridge: Cambridge University Press, 2009).
Lazer, Hank, 'The Lyricism of the Swerve: The Poetry of Rae Armantrout', in *A Wild Salience: The Writing of Rae Armantrout,* ed. Tom Beckett, Bobbie West and Robert Drake, pp. 131–54.
Lerner, Ben, 'Rae Armantrout by Ben Lerner', *BOMB* 114 (Winter 2011), <https://bombmagazine.org/articles/rae-armantrout/> (last accessed 14 July 2019).
Longenbach, James, *The Art of the Poetic Line* (Minneapolis: Graywolf, 2008).
Luck, Jessica Lewis, 'Larry Eigner and the Phenomenology of Projected Verse', *Contemporary Literature* 53 (2012): 461–92.
Mackail, J. W., *Select Epigrams from the Greek Anthology* (London and New York: Longmans, Green, 1906).
Mariani, Paul, ' "Fire of a very Real Order": Creeley and Williams', *Boundary 2* 6 (1978), pp. 173–92.
Messerli, Douglas, *'Language' Poetries: An Anthology* (New York: New Directions, 1987).
Middleton, Peter, *Physics Envy: American Poetry and Science in the Cold War and After* (Chicago: University of Chicago Press, 2015).
— 'The British Niedecker', in *Radical Vernacular*, ed. Elizabeth Willis, pp. 247–70.
Monro, Harold, 'The Imagists Discussed', *The Egoist* (1915): 77–80.
Montgomery, Will, 'Sound Leads to Structure: Dissonant Lyricism in Barbara Guest's *Miniatures*', *Jacket* 36 (2008) <http://jacketmagazine.com/36/guest-montgomery.shtml> (last accessed 12 August 2019).
Nadel, Ira B. and Ezra Pound, *Cathay: Ezra Pound's Orient* (London: Penguin, 2016).
Nicholls, Peter, 'Of Being Ethical: Reflections on George Oppen', *Journal of American Studies* 31 (1997): 153–70.
— *George Oppen and the Fate of Modernism* (Oxford: Oxford University Press, 2013).
— 'A Necessary Blindness', *Journal of Philosophy: A Cross-Disciplinary Inquiry* 6 (2010), pp. 28–40.
— 'The Poetics of Modernism', in *The Cambridge Companion to Modernist Poetry*, ed. Alex Davis and Lee M. Jenkins (Cambridge University Press, Cambridge, 2007), pp. 51–67.
Niedecker, Lorine, *'Between Your House and Mine': The Letters of Lorine Niedecker to Cid Corman, 1960 to 1970*, ed. Lisa Faranda (Durham, NC: Duke University Press, 1986).
— *Collected Works*, ed. Jenny Penberthy (Berkeley: University of California Press, 2004).
— *Lake Superior: Lorine Niedecker's Poem and Journal, Along with Other Sources, Documents, and Readings* (Seattle: Wave Books, 2013).
— MS of 'Darwin', University of Wisconsin Digital Collections, local identifier: WI.hfad0120.bib, <https://uwdc.library.wisc.edu/collections/> (last accessed 12 June 2019).
— *North Central* (London: Fulcrum, 1968).
— 'The Poetry of Cid Corman', *Arts in Society* (1965): 558–60, <https://

writing.upenn.edu/epc/authors/niedecker/three-essays.pdf> (last accessed 27 September 2019).
— Undated letter to Mary Hoard, Lorine Niedecker documents, University of Wisconsin Digital Collections, identifier WI.hfad0208.bib, <https://uwdc.library.wisc.edu/collections/> (last accessed 12 August 2019).
O'Leary, Peter, 'The Energies of Words', Poetry Foundation website, June 2008, <https://www.poetryfoundation.org/articles/69068/the-energies-of-words> (last accessed 12 July 2019).
Olson, Charles, 'Projective Verse', in *Collected Prose*, ed. Donald M. Allen (Berkeley: University of California Press, 2007), pp. 239–49.
Olson, Charles and Robert Creeley, *Charles Olson & Robert Creeley: The Complete Correspondence*, Vols 2 and 8, ed. George Butterick (Santa Rosa, CA: Black Sparrow, 1987).
Oppen, George, *New Collected Poems*, ed. Michael Davidson (New York: New Directions, 2008).
— *The Selected Letters of George Oppen* (Durham, NC: Duke University Press, 1990).
— *Selected Prose, Daybooks and Papers*, ed. Stephen Cope (Berkeley: University of California Press, 2007).
— *Speaking with George Oppen: Interviews with the Poet and Mary Oppen, 1968–1987*, ed. Richard Swigg (Jefferson, NC: McFarland, 2012).
Oppen, George and L. S. Dembo, 'George Oppen (Interview)', *Contemporary Literature* 10 (1969): 159–77.
Oppen, George, Charles Amirkhanian and David Gitin, 'Interview, 1970', in *Speaking with George Oppen*, ed. Richard Swigg, pp. 35–44.
Oppen, George, Charles Amirkhanian and Don Branning, 'Interview, 1973', in *Speaking with George Oppen*, ed. Richard Swigg, pp. 45–56.
Oppen, George and Charles Tomlinson, 'Interview, 1973', in *Speaking with George Oppen*, ed. Richard Swigg, pp. 57–61.
Oppen, George, Mary Oppen, Burton Hatlen and Tom Mandel, 'Interview, 1980', in *Speaking with George Oppen*, ed. Richard Swigg, pp. 216–39.
Osborne, Peter, *Anywhere Or Not at All: Philosophy of Contemporary Art* (London: Verso, 2013).
Penberthy, Jenny, 'A Little Too Little: Re-Reading Lorine Niedecker', *How 2* 1 (1999), <https://www.asu.edu/pipercwcenter/how2journal/archive/online_archive/v1_1_1999/jplittle.html> (last accessed 10 August 2019).
Penberthy, Jenny (ed.), *Lorine Niedecker: Woman and Poet* (Orono, ME: National Poetry Foundation, University of Maine, 1996).
— *Niedecker and the Correspondence with Zukofsky, 1931–1970* (Cambridge and New York: Cambridge University Press, 1993).
Perloff, Marjorie, 'Afterword for Rae', *Poems and Poetics* blog (3 March 2010), <http://poemsandpoetics.blogspot.co.uk/> (last accessed 14 September 2019).
— 'Robert Creeley's Radical Poetics', *Electronic Book Review* (2007), <http://electronicbookreview.com/essay/robert-creeleys-radical-poetics/> (last accessed 15 August 2019).
Perloff, Marjorie and Craig Dworkin (eds), *The Sound of Poetry, the Poetry of Sound* (Chicago and London: University of Chicago Press, 2009).
Peters, Margot, *Lorine Niedecker: A Poet's Life* (Madison: The University of Wisconsin Press, 2011).

Peterson, Jeffrey, 'Lorine Niedecker: Before Machines', in *Lorine Niedecker: Woman and Poet*, ed. Jenny Penberthy, pp. 245–79.
Pinard, Mary, 'Niedecker's Grammar of Flooding', in *Radical Vernacular*, ed. Elizabeth Willis, pp. 21–30.
Pondrom, Cyrena, 'H.D. and the Origins of Imagism', in *Signets: Reading H.D.*, ed. Susan Stanford Friedman and Rachel Blau DuPlessis, pp. 85–110.
Pondrom, Cyrena and H.D., 'Selected Letters from H.D. to F. S. Flint: A Commentary on the Imagist Period', *Contemporary Literature* 10 (1969): 557–86.
Pound, Ezra, *ABC of Reading* (New York: New Directions, 2010).
— 'Affirmations: As for Imagisme', in *Selected Prose, 1909–1965*.
— 'Cavalcanti', in *Literary Essays of Ezra Pound*, pp. 149–200.
— 'Date Line', in *Literary Essays of Ezra Pound*, pp. 74–87.
— *Early Writings: Poems and Prose*, ed. Ira B Nadel (New York: Penguin Books, 2005).
— 'How to Read', in *Literary Essays*, pp. 13–40.
— 'Introduction to Cavalcanti Poems', in *Translations*, pp. 17–25.
— *Literary Essays of Ezra Pound*, ed. T. S. Eliot (New York: New Directions, 2007 [1954]).
— *Personae: The Shorter Poems of Ezra Pound* (New York: New Directions, 1990 [1926]).
— *The Pisan Cantos* (New York: New Directions, 2003).
— 'A Retrospect', *Literary Essays* (New York: New Directions, 2007), pp. 3–14.
— *Selected Letters of Ezra Pound, 1907–1941* (New York: New Directions, 1971).
— *Selected Prose, 1909–1965*, ed. William Cookson (New York: New Directions, 1973).
— *The Translations of Ezra Pound*, ed. Hugh Kenner (London: Faber, 1984).
— 'TS Eliot', *Literary Essays*, pp. 418–22.
— 'Vorticism', in *Gaudier-Brzeska* (New York: New Directions, 1974), pp. 81–94.
Pound, Ezra (ed.), *Des Imagistes: An Anthology* (London and New York: Poetry Bookshop; Albert & Charles Boni, 1914).
Qian, Zhaoming, *Ezra Pound and China* (Ann Arbor: University of Michigan Press, 2006).
Quartermain, Peter, *Disjunctive Poetics: From Gertrude Stein and Louis Zukofsky to Susan Howe* (Cambridge: Cambridge University Press, 1992).
— 'Take Oil / and Hum: Niedecker/ Bunting', in *Radical Vernacular*, ed. Elizabeth Willis, pp. 271–83.
Reed, Brian M., *Phenomenal Reading: Essays on Modern and Contemporary Poetics* (Tuscaloosa: University of Alabama Press, 2012).
Reznikoff, Charles, *The Poems of Charles Reznikoff, 1918–1975* (Boston, MA: D. R. Godine, 2005).
Riley, Denise, *The Words of Selves: Identification, Solidarity, Irony* (Stanford: Stanford University Press, 2000).
Robertson, Lisa, 'In Phonographic Deep Song: Sounding Niedecker', in *Radical Vernacular*, ed. Elizabeth Willis, pp. 83–90.

Robinson, Kit, 'What do You Know: A Read on Larry Eigner', *Passages 5* (1996), <http://writing.upenn.edu/epc/ezines/passages/passages5/p5entry.html> (last accessed 20 August 2019).

Roub, Gail, 'Getting to Know Lorine Niedecker', in *Lorine Niedecker, Woman and Poet*, ed. Jenny Penberthy, pp. 79–86.

Scott Snelson, Daniel, '*Alcheringa*, "The Dwelling Place" and Structuralist Tendencies', *Mimeo Mimeo* (2009): 18–32.

Scroggins, Mark, *The Poem of A Life: A Biography of Louis Zukofsky* (Berkeley: Counterpoint, 2009).

Shaw, Lytle, *Narrowcast Poetry and Audio Research* (Stanford: Stanford University Press, 2018).

Sieburth, Richard, 'In Pound we Trust: The Economy of Poetry/ the Poetry of Economics', *Critical Inquiry* 14 (1987): 142–72.

Silliman, Ron, 'Asterisk: Separation at the Threshold of Meaning in the Poetry of Rae Armantrout', in *A Wild Salience: The Writing of Rae Armantrout*, ed. Tom Beckett, Bobbie West and Robert Drake, pp. 162–75.

— 'The New Sentence', in *The New Sentence* (New York: The Segue Foundation, 1987), pp. 63–93.

— 'Third Phase Objectivism', *Paideuma* 10 (1981): pp. 85–9.

— Untitled blog post, 7 January 2019, <https://ronsilliman.blogspot.com/2019/01/ben-friedlander-jokingly-introduced-me.html> (last accessed 14 August 2019).

Silliman, Ron (ed.), 'The Dwelling Place (Special Issue)', *Alcheringa* (1975), <http://eclipsearchive.org/projects/ALCHERINGA/alcheringa.html> (last accessed 12 July 2019).

— *In the American Tree* (Orono: National Poetry Foundation, University of Maine at Orono, 1986).

— *Tottel's* 15, Larry Eigner Special Issue (undated early 1970s), <http://eclipsearchive.org/projects/TOTTELS> (last accessed 6 July 2019).

Skinner, Jonathan, 'Birds in Dickinson's Words', *The Emily Dickinson Journal* 20 (2011): 106–10.

— 'Particular Attention: Lorine Niedecker's Natural Histories', in *Radical Vernacular*, ed. Elizabeth Willis, pp. 41–60.

Sorrentino, Gilbert, 'Misconstruing Lorine Niedecker', in *Lorine Niedecker: Woman and Poet*, ed. Jenny Penberthy, pp. 287–92.

Stein, Gertrude, 'Composition as Explanation', in *Look at Me Now and Here I Am: Writings and Lectures, 1911–1945*, ed. Patricia Meyerowitz (London: Peter Owen, 2004), pp. 21–30.

— 'Portraits and Repetition', in *Look at Me Now and Here I Am: Writings and Lectures, 1911–1945*, ed. Patricia Meyerowitz, pp. 98–122.

Stephens, Paul, '"Really 'Reading in'": A Media-Archival History of Robert Grenier's *Sentences*', *American Literary History*, 30 (2018), 278–303.

Stevens, Wallace, *Collected Poems* (New York: Knopf, 1971).

— *Collected Poetry and Prose* (New York: The Library of America, 2010).

— *Letters of Wallace Stevens* (New York: Knopf, 1981).

Stewart, Susan, 'Rhyme and Freedom', in *The Sound of Poetry, the Poetry of Sound*, ed. Marjorie Perloff, Craig Dworkin (Chicago: University of Chicago Press, 2009), pp. 29–48.

Symons, Arthur, *The Symbolist Movement in Literature* (London: Heinemann, 1899).
Thinking Verse, ed. David Nowell Smith, <http://www.thinkingverse.org> (last accessed 14 December 2019).
Thoreau, Henry D., *The Maine Woods: A Fully Annotated Edition* (New Haven; London: Yale University Press, 2010).
Tichy, Susan, 'Susan Tichy's Field Guide to the Birds of Lorine Niedecker's *Collected Works*', <http://mason.gmu.edu/~stichy/Niedecker%27s%20Birds.html> (last accessed 12 August 2019).
Twitchell-Waas, Jeffrey, 'What were the "Objectivist" Poets?', *Modernism/Modernity* 22 (2015): 315–41.
Watten, Barrett, 'Missing "X": Formal Meaning in Crane and Eigner', in *Poetics Journal Digital Archive*, ed. Lyn Hejinian and Barrett Watten (Middletown, CT: Wesleyan University Press, 2014), Epub edn.
White, Gillian C., *Lyric Shame: The "Lyric" Subject of Contemporary American Poetry* (Cambridge, MA and London: Harvard University Press, 2014).
Wilkinson, John, *The Lyric Touch* (Cambridge: Salt, 2007).
— 'The Weight of Words: W. S. Graham's Lyric Poetry', *Chicago Review* 62.1/2/3 (2018–19): 40.
Williams, William Carlos, *The Autobiography of William Carlos Williams* (New York: New Directions, 1967).
— 'Caviar and Bread Again', in *Selected Essays* (New York: New Directions, 1969), pp. 102–4.
— *The Collected Earlier Poems* (New York: New Directions, 1973).
— *The Collected Poems of William Carlos Williams, Volume 1* (New York: New Directions, 1986).
— *The Collected Poems of William Carlos Williams, Volume 2* (New York: New Directions, 1988).
— 'Excerpts from a Critical Sketch: A Draft of XXX Cantos', in *Selected Essays* (New York: New Directions, 1969), pp. 105–12.
— *Imaginations: Kora in Hell; Spring and all; the Great American Novel; the Descent of Winter; a Novelette and Other Prose* (New York: New Directions, 1979).
— *In the American Grain: Essays* (New York: New Directions, 1956).
— *I Wanted to Write a Poem: The Autobiography of the Works of a Poet* (New York: New Directions, 1978).
— 'Letter to an Australian Editor', *William Carlos Williams Review* 17 (1991): 8–12.
— 'The New Poetical Economy', *Poetry* 44 (1934): 220–5.
— 'A Note on Poetry', in *The Oxford Anthology of American Literature*, ed. William Rose Benét and Norman Holmes Pearson (New York: Oxford University Press, 1938).
— 'The Poem as a Field of Action', *Selected Essays*, pp. 280–91.
— *A Recognizable Image: William Carlos Williams on Art and Artists* (New York: New Directions, 1978).
— *Selected Essays* (New York: New Directions, 1969).
— 'The Work of Gertrude Stein', in *Selected Essays*, pp. 113–20.
Willis, Elizabeth, 'The Poetics of Affinity: Niedecker, Morris, and the Art of Work', in *Radical Vernacular*, ed. Elizabeth Willis, pp. 223–46.

— 'Who was Lorine Niedecker?' (2006), <https://poets.org/text/who-was-lorine-niedecker> (last accessed 24 August 2018).
Willis, Elizabeth (ed.), *Radical Vernacular: Lorine Niedecker and the Poetics of Place* (Iowa City: University of Iowa Press, 2008).
Woods, Tim, 'Cid Corman: Editor, Translator, Poet', *Paideuma* 41 (2014): 49–78.
— *The Poetics of the Limit: Ethics and Politics in Modern and Contemporary American Poetry* (New York: Palgrave Macmillan, 2002).
Xie, Ming, *Ezra Pound and the Appropriation of Chinese Poetry: Cathay, Translation, and Imagism* (London: Routledge, 2014).
Zukofsky, Louis, *Anew: Complete Shorter Poetry* (New York: New Directions, 2011).
— 'An Objective', in *Prepositions*, pp. 12–18
— *Prepositions: The Collected Critical Essays of Louis Zukofsky* (Berkeley: University of California Press, 1981).
— 'Sincerity and Objectification: With Special Reference to the Work of Charles Reznikoff', *Poetry* 37 (1931): 272–85.
— *A Test of Poetry* (Hanover: University Press of New Hampshire, 2000).
Zukofsky, Louis and L. S. Dembo, 'Louis Zukofsky (Interview)', *Contemporary Literature* 10 (1969): 203–19.

Index

Agamben, Giorgio, 8
Alcheringa magazine, 160
Aldington, Richard
   'Beauty Thou Hast Hurt Me
      Overmuch', 32
   'Choriços', 23
   'The River', 23
Aldington, Richard and H.D. (ed.),
   Some Imagist Poets, 16, 19, 32,
   40n
Allen, Don (ed.), *The New American
   Poetry* (anthology), 139, 141, 159,
   177n
Altieri, Charles, 1, 2, 5, 6, 119, 121,
   127, 136n
ancient Chinese literature, 21, 25–6,
   30–1, 39–40n
ancient Greek literature, 9, 29–31
anti-metaphorical impulse, in poetry,
   49, 50, 58, 153, 175
Armantrout, Rae, 3, 7, 13, 107,
   180–201
   'Anti-short Story', 186
   'Around', 195
   'Box', 194
   'Cheshire Poetics' (prose), 183
   'Darkinfested' (prose), 201n
   'En Route', 194
   Entanglements, 188
   Extremities, 185–6
   'Grace', 185
   'Homer', 198
   'Like', 196
   Money Shot, 197–8
   Next Life, 190, 192
   'Pinocchio', 181–2
   'The Short Poem' (prose), 183
   'The Vescicle', 198
   'The Vessels', 198–200
   'Translation', 195–6
   'Two, Three', 190
   Up to Speed, 187–9, 193–4
   'Upper World', 193, 206
   Versed, 195–7
   'View', 186
   'Visualizations', 189, 190
   'Us', 192
   Wobble, 198
Ashbery, John, 2, 165, 186

Balso, Judith, 6
Bashō, 104, 111, 146
Beat Generation, 118, 122
Bernstein, Charles, 9–10, 139, 140,
   148, 152, 164
Billy the Kid, 180
birds, 7, 12, 34, 61–2, 79, 98, 101–3,
   105, 111, 144–5, 147, 148, 153,
   164, 178, 185, 195
Black Mountain poets, 12, 118, 139,
   159–60
Blake, William, 58, 84, 89n
Blasing, Mutlu Konuk, 7, 10
Blau DuPlessis, Rachel, 14n, 40n, 69,
   72, 90, 97, 116n
Brecht, George, *Water Yam*, 166–71

Cage, John, 166, 168, 171
Carr, Helen, 31, 39n
Catullus, 95

citation, 46, 106–7, 110–11, 112–13, 206
clarity, 3, 5–6, 12, 15–16, 19, 32, 34, 71–2, 74, 77, 81–3, 86, 161, 188, 207
Close Listening (radio show), 164
cognition, 2, 4, 22, 34, 62, 64, 70, 72, 82, 112, 119–21, 126, 134, 142, 145, 150, 168, 183, 189, 198, 200
compression, 9, 16, 18, 33, 37, 38, 57–9, 69–70, 74–5, 79, 90, 92, 93, 103, 105, 119, 122, 128, 130–1, 134, 139, 142, 152, 164, 182, 183, 186, 189, 206; *see also* condensation
condensare (Poundian), 28, 37, 70, 93, 118, 119, 122–3, 130, 206
condensation, 3, 6, 8, 10, 11, 25, 28, 35, 38, 62, 64, 70, 81, 90, 92–3, 96–100, 102, 107, 114, 115n, 116n, 118, 119, 137n, 151, 156, 167, 191, 194, 206
consciousness, 1, 42, 74, 77, 78, 80, 83–4, 89n, 120, 123, 140, 145, 153, 161, 184; *see also* self-consciousness in poetry
Coolidge, Clark, 10, 100
Corman, Cid, 10, 92, 98–9, 104–5, 106, 107, 116n, 117n, 139, 141, 146
Couchoud, Paul-Louis, 22, 25, 26
Cournos, John, 'The Rose', 24
Creeley, Robert, 1–2, 7, 9–10, 53, 55, 63, 70, 118–35, 141, 142, 156, 160, 161–2, 164, 169, 172–3, 182, 184, 186, 190, 204, 206, 207
  'A Piece', 7, 128, 129, 169, 190, 205
  'A Sense of Measure' (prose), 120, 132
  Complete Correspondence (with Charles Olson), 123–4
  'Echo', 133
  For Love, 118, 119, 120, 126
  'For W.C.W.' (*For Love*), 124
  'For W.C.W.' (*Words*), 126–8
  I Know a Man', 63
  Pieces, 9, 119, 120, 129, 133, 161, 163, 207
  'Poems are a Complex' (prose), 132, 136n, 138n

  'The', 132–3
  '"Time" is some sort of hindsight', 64, 129–30, 179n, 207
  Words, 9, 119, 120, 126, 136n
Crozier, Andrew, 72, 75
Culler, Jonathan, 7, 14n
custard, 25; *see also* slither

Darwin, Charles, 110, 112–14
Davidson, Michael, 70, 74, 78, 127, 137n, 140, 142, 156
Demuth, Charles, 47
Dickinson, Emily, 58, 90, 94, 97, 144, 145, 183
directness, 3–4, 6–7, 15–21, 26, 27, 31–2, 37–8, 54–5, 59, 61, 74, 77, 84, 91, 114, 119–21, 200, 204, 207
discontinuity, 4, 54, 134, 164, 175, 177, 205
disjunction, 61, 64, 73, 101, 131, 139, 156
Duchamp, Marcel, 47, 48, 51–2, 170–1
Dworkin, Craig, 179n, 205

economy (poetic), 6, 11, 16, 19, 23, 27, 50, 62, 68–9, 78, 93, 110, 115n, 171
Eigner, Larry, 12, 139–56, 159, 160, 164, 167, 171, 176, 182, 184, 186, 204–5
  #237 ('A bird from somewhere'), 144
  #292 ('in the air'), 145
  #371 ('co-op'), 151
  #423 ('rain'), 152
  #427 ('You ride for some hours'), 149
  #448 ('u n k n o w n'), 146
  #473 ('Common sense'), 146
  #478 ('motor'), 154
  #769 ('i// mean'), 155
  #1741 'd e a d l y e n o u g h', 143
  Air the Trees, 143
  Another Time in Fragments, 139
  'Here and There' (prose), 143
  'Like a Dog Bark in Music' (prose), 148
  'not forever serious' (prose), 150–1

Eliot, T. S., 46, 47, 52, 54, 70, 92, 121, 147
  'The Love Song of Alfred J. Prufrock', 73, 83, 89n
  The Waste Land, 30, 44, 109, 191
ellipsis, 12, 15–16, 37, 44, 61, 70, 71, 74, 77–8, 81, 96, 122, 130, 139, 142, 150, 156, 183, 205, 206
Emmerson, Stephen, 205
emotion, 9–10, 15, 16, 17, 20, 21, 24, 26–8, 32, 37, 51, 54, 59, 71, 92, 100, 118, 119–22, 125, 126, 131, 132, 134–6, 204
empirical ambitions of poetry, 6, 15, 55, 71–5, 81, 127
epic, 1, 4, 56, 117n, 118
experience, 1–2, 3, 4, 13, 17, 34, 46, 49, 54, 71, 74, 83, 104, 106–7, 119–22, 126–7, 140, 142, 146–7, 148, 153, 156, 161, 164–7, 170–1, 182, 183, 186, 192, 205
Eyers, Tom, 2–3, 4, 10

femininity, 25, 31, 33, 39n, 119
Flint, F. S., 17, 21–3, 25, 26, 28–9, 32, 34, 40n
  'A Swan Song' and 'The Swan', 20–1
  'The Poetry of H.D.' (prose), 28–9
flowers, 22–6, 32–6, 46, 57–8, 59, 60, 84, 104, 110, 124, 199–200
form, social ramifications of, 2, 3, 6–7, 54, 56–7, 67–8, 76–7, 85, 118, 121–4, 127–31, 135, 149, 177, 187, 190, 198, 205
Forrest, Seth, 142, 156n
Foust, Graham, 183, 205
Friedlander, Ben, 136n, 137n, 139, 140
fullness, 10, 22, 28, 33, 99, 114, 119, 122, 151

Giles, Herbert, *History of Chinese Literature*, 21, 25–7
Graham, W. S., 5
Grenier, Robert, 12, 139, 159–77, 183, 184, 186, 205, 206
  'drawing poems', 161
  Farming the Words: Talking with Robert Grenier, 163
  'On Speech' (prose), 159–61, 179n
  'Robert Creeley: Pieces, Scribners 1969' (prose), 162
  Sentences, 160–77
Guest, Barbara, 11, 41n

H.D. (Hilda Doolittle), 15, 16, 25, 28–38, 43, 47, 48, 57, 198–200
  '*Goblins and Pagodas*' (prose), 31–2
  'Hermes of the Ways', 29–30, 37
  Sea Garden, 16, 32–4, 198
  'Sea Iris', 36
  'Sea Lily', 35
  'Sea Poppies', 34–5, 199–200
  'Sea Rose', 32–4, 199
  'Storm', 36
  'The Sheltered Garden', 36
haiku, 10, 22, 23, 25, 28, 103–5, 106–7, 111, 145, 146, 151, 153, 174, 186
Hartley, Marsden, 47
hesitancy, 4, 5, 10, 12, 14n, 78, 84, 99–100, 118, 126, 127, 130, 204
holes, 8, 79–81, 84, 86, 134, 138n, 149
Hulme, T. E., 6, 16, 17–19, 25, 28, 31, 34, 38, 39, 54, 65n, 119

Imagism, 11, 15–38, 42–3, 56, 62, 68–9, 71, 77, 91, 102, 104, 105, 107, 119, 135n, 164
impasse, 3–4, 8, 10, 13, 206
incompletion, 8–9, 13, 19, 27, 32, 33, 37, 38, 73, 81, 96, 119, 120, 122, 126, 130, 132, 140, 149, 156, 204, 205–6
ineffability, 16, 19, 38n, 189
inexpressibility, 10, 15, 16, 23, 24, 28, 37, 183, 206
insufficiency, 18–19, 24–5, 28, 94–7, 104, 109, 124, 127, 147, 177, 184, 187, 194
  insufficiency, pathos of, 11, 22–8, 30, 32, 34
interruption, 4, 5, 8, 10, 38, 54, 64, 84, 98, 101, 114, 149, 155, 177, 189, 206, 207

Japanese literature, 21–3, 25, 28, 31, 39n, 104–6, 146

Joglars magazine, 100
Joyce, James, 19–20, 21

Keats, John, 44, 49, 65n, 143, 146
Kermode, Frank, 18–19, 39n
Kerouac, Jack, 122

L=A=N=G=U=A=G=E magazine, 139, 156n
Language writing, 12–13, 67, 139, 141–2, 159, 162, 165, 166, 182
Lazer, Hank, 186
Levertov, Denise, 182, 201n
linebreaks, 8, 9, 12, 15, 32, 43–5, 48, 50–3, 59–60, 62–4, 74–5, 84, 86, 93, 98, 101, 104, 110, 114, 125–30, 132, 134, 150, 160, 163–5, 176, 182, 194, 198, 204, 206, 207
Loy, Mina, 47
Luck, Jessica Lewis, 140, 142
lyric, 4, 7, 9, 86, 102, 105, 107, 116n, 118, 127, 130, 131, 135, 177, 182, 186, 190, 192, 193, 194

Maciunas, George, 166, 170
Mackail, J. W., 9, 30
Mallarmé, Stephane, 18–19, 22, 29, 37
masculinity, 19, 25–7, 31–2, 34, 123, 137n, 180
measure, 46, 92, 120–1, 132, 135, 136n, 163, 174
Messerli, Douglas (ed.), *'Language' Poetries, an Anthology*, 182
Mica magazine, 147
mind, self-reflexive activity of, 1, 4, 58, 64, 75, 78, 84, 93, 103, 120, 122, 127, 141–2, 194
minimalism, 9–10, 13, 86, 104, 160
mise-en-page, 12, 51, 52, 94, 102, 142, 149, 160, 172
Monroe, Harriet, 31, 45, 65n, 69
Moore, Marianne, 47, 70

narrative, 4–5, 22, 64, 99, 114, 123, 159, 169, 176–7, 183, 188, 200, 205–6, 207
Nicholls, Peter, 6, 14n, 54, 81, 86, 88n, 120, 131, 137n

Niedecker, Lorine, 5, 10, 11, 70, 90–114, 135, 143, 144, 146, 155, 167, 176, 201n, 204, 206
'Foreclosure', 96–7
Harpsichord and Salt Fish, 112
'July, waxwings', 105
'Lake Superior', 98, 107–11, 117n
'My Life by Water', 105, 107, 109, 111
My Life by Water, 105
North Central, 106–12
'Now in one year', 99, 101
'Paean to Place', 98, 105, 106, 117n
'Property is poverty', 94, 99
T&G: Collected Poems, 105
'The Poetry of Cid Corman' (prose), 104
'To my pres-/sure pump', 101–3
'To my small/ electric pump', 100–1
'Traces of Living Things', 109
'Wintergreen Ridge', 107, 109–11, 112, 113
'You see here', 106
non-discursive (aspect of poetry), 18, 27, 177, 206
non-sense, 10, 134
non-statement, 3, 9, 26, 134

O'Leary, Peter, 69
Objectivism, 1, 5, 6, 10, 13, 48, 57, 67, 69, 70–2, 75, 83, 86n, 87n, 88n, 90–2, 115n, 142, 182
objects, 2–7, 11, 15, 17, 18, 26, 27, 32, 42, 51, 57, 64, 68, 69–70, 72–9, 85–6, 119–20, 125, 127, 142, 147–8, 153, 156, 167, 168, 177, 178n, 183–4, 200; *see also* poem-as-object; things
Olson, Charles, 1, 71, 121, 122, 128, 129, 132, 140, 141, 142, 144, 151, 160, 163
opacity, 3, 7, 16, 35, 71, 81, 107
open-field poetics *see* Projective Verse
Oppen, George, 10, 67–86, 105, 107, 108, 135, 156, 187, 192–4, 206
'As I saw', 79
Discrete Series, 67, 72–80
'Five Poems about Poetry', 80
'If it all Went up in Smoke', 85–6

'Latitude, Longitude' (draft of), 71
Myth of the Blaze, 85
'Neighbours', 86
'Of Being Numerous', 77, 81, 83, 85, 192
Of Being Numerous, 75
'Parousia', 80
'Party on Shipboard', 73, 79, 85
Primitive, 84–6
'Psalm', 78
'Route', 81–3
'Statement on Poetics' (prose), 74, 83
'The Little Pin: Fragment', 84
'The Natural', 85
This in Which, 80
'White. From the', 76–7
'Who Shall Doubt', 83–4
Osborne, Peter, 14n

Parker, Charlie, 122
pathos, 5, 11, 43, 46, 104; *see also* insufficiency, pathos of
Penberthy, Jenny, 115n
Perelman, Bob, 164, 182
Pinard, Mary, 98–9
poem-as-object, 69–70, 75, 92, 120, 142, 184
poetic thinking, 1, 3, 4, 6–7, 12–13, 56, 63, 68, 78, 109, 114, 121, 141–2, 143–4, 149, 156, 200, 204–6
Poetry magazine, 43, 67, 69, 90
Pondrom, Cynthia, 34, 39n
Pound, Ezra, 5, 6, 10, 11, 15–28, 31, 34, 36, 42–3, 47, 51, 53–7, 59, 62, 69. 71, 73, 75, 78, 91, 92, 93, 110, 118–22, 130, 131, 132, 143, 145, 147, 163, 164, 184, 206
'Δώρια', 24, 143
'A Few Don'ts by an Imagiste' (prose), 42
Cathay, 16, 26, 28, 32, 35, 37, 40n
'Credo' (prose), 87n
'Date Line' (prose), 16
Des Imagistes (editor), 16, 19, 20, 23, 24, 27, 43
'Fan-Piece for her Imperial Lord', 27
'In a Station of the Metro', 24–5, 34, 43, 145, 157

'Lament of the Frontier Guard', 28
'Liu Ch'e', 25–6, 27, 34
'Papyrus', 9
Ripostes, 17
'The Jewel Stairs' Grievance', 28
The Pisan Cantos, 120, 136n
'The Return', 37, 60n
'The River Merchant's Wife: a Letter', 23, 28
'Vorticism' (prose), 25, 28
precision, 15, 19, 34, 161
Projective Verse (and open-field poetics), 121, 139, 141–2, 144, 151, 156, 159, 162, 178n
prosody, 9, 45, 57, 74, 81, 111, 132, 138n, 140
Prynne, J. H., 147

Qian, Zhaoming, 40n
Quartermain, Peter, 14n, 48, 106

reduction (poetics of), 10, 22, 25, 28, 43, 69, 71, 77, 81, 86, 93, 97, 128, 130, 131, 162, 168, 177
Reed, Brian, 161
repetition, 63, 125, 127, 131, 133–4, 137n, 168, 169, 182, 188, 189, 200
Reznikoff, Charles, 70, 71
Rich, Adrienne, 2
Riley, Denise, 32
Robinson, Kit, 145
romanticism, 6, 9, 14, 17, 26, 31, 68, 116n
Russell, Bertrand, 110

Sappho, 9
Saroyam, Aram, 10, 179n
Satie, Erik, 137n
Schlegel, Friedrich, 9, 14n
self-consciousness in poetry, 83–4, 103, 194, 197
Shaw, Lytle, 141
Shelley, Percy Bysshe, 84
Sieburth, Richard, 18, 38–9n
Silliman, Ron, 67, 160, 161, 163, 172, 184, 187
Silliman, Ron (ed), *In the American Tree* (anthology), 139, 141, 159, 177n, 182

Skinner, Jonathan, 101, 157n
slither (emotional), 17, 18, 20, 25, 28, 31, 37, 39n, 54
Stein, Gertrude, 48–9, 52, 57, 64, 127, 160, 179n
Stephens, Paul, 166
Stevens, Wallace, 68, 87n
   'Anecdote of the Jar', 145, 199
   'Nuances on a Theme by Williams', 65n
   'Thirteen Ways of Looking at a Blackbird', 7
Stewart, Susan, 125
Stieglitz, Alfred, 47
Storer, Edward, 25
surrealism, 91, 92, 98, 113, 116n
symbolism, 11, 15, 18–21, 26, 54, 62, 116n, 119
Symons, Arthur, *The Symbolist Movement in Literature*, 19, 22, 36
syntax, 8, 10, 12, 16, 43, 53, 59, 60, 61, 66n, 71–5, 79, 101, 102, 112, 122, 125–6, 129–30, 132, 135, 140, 149, 151, 168, 172, 185, 204, 206, 207

technique (poetic), 9, 12–13, 55–6, 67–8, 87n, 93, 96–8, 108, 131, 137n, 140, 142, 205
temporality, 3–4, 75, 125–6, 130, 132, 134, 141, 143, 151, 155–6, 176–7, 193, 194
Terrell, Carroll F., 141, 142
things, 3, 5, 11, 15, 25, 42, 46, 47, 48, 54–6, 62, 78, 82, 101, 119–21, 127, 141–2, 164, 183–4, 188
'Thing', the (in Pound's thinking), 6, 25, 42, 120, 122, 131, 157n
This magazine, 139, 159
Thoreau, Henry David, 21, 90, 102, 110, 144
Tottels magazine, 139, 156n, 160
trees, 30, 34, 36, 59–63, 110, 116, 144–5, 183
Twitchell Waas, Jeffrey, 69, 86n

unsayability *see* inexpressibility

Watten, Barrett, 140, 141, 157n
Webern, Anton, 137n
Wilkinson, John, 5
Williams, William Carlos, 7, 13, 42–64, 67–71, 76–7, 78, 80, 87n, 121–2, 127, 136n, 141, 149, 156, 161, 171, 174, 182, 183, 185, 198, 201n, 204
   '10/10', 57–8
   'A Note on Poetry' (prose), 55
   Al Que Quiere, 44
   Autobiography, 42, 48, 65
   'Aux Imagistes', 43
   'Broken Windows', 44
   'Caviar and Bread Again: A Warning to the New Writer' (prose), 87
   'El Hombre', 44
   'Excerpts from a Critical Sketch: A Draft of XXX Cantos' (prose), 53–4
   In the American Grain, 66n
   Introduction to *The Wedge* (prose), 55, 56, 122
   'Lines', 44–5
   Paterson, 45, 54, 65, 71
   'Portent', 43
   'Postlude', 43, 65n
   Prologue to *Kora in Hell*, 42, 47
   'Shadows', 80
   'Silence', 61
   Sour Grapes, 46
   'Spirit of '76', 45, 65n
   'Spring and All', 44, 52, 88n, 185
   Spring and All, 47–52, 54, 57, 185
   The Clouds, 63
   'The crowd at the ball game', 52, 53
   The Descent of Winter, 57
   'The Great Figure', 46–7
   'The Hurricane', 63
   'The Locust Tree in Flower' (*first version*), 59
   'The Locust Tree in Flower' (*second version*), 60–1
   'The New Poetical Economy' (prose), 67–9
   'The Red Wheelbarrow', 7, 50–2, 64, 71, 77, 79, 104, 174, 184
   'The rose is obsolete', 40n, 52, 53
   The Tempers, 43

'The Work of Gertrude Stein' (prose), 48–9
The Wedge, 61, 136n
'To an Australian Editor' (prose), 121, 136n
'To be Closely Written on a Small Piece of Paper…', 44
'To Daphne and Virginia', 121
'To Elsie', 52
windows, 47, 75, 86, 144, 153
Woods, Tim, 117n
wounding, 27, 32, 34, 35, 37

Zukofsky, Louis, 10, 11–12, 48, 69–71, 75, 80, 87n, 88n, 90–1, 95, 98, 105, 110, 115n, 119, 138n, 144
80 Flowers, 144
A Test of Poetry (prose), 115n
An 'Objectivists' Anthology (editor), 67
Objectification (Zukofsky's concept of), 69–70, 80
'Sincerity and Objectification' (prose), 69–70
'Songs of Degree', 70

EU representative:
Easy Access System Europe
Mustamäe tee 50, 10621 Tallinn, Estonia
Gpsr.requests@easproject.com